CONTEMPORARY PERSPECTIVES ON PSYCHOTHERAPY AND HOMOSEXUALITIES

CONTEMPORARY PERSPECTIVES ON PSYCHOTHERAPY AND HOMOSEXUALITIES

Edited by

Christopher Shelley

FREE ASSOCIATION BOOKS / LONDON / NEW YORK

First published in 1998 by
Free Association Books Ltd
57 Warren Street, London W1P 5PA
and 70 Washington Square South,
New York, NY 10012–1091

© Christopher Shelley 1998

The right of the contributors to be identified as the authors
of this work has been asserted by them in accordance with
the Copyright, Designs and Patents Act 1988.

ISBN 1 85343 403 5 (hbk); 1 85343 404 3 (pbk)

A CIP catalogue record for this book is available from
the British Library.

Designed, typeset and produced for the publisher by
Chase Production Services, Chadlington, OX7 3LN
Printed in the EC by J.W. Arrowsmith Ltd, Bristol

Contents

Acknowledgements

The pursuit of this volume would not have been possible without the kindness, support and encouragement I have received from the following individuals: special thanks to Dr John Head and the 'gender group' at King's College, University of London; Professor Richard Royal Kopp, the California School of Professional Psychology, Los Angeles; Dr Linda Page, Adler School of Professional Psychology, Toronto; Dr Leo Gold, Alfred Adler Institute of New York; Professor Andrew Samuels, University of Essex (UK); Dr Pascal Perrodo, Annecy (France); Paola Prina, Don Smart and Rivka Pomson of the Adlerian Society (UK); and the Association of Lesbian, Gay and Bisexual Psychologies – ALGBP (UK). Most of all, I wish to thank each of the contributors in this volume for their collective support, suggestions and encouragement.

Christopher Shelley,
London

Notes on Contributors

Chess Denman, PhD is a consultant psychotherapist and head of department at Addenbrooke's Hospital, Cambridge (UK). She is Vice-Chair of Training of the Association of Cognitive Analytic Therapists and a training and supervising therapist with that organisation. Dr Denman maintains an interest in sexuality and psychotherapy and has written extensively in this field. She also maintains an interest in Cognitive Analytic Therapy and integrations between Cognitive and Analytic Therapies, and has written in this area as well.

Petrus de Vries, MRCPsych is a clinical research associate in developmental psychiatry at the University of Cambridge (UK). His main research focus is on localization strategies in the developmental psychopathologies. Dr de Vries also maintains an active interest in the psychotherapies and works using a Cognitive Analytic Therapy model.

Roger Horrocks, PhD was formerly a lecturer in psycholinguistics at the University of Hertfordshire (UK). He also carried out research into aphasia, metaphoric language and schizophrenic language. He then became a psychotherapist, working in London. He is the author of *Masculinity in Crisis* (1994), *Male Myths and Icons* (1995) and *An Introduction to the Study of Sexuality* (1997) all published by Macmillan.

Claudette Kulkarni, PhD is a Jungian psychotherapist in private practice at Persad Center in Pittsburgh (USA), a mental health agency serving the 'lesbigay', transgendered, and HIV/AIDS communities and their families. She is a contributing editor to the *Round Table Review of Contemporary Contributions to Jungian Psychology*, an active member of the Association for Women in Psychology (an organization of feminist psychologists), a practising astrologer, and author of *Lesbians and Lesbianisms: A Post-Jungian Perspective* (Routledge, 1997).

Bernard Ratigan, PhD is Consultant Adult Psychotherapist and Director of Training in the National Health Service Nottingham Psychotherapy Unit. He is a Medical Science Teacher in the Division of Psychiatry and Behavioural Sciences in the Faculty of Medicine and

Health Sciences in the University of Nottingham. He is a registered psychoanalytic psychotherapist with the United Kingdom Council for Psychotherapy and a Fellow of the British Association for Counselling.

Joanna Ryan, PhD is a psychoanalytic psychotherapist in practice in London. She trained at the Philadelphia Association (London) where she now teaches. She is co-author of *Wild Desires and Mistaken Identities: Lesbianism and Psychoanalysis* with Noreen O'Connor (Virago, 1993). Her other publications include *The Politics of Mental Handicap* (Free Association Books, 1987).

Christopher Shelley, MA is co-ordinator and faculty member at the Institute for Individual Psychology, London (the training division of the Adlerian Society, UK). A former psychotherapist and group facilitator at the Toronto Counselling Center for Lesbians and Gays; he is currently completing a PhD at King's College, London, researching gender and psychology. Also a violist, he continues to perform with orchestral and chamber music groups in addition to managing a small private practice in psychotherapy. He is co-editor of the *Adlerian Yearbook*, an international journal of Adlerian theory, research and practice.

Emmett Velten, PhD has been a staff psychologist at the University of Alabama School of Medicine; chief psychologist at Yuma County Behavioral Health Services in Arizona; school psychologist at the Memphis City Schools and staff psychologist at the inpatient psychiatric unit of the Desert Hospital in Palm Springs. He was also an instructor in the Department of Psychiatry at California Pacific Medical Center; assistant clinical professor at the University of California, San Francisco; clinical development director of Bay Area Addiction Research & Treatment (BAART) and California Detoxification Programs; past president of the Association for Behavioral and Cognitive Therapy (USA). He is a member of the Board of Professional Advisors of the Albert Ellis Institute for Rational Emotive Behavior Therapy in New York; and has co-authored, with Carlene Sampson, *Rx for Learning Disability* (Nelson-Hall, 1978) and, with Albert Ellis, *When AA Doesn't Work for You* (Barricade Books, 1992) and *Optimal Aging* (Open Court, 1998).

Introduction

omnia ex opinione suspensa sunt – Seneca

(everything depends on one's opinion)

HOMOSEXUALITY AND ITS DISCONTENTS

Same-sex desire and behaviour occurs across historical and cultural boundaries and with great regularity in a significant number of people.[1] Within industrial and non-industrial cultures, homosexual behaviour continues to fall on a spectrum from being widely contested through to being institutionalized and accepted, usually in a ritualized manner as in various gender-mixing forms, such as in the Hijras of India or the native Berdache of the American plain. Indeed, anthropological investigations continue to reveal a wide range of attitudes and institutional variations towards sex and gender consistent with Ford and Beach's (1951) classic study and sustained through more contemporary analyses (see, for example, Blackwood 1986). But what exactly do we mean by the term 'homosexuality'? Admittedly, problems of terminology have permeated the literature on homosexuality since the word was first coined in the nineteenth century. In particular, homosexuality has not been adequately defined, with the impression being that it is somehow merely a uni-dimensional phenomenon. Moreover, a significant minority of individuals continue to associate the word with sex between men, excluding sex between women (Wellings et al. 1994). The deeper moral, political and stereotypic views on homosexuality that the wider population adheres to are overwhelmingly posited against same-sex practice.[2] My argument is that instead of pursuing monolithic representations of homosexuality, why not abandon the dogma associated with this word of contention and, pursue a concept of *homosexualities*? I am not suggesting the final word on this matter; rather, I am trying to make the best out of an unsatisfactory linguistic situation, as others have also attempted (Tripp 1987). In this regard, the historic implication of Kinsey's (1948) team research was to begin to elucidate a number of important points about sexual *behaviour*. Among the most important of these points were the beginnings of a view of sexuality on a continuum (Kinsey's rather crude and linear scale of 0–6) rather than as discrete categories (for example, heterosexual/bisexual/homosexual), and that many people engage in a fluidity of sexual behaviours which resist a fixed label. However, while the Kinsey data opened the door towards a pluralistic understanding of sexuality in the US, we must also remember that this data has been widely criticized for failure to employ random sampling of the subjects interviewed, and Kinsey himself has been criticized for his underlying essentialism, particularly in regard to his subscription to biological drive theory (O'Connell Davidson and Layder 1994). However, by rating sexual behaviour on a linear continuum Kinsey also allowed us to see the marginality of people who express *exclusive* same-sex acts while also exposing the striking numbers of so-called *heterosexuals* who have engaged in homosexual acts. This brings us to the axis of identity[3] and behaviour. By focusing on the 'objectivity' of sexual behaviour, Kinsey selectively ignored the interplay of behaviour, politics and identity. To illustrate, under the right circumstances individuals may engage in homosexual acts but not identify themselves or be regarded by others as 'homosexual' (Berger 1983); such individuals thus avoid the opprobrium which the status of homosexuality implies. For example, a man may regard himself as 'heterosexual', practice regular 'heterosexual' intercourse and simultaneously engage in secretive 'homosexual' acts (Herdt 1988); being labelled homosexual by others may be independent of a homosexual identity (usually gay or lesbian); and cultural sanctioning of same-sex acts (as found in the Sambia of the eastern New Guinea highlands) may even be deemed essential in the construction of a *heterosexual* identity, as Herdt and Stoller (1985) have documented in their anthropological and psychoanalytic work.

The assertion of a *bisexual* identity (see Tucker 1995) by those who identify as such is clearly related to the topic of homosexualities, inasmuch as same-sex desire and sexual practice are usually implicit within this identity (but not necessarily mandatory!). This text is by definition one which focuses on homosexualities rather than bisexuality *per se*. This exclusion should not necessarily be misunderstood as an argument against the maintenance or utility of a bisexual identity or those who identify as such. Rather, it is beyond the scope of this text to adequately address all of the issues surrounding bisexuality. However, whether or not one identifies as, lesbian, gay, bisexual, transgendered or heterosexual, as long as we live in a culture that places the value of one dimension of sexual behaviour/identity (that is, heterosexism) over another, we will continue to be able to identify the sexual orientations of people as simultaneously occupying a hierarchical status. For my purposes here, I wish to state clearly that my usage of *homosexual* – pertaining to same-sex desire, eroticism, identity, limerance (romantic love) and behaviour – is regardless of one's particular identity (or lack of) or movement between or beyond such an identity. I am cautious about this usage: for example, the label 'homosexual' carries with it the historical stigma of illness (see Chapter 1), and the word 'homosexuality' is often confused with its historical predecessors which carry even worse stigma (such as sodomy, pederasty, buggery and the Black Mass) or is sometimes confused with paraphillia (for example, paedophilia). Moreover, homosexuality has been principally associated and identified with male sexual behaviour while lesbianism has, until recently, been scarcely considered. This was reflected in criminal legislation (where it existed) which prohibited homosexual acts between men. Indeed, the historical legal position of punishing 'sexual aberration' among men has simultaneously and adversely delegated lesbianism to near invisibility, not at all a pleasant alternative to the more explicit (and equally oppressive) treatment of many male homosexuals. Nevertheless, my representation of the term 'homosexuality' in this short introduction has been intended to refer collectively to the range of behaviours which cut across constructed sexual identities and which can differentiate the network of attributes and values that provide a deeper richness to gay and lesbian cultures, without focusing solely on the sexual acts and desires bound with these identities. In recognizing that homosexual behaviour also occurs independently of a gay, lesbian or bisexual identity I have attempted to clarify this issue to a greater degree, but it does not solve the problem that it is a poorly understood word laden with stigma and stereotype.

A MATTER OF CONTROVERSY AND ETHICS

In the UK, a recent report published by the National Institute for Mental Health (MIND) revealed that gay men, lesbian and bisexual people are subject to a wide range of discrimination and intolerance within the British mental health system (Golding 1997). Similar problems of bias have been recorded in the US where, for example, the 1990 American Psychological Task Force on lesbians and gay men revealed a significant number of qualitative aspects of bias against homosexuals within the report. The consequences of this pervasive bias lead to significant stress for many of those lesbians, gay men and bisexuals who have turned to the mental health system, inclusive of psychiatric care, psychotherapy and counselling, in order to make sense of and mitigate the effects of stress and to address other psychological issues (such as anxiety, depression, substance abuse, and so on). Of the respondents to the MIND research initiative, 51% claimed that their sexuality 'had been inappropriately used by mental health workers in order to explain the causes of their mental distress' (Golding 1997, p. 13). Nevertheless, the extent to which some members of the gay and lesbian community have sought therapy has been as high as three-quarters of those surveyed (Rothblum and Bond 1996). Although gay men and lesbians continue to use psychotherapy and counselling services, many remain deeply and justifiably suspicious; the MIND report indicates that 73% of the respondents 'said they had experienced some form of prejudice or discrimination in connection with their sexuality within mainstream mental health services' (ibid., p. 10). It is clear that psychotherapists (amongst other community members) must address the concerns of gay men, lesbian, bisexual and transgendered people.

In the US, national surveys of mental health care providers have revealed that most therapists (nearly all surveyed) have seen at least one gay or lesbian client of which they were aware (Hancock 1995). The likelihood that a given psychotherapist will encounter a gay man, lesbian (or homosexuality as a therapeutic issue) in his or her work appears to be a given. However, most psychotherapy training programmes do not incorporate training elements which examine the special needs of the gay and lesbian populations. This insufficiency of training appears to relate to an even deeper issue: that in contemporary Western cultures, sex in general still carries with it certain taboo elements. We can clearly see these taboos in a number of spheres. For example, in mental health training courses, most psychology, psychiatry and psychotherapy programmes spend an inadequate amount of time teaching future practitioners about human sexuality in general (Forstein 1988). As a result, it is questionable whether many students/ therapists possess, upon completion of their studies, the basic and necessary skills for assessing sexual issues and employing interventions based on sexually sensitive material. Moreover, in the absence of training in sexuality issues, there is little to prevent the practitioner's own private logic from entering the clinical picture, and as a consequence it becomes much easier to act on the basis of one's private opinion rather than methods derived from research or informed from adequate experience. Even when these opinions are favourably disposed towards homosexualities, this does not always mean that adequate service will follow suit. As Hancock (1995) points out, those practitioners who hold positive attitudes towards gay and lesbian people have frequently been found to give 'mixed messages' to their clients. This is obviously quite separate from those practitioners who have *never* examined their own private opinions and attitudes towards same-sex love, heterosexism and homophobia.

The varied therapeutic consequences are often more severe for those 'homosexuals' who receive treatment from therapists who practise with the assumption that homosexuality is an illness or a product of psychopathology. On the extreme end of the illness paradigm we find concordant treatment methods, such as *reparative* or *conversion* treatment. In the US, reparative therapy is offered through networks such as the National Association for Research and Therapy of Homosexuality (NARTH), and is consistent with the therapeutic approaches advocated by Nicolosi (1991) and Bieber (1988). The principal argument put forward by the reparative approach is that if a 'homosexual' person has attempted to adopt a gay or lesbian identity and is dissatisfied or distressed with this 'way of life', he or she should have the right to change his or her sexual orientation to heterosexuality, and the reparative approach is able to facilitate such change. However, the danger of this approach is that it doesn't necessarily do what it purports to do (convert homosexuals into heterosexuals): for example, Money (1988) found that upon closer scrutiny, the majority of successful 'conversions' were carried out on those who clearly had significant 'bisexual' feelings with which to capitalize on. Moreover, Haldemann (1991) was unable to find any evidence to support the conversion claims made by reparative advocates. Indeed, Hancock (1995) reports that homosexuals who receive treatment from 'illness adherents', are at a greater risk from mental health problems than are those who receive treatment for non-illness adherents. Arguably, what is of greater concern to those of us opposed to reparative practices are the underlying ideologies, such as being consistent with certain strands of conservatism, Judeo-Christian and Islamic fundamentalism, and so on. Such ideologies pervade reparative approaches. This is intertwined with the failure of reparative practitioners to examine the pervasive heterosexism which sustains their standpoint and clearly puts into question the entire nature of their task (for an alternative discussion, see Kitzinger 1996).

Moving away from reparative therapy to the other end of the spectrum, we find those who argue that the institutions of psychology, psychiatry and their applied methods (therapy) have colluded with and are pervaded by those very forces and ideologies which have initially brought so many gays and lesbians into therapy (Hodges and Hutter 1979). For example, this approach views a lesbian existence and therapeutic experience as fundamentally irreconcilable (Kitzinger and Perkins 1993). While the contributors in this volume are informed of the diversity and controversy of opinion surrounding the entire question of psychotherapy and homosexualities, we obviously share a fundamental conviction that the therapeutic process is a valid means by which lesbians and gay men may choose to address the myriad issues, internalized homophobia (or heterosexism), external oppression and the experiences of pain and stress involved in living at the end of the millennium while moving into a postmodern world. There remains little question that psychotherapy in general is an effective method of treatment for mental distress as meta-analyses and various replications have demonstrated (Shapiro and Shapiro 1982). What may be necessary here is for psychotherapists to increase their political awareness (Samuels 1993) so as not to avoid the concomitant pressures that social institutions exert on to the individuals concerned.

An important impetus which led me to organize this book is the trend for psychotherapy training organizations to dismiss or hide the topic of homosexuality and therapy under the liberal political trend: 'I promise to abide by the directive which forbids discrimination on the grounds of race, colour, sex, gender, sexual orientation ....' While there are many benefits to the construction of these legislative guidelines, I remain concerned with this approach, especially when applied as a convenient solution to what is a much deeper problem. For example, I recall attending a training workshop (not too many years ago) with an organization that clearly subscribed (in print) to an anti-discrimination policy which included sexual orientation. However, one of their principal tutors actively represented all forms of homosexuality as 'psychopathological'. This is consistent with structural models of homosexuality which, for example, may view such behaviour as stemming from a developmental character disorder. Such a viewpoint has permeated depth psychology and is not easily solved by adherence (or lack of) to liberal codes. While many organizations do practise the codes to which they subscribe, others clearly do not enforce these codes as a solution to heterosexism, or they dodge the issue completely. In psychoanalytic training, Drescher (1995) offers his own account of the 'don't ask – don't tell' 'solution' to the issue of gays and lesbians who seek a psychoanalytic training.

These liberal solutions to the problem of heterosexism in psychotherapy training are like wet bandages, threatening to fall off and expose the deeper wounds beneath. I argue that this problem cannot be adequately resolved without painfully challenging and working through the experience of 'how did we arrive at this position to begin with?' These liberal codes also beg more fundamental questions: for example, is it possible to agree to an anti-discrimination code and work with homosexuals effectively while simultaneously maintaining a private opinion that the behaviours in question are wrong, disgusting or immoral? Asking such questions, particularly within the theoretical divisions of psychotherapy, has become imperative. Anti-discrimination measures, while welcomed by many concerned with these issues, are not enough, as Kitzinger and Perkins (1993) have also argued. An unexamined and untrained approach to working with sexual minorities can no longer be tolerated within the psychotherapeutic domain; indeed, it arguably constitutes an ethical violation, particularly in terms of practising within one's sphere of competency. As Brown (1996) has also argued, practising psychotherapy with gay men, lesbians and bisexuals without sufficient training of the myriad issues of relevance involved, is a serious ethical problem.[4]

PSYCHOTHERAPIES AND SHIFTING CONVICTIONS: 'AFFIRMATIVE' AND BEYOND

More than 15 years ago, Corsini (1981) identified 250 different schools of counselling and psychotherapy. In Britain today, mainstream schools constitute a large number of contrasting approaches, as apparent in the 75 different schools accredited by the United Kingdom Council for Psychotherapy (UKCP). Many of these schools subscribe to anti-discrimination directives which include sexual orientation. Nevertheless, some of these schools have in the past actively supported and sustained the often grotesque and barbaric measures brought against homosexuals in failed attempts to 'cure' them. These schools created and endorsed a system designed to rehabilitate homosexual 'patients' into morally abiding citizens who would conform to their assigned gender roles and to the compulsory heterosexuality expected within those roles. Many of these very schools now support the idea of 'affirmative therapy' for homosexual clients and safeguard their positions under the protective guise of anti-discrimination measures. That these schools of psychotherapy train professionals to provide a service for gay men and lesbians may, under the circumstances, seem rather incoherent; in some cases even duplicitous. Is it possible to relent on such a matter, like changing the wallpaper scheme just to suit the times? I believe that adequate theoretical revision or transformation is necessary within many of these schools in order to address what Gonsiorek (1995) has argued,

> It is important to note that the demise of the illness model of homosexuality created a theoretical and clinical vacuum for understanding sexual orientation as well as responding to Lesbian and Gay clients who seek psychological services. (p. 25)

I assert that this theoretical vacuum has been sustained by means of a shift from illness to affirmation. The purpose of this book is to address some of the incoherence which has resulted from this shift towards 'affirmative therapy', a shift which I believe has been a 'reaction to' rather than a 'working through' of the preceding illness models. While some schools, particularly the Humanistic models, are beginning to use (rather than just subscribe to) a well intentioned affirmative position (see Davies and Neal 1996), is this necessarily the best concept with which to fill this 'theoretical vacuum'? For example, the word 'affirmative' seems to lack a kind of dialectic or, better yet, a reflexiveness within its uni-dimensionality. Affirmative means certitude, an absolute 'yes', with synonyms for 'affirmative' including: unequivocal, undeniable, definite, indubitable, categorical, sure and absolute. I admit that affirmative may also take the form of an attitude I have adopted under certain circumstances (it has long been a popular catchword among many gays and lesbians); however, I also argue that it is not the best word to describe therapeutic work with sexual minorities from a non-pathology position; not only because I would, as an Adlerian, normally subsume *affirmative* under the concept of *Gemeinschaftsgefühl*[5] but also because I am aware that the term may antagonize other non-pathology positions, such as the stance of neutrality taken in psychoanalytic practice. Moreover, political objections to 'affirmative therapy' have also been argued by Kitzinger (1997) who suggests that the term undermines the subversive potential of gays and lesbians to transform society.

In the spirit of diversity and pluralities, and with recognition of the vast numbers of existing schools of psychotherapy, I have had the difficult task of selecting seven differing accounts. This allows the reader to make dialectical comparisons and stimulates greater debate. It also makes room for the obvious commonalities to shine through. These accounts include a historical, two psychoanalytic, a post-Jungian, an Adlerian, a Cognitive Analytic Therapy and a Rational Emotive Behaviour Therapy standpoint. The issue of homosexuality from the perspectives of the Humanistic-Existential models has been sufficiently addressed elsewhere (Davies and Neal, forthcoming). Instead, this volume examines a selection of perspectives from models which emphasize psychodynamic, 'analytic',[6] and/or cognitive structures and processes. Many of these approaches maintain fundamental disagreements on the topic. Also, the views expressed by each writer do not necessarily represent those of the school under discussion and in some cases the views argued here are quite the contrary! In this regard, we are all largely advocating an ideal – how a given therapeutic model can accommodate a homosexual client outside of an illness paradigm. Furthermore, we aim to demonstrate how it is that the theory and practice of a given model may be beneficial to the therapeutic needs of clients who are lesbian and gay or otherwise concerned with their sexuality. The inclusion of contrasting models reflects what I believe are three important features of psychotherapy in general:

1. *Across the various schools there is no consensual definition of what psychotherapy is or does.* By encouraging pluralities through the contrasting accounts presented here, I am also advocating a greater appreciation of difference and diversity within and across the psychotherapies. There is no one school of psychology or psychotherapy which is able to answer conclusively all questions pertaining to homosexualities. Nor, I suggest, can we in psychology continue to ignore the social, political and institutional aspects to these problems any longer.

2. *Psychotherapists usually practise from a certain theoretical base, grounded by their training in the values of a certain school. Many people are unaware of the ideologies and values advocated within these schools.* In my experience, a significant number of people (inclusive of gay men and lesbians) know little and sometimes nothing about the differences between various psychotherapeutic approaches. Nevertheless, it is the *individual practitioner* who represents his or her theory through practice. Exemplary practice therefore lies with the individual practitioner. We meet the particular school through our interactions with textual and/or narrative representations or by individual engagement on an implicit encounter-based experience, the therapist as agent of his or her position(s).

3. *All systems of psychotherapy are value laden.* The schools of psychotherapy were created by individuals who brought the stamp of their historical period(s) and their own values and subjective biases to the creation of their systems. These are created traditions. If these schools, and the theories and practices they reproduce, are to survive at all, they will need to evolve through history as history is created, to shed what is no longer relevant or useful and to acquire a meaningful connection with the emerging historical moment. Beyond this, the psychotherapies as a whole may also be considered both art and science in design and service of healing for the psyche; it is, like the human beings who facilitate the process or the critics who admonish these practices, imperfect.

In this volume, Roger Horrocks explores historical issues through discussion of the paradigms which have emerged and brought shape to our understanding of same-sex behaviour. He demonstrates how various cross-cutting influences have infected, for example, psycho-analytic discourse on homosexuality. Throughout he focuses on the cultural, religious, political, philosophical, and psychological dimensions to understanding homosexuality and psychotherapy.

Joanna Ryan explores issues relevant to psychoanalysis and lesbian-ism. In particular, she makes a strong case of the need for psychoanalysts to explore countertransferential issues in relation to homosexuality while drawing on clinical material to support her arguments.

Bernard Ratigan examines psychoanalytic theorizing on male homosexuality by acknowledging the radical implications of the Freudian unconscious and, particularly, a rethinking of the Kleinian approach and how this approach can assist those with psychopathology who are also gay or lesbian. While recognizing a bias towards an illness model of homosexuality in many psychoanalytic writings, he nevertheless draws our attention to the benefits that psychoanalytic psychotherapy has to offer gay and lesbian patients.

Claudette Kulkarni brings her experience as a post-Jungian therapist and feminist to her analysis of the issues and concepts in analytical psychology which sustain heterosexist views. She argues the need for Jungian practitioners to adopt and utilize a radical view in order to leave behind Jung's heterosexism while retaining his respect for psyche and soul. Through case vignettes, she demonstrates how post-Jungian practice can form the basis of transformative experiences in psychotherapy for lesbian and gay clients.

In my own chapter, I survey Adlerian thinking on homosexualities and offer a critique of traditional Adlerian ideas of same-sex behaviour and gender. A solidly laid theory, Individual Psychology has a tradition of viewing homosexuality as neurosis. But I remain confident that this modality is able to provide support to gays and lesbians who experience mental distress without the need to preserve an illness paradigm. Instead, a replacement goal of a broader manifestation of *community feeling* with an eye and ear on social contexts and prevention of mental distress is just the replacement needed.

Chess Denman and Petrus de Vries outline the integration of cognitive and psychoanalytic therapies through the modality of Cognitive Analytic Therapy (CAT). They outline the central tenets of CAT and then contrast this approach to other models such as Cognitive Behaviour Therapy (CBT). In addition, they cogently illustrate the theory of CAT with a case study which argues the effectiveness of this modality in treating gay and lesbian patients.

Emmett Velten explores the history of Rational Emotive Behaviour Therapy (REBT) through its founder, Albert Ellis, who has long been a leading figure on human sexual matters and has been an influential theorist in both psychology and sexology. By drawing on the historical context of American social and political views towards same-sex behaviour, Velten succeeds in contextualizing REBT's evolution in viewing homosexuality. Velten also demonstrates how REBT can be an effective and constructive tool for working with gay men and lesbians without pathologizing their identities.

NOTES

1   The Kinsey data reported in 1948 that 38.7% of American males between the ages of 36 and 40 have had at least one homosexual experience, while 4% were exclusively homosexual in terms of their sexual behaviour with others. Later surveys based on this method (for example, Wellings et al. 1994) have been more conservative in their findings but acknowledge that due to social stigma and bias 'all prevalence figures relating to homosexual activity should be regarded as minimum estimates ... it can be expected to be under- rather than over-reported' (p. 180).

2   Wellings et al. (1994) found that 70.2% of British males and 57.9% of British females randomly surveyed believe that sex between two men is always or mostly wrong while 64.5% of males and 58.8% of females surveyed believe sex between females is wrong or mostly wrong. These findings are very similar to the 1989 General Social Survey in the US where roughly three-quarters of Americans surveyed found homosexual relations always or almost always wrong (ibid.).

3   Within lesbian and gay literature there is controversy over the issue of identity. For example, many postmodern accounts reject the very idea of identity. An excellent account of how this debate relates to psychoanalysis can be found in Decker (1995) and Domenici and Lesser (1995).

4   Both the American Psychological and Psychiatric Associations have failed to pass tabled resolutions declaring that conversion 'treatment' is unethical. Consequently, their position – that homosexuality is not pathological – remains highly contradictory and in need of attention.

5   Translated into English as either 'social interest' or 'feeling of community'.

6   I do not take the traditional psychodynamic meaning of 'analytic' here but refer instead to a more inclusive definition in order to include the Rational Emotive Behaviour Therapy approach which advocates active, directive and conscious analysis of irrational cognitions independent of a psychodynamic framework. Moreover, Albert Ellis – the founder of REBT – has always maintained that the REBT approach has its founding roots in Adler's Individual Psychology and Karen Horney's version of Psychoanalysis although it is not a psychodynamic model (Velten 1997, personal communication).

REFERENCES

Berger, R. M. (1983) 'What is a homosexual? A definitional model', *Social Work*, March–April 1983.

Bieber, I. (1988) *Homosexuality: A Psychoanalytic Study of Male Homosexuals*, London: Aronson.

Blackwood, E. (ed.) (1986) *The Many Faces of Homosexuality: Anthropological Approaches to Homosexual Behaviour*, New York: Harrington Park Press.

Brown, L. S. (1996) 'Preventing heterosexism and bias in psychotherapy and counselling', in Rothblum, E. D. and Bond, L. A. (eds) *Preventing Heterosexism and Homophobia*, London: Sage.

Corsini, R. J. (ed.) (1981) *Handbook of Innovative Psychotherapies*, New York: John Wiley.

Davies, D. and Neal, C. (1996) *Pink Therapy: A Guide for Counsellors and Therapists Working with Lesbian, Gay and Bisexual Clients*, Buckingham: Open University Press.

Decker, B. (1995) 'How to have your Phallus and Be it too', in Glassgold, J. M. and Iasenza, S. (eds) *Lesbians and Psychoanalysis: Revolutions in Theory and Practice*, New York: The Free Press.

Domenici, T. and Lesser, R. C. (eds) (1995) *Disorienting Sexuality: Psychoanalytic Reappraisals of Sexual Identities*, London: Routledge.

Drescher, J. (1995) 'Anti-Homosexual Bias in Training', in Domenici, T. and Ronnie, R. C. (eds) *Disorienting Sexuality: Psychoanalytic Reappraisals of Sexual Identities*, London: Routledge.

Ford, C. S. and Beach, F. A. (1951) *Patterns of Sexual Behaviour*, New York: Harper and Row.

Forstein, M. (1988) 'Homophobia: An overview', *Psychiatric Annals*, 18 (1).

Golding, J. (1997) *Without Prejudice: MIND Lesbian, Gay and Bisexual Mental Health Awareness Research*, London: MIND Publications.

Gonsiorek, J. C. (1995) 'Gay male identities: Concepts and issues', in D'Augelli, A. R. and Patterson, C. J. (eds) *Lesbian, Gay and Bisexual Identities over the Lifespan: Psychological perspectives*, Oxford: Oxford University Press.

Haldemann, D. (1991) 'Sexual orientation conversion therapy for gay men and lesbians: A scientific examination', in Gonsiorek, J. and Weinrich, J. (eds) *Homosexuality: Research Implications for Public Policy*, Newbury Park, CA: Sage.

Hancock, K. A. (1995) 'Psychotherapy with lesbians and gay men', in D'Augelli, A. R. and Patterson, C. J. (eds) *Lesbian, Gay and Bisexual Identities Over the Lifespan: Psychological perspectives*, Oxford: Oxford University Press.

Herdt, G. H. (1988) 'Cross-cultural forms of homosexuality and the concept "Gay"', *Psychiatric Annals*, 18(1): 60–91.

Herdt, G. H. and Stoller, R. J. (1985) 'Theories of origins of male homosexuality', *Archives of General Psychiatry*, 42: 12–31.

Hodges, A. and Hutter, D. (1979) *With Downcast Gays: Aspects of Homosexual Self-Oppression*, Toronto: Pink Triangle Press.

Kinsey, A., Pomeroy, W. and Martin C. (1948) *Sexual Behaviour in the Human Male*, Philadelphia, PA: W.B. Saunders.

Kitzinger, C. (1996) 'Speaking of Oppression: Psychology, Politics, and the Language of Power', in Rothblum, E. D. and Bond L. A. (eds) *Preventing Heterosexism and Homophobia*, London: Sage.

Kitzinger, C. (1997) 'Lesbian and Gay Psychology', in Fox, D. and Prilleltensky, I. (eds) *Critical Psychology: An Introduction*, London: Sage.

Kitzinger, C., and Perkins, R. (1993) *Changing Our Minds: Lesbian Feminism and Psychology*, New York: New York University Press.

Money, J. (1988) *Gay, Straight And Inbetween: The Sexology of Erotic Orientation*, New York: Oxford University Press.

Nicolosi, J. (1991) *Reparative Therapy of Male Homosexuality*, New York: Aronson Inc.

O'Connell Davidson, J. and Layder, D. (1994) *Methods: Sex and Madness*, London: Routledge.

Rothblum, E. D., and Bond, L. A. (eds) (1996) 'Introduction', in *Preventing Heterosexism and Homophobia*, London: Sage.

Samuels, A. (1993) *The Political Psyche*, London: Routledge.

Shapiro, D. A. and Shapiro, D. (1982) 'Meta-analysis of Comparative Therapy Outcomes: A replication and refinement', *Psychology Bulletin*, 92: 581–604.

Tripp, C. A. (1987) *The Homosexual Matrix*, New York: New American Library.

Tucker, N. (ed.) (1995) *Bisexual Politics: Theories, Queries, and Visions*, Binghamton, NY: Harrington Park Press.

Wellings, K., Field, J., Johnson, A. M. and Wadsworth, J. (1994) *Sexual Behaviour in Britain*, London: Penguin.

1 Historical Issues:
Paradigms of Homosexuality

Roger Horrocks

For the whole of the twentieth century, the treatment of homosexuality in the psychological disciplines – psychiatry, psychotherapy, psychoanalysis, and so on – has operated under the paradigm of 'sickness' and 'cure'. That is, it has been assumed that homosexuality is pathological, and through psychological investigation (and in the case of psychiatry, other, more physical procedures) can be dissolved, so that the sick patient can be returned to full heterosexual health.

The ways in which this paradigm has been expressed have varied widely. Psychoanalysis has taken a keen interest in homosexuality, and has often preached a militant line against it; not simply pointing out its 'immaturity', indicative of 'arrested development' or 'fixation', but also taking a more moral line, and even suggesting that homosexuality is corrupt and malign (Lewes 1989). One indication of this in Britain could be found at the time of the furore over Clause 28 of the 1988 Local Government Bill, which attempted to ban the discussion of homosexuality in schools. Many non-analytic psychotherapists were staggered to find that a number of psychoanalysts were actively campaigning for the Bill.[1] One can also cite here the view put forward by the famous British analyst, W. D. R. Fairbairn, that homosexuals should be put into 'settlement camps' (Domenici 1995).

But the US has probably seen the most militant homophobic stance within psychoanalysis – at times, it seemed as if homosexuality ranked with communism as the most un-American of activities. Lacan's comment about '... the degradation of psychoanalysis consequent on its American transplantation' seems apposite in this case (Mitchell and Rose 1982, p. 77). However, the psychoanalytic stance is more complex than that, since, as is well known, Freud himself adopted a fairly relaxed, tolerant attitude to homosexuality, and notably did not object to the idea of homosexuals undertaking training as analysts. However, Freud's stance towards homosexuality is complex and contradictory, since in his more formal documents he generally described it as an 'aberration' or an indication of arrested development (Abelove 1993).

Certainly psychoanalysis has taken an active interest in homosexuality – for example, it is a remarkable fact that Freud's famous case studies all contain it as a major theme. One can contrast Jungian psychology here, for generally homosexuality has been ignored, both by Jung and post-Jungians. Thus Samuels (1985) states in his well known review of Jungian psychotherapy, *Jung and the Post-Jungians*: 'Homosexuality has received little attention in analytical psychology' (p. 228). It also strikes me that the world of Humanistic psychotherapy has not fared much better – while purporting to be more liberal than analytic therapy, its discussion of homosexuality has been minimal.

Gay men and lesbians are familiar with this approach in Western society and culture as a whole: it can be termed 'erasure'. They are simply wiped out from the historical record; they are non-persons.[2] It is a moot point which is worse – the militant homophobia of certain psychoanalysts, or the enigmatic silence of analytical psychologists and certain other schools.

However, so far in this historical sketch I have myself ignored one of the most important protagonists – the gay movement itself. In the last 30 years, this movement has not only been able to generate great enthusiasm, energy, creativity and self-support, but has begun to change attitudes outside the gay movement. The most obvious indications of this are the various decriminalizations that have taken place in Western countries – for example, the 1967 Sexual Offences Act in Britain – but psychotherapy and psychiatry themselves have not been immune. Thus in the US the removal of homosexuality from the DSM (Diagnostic and Statistical Manual of Mental Disorders) register of psychological pathologies in 1973 was a significant step (Lewes 1989). Currently in Britain a struggle is being waged against the block on gay men and lesbians within the analytic training organizations.

But these are outward political manifestations of a 'gay affirmative' shift. In more psychological terms, the growth of the gay movement has led to the partial depathologization of homosexuality. This has led to 'gay affirmative' therapy, which begins with the premise that homosexuality is not perverse and that it is homophobia that is pathological; or, to put it another way, homophobia is indicative of an unprocessed personal complex (Davies and Neal 1996). However, one has to express some caution towards this movement, as many therapists might feel loath to become too 'affirmative', since this infringes the notion of therapeutic 'neutrality'.

One can argue therefore that we are witnessing today a clash of paradigms concerning homosexuality. As against the paradigm of 'sickness and cure', there is the paradigm of 'gay affirmation'.

However, the situation is more complex than that. For example, the moral stance taken by some analysts reminds us of the ancient religious objections to homosexuality, which may be assumed to be still functioning, even if unconsciously, within psychotherapy as in society at large. Other paradigms have been influential in the twentieth century: for example, feminism has carried out a massive theoretical deconstruction of patriarchy, and this analysis is extremely valuable for a socio-political understanding of homosexuality and homophobia. In fact, one of the arguments put forward by feminism is that human sexuality itself is a political structure, and is neither 'natural' nor unchangeable.

This connects with the body of ideas known as 'social constructionism', which has taken the very radical line that the notion of homosexual identity, or 'the homosexual' as a 'species', in the words of the French philosopher Michel Foucault (1990, p. 43), is a comparatively recent invention. Historical and anthropological research seems to bear this out, demonstrating a very wide spectrum of attitudes towards homosexual behaviour in human societies, and a great variety of social 'niches' for it (Horrocks 1997).

One must also mention the increasing influence of genetic research, and particularly the indications that homosexuality is inherited. This has raised the familiar arguments about nature/ nurture: is homosexuality inborn, or does it arise out of environmental influences? These arguments are fiercely contested, since they have direct political connotations: some gay men and lesbians express relief at the idea of 'the gay gene', since it promises to absolve the homosexual person (and his or her family) of any aberration. On the other hand, some gay activists dismiss the genetic arguments, since this seems to them to elide the political agitation against homophobia.

In short, we find today a contestation of different paradigms about homosexuality; some of them very old, some very recent. This makes the 'history of homosexuality' very interesting, and in some ways a topic which goes beyond homosexuality itself. It can be seen as a site of political struggle about the nature of human sexuality, identity and freedom. The study of homosexuality is at the cutting edge of radical theorizing about sexuality, the family, and the connection between sexual relationships and larger socio-political structures (patriarchy).

In this chapter, I intend to outline a historical overview of these paradigms, and indicate some of their interrelationships. I see this not simply as a matter of historical interest, but also as a way into the inner world, and the complex attitudes towards homosexuality which we all possess. The 'clash of paradigms', which can be observed going on externally in society at large, can be assumed partly to echo an internal clash within individuals.

AN OPEN LETTER

An event took place in the mid-1990s which seemed to encapsulate the confusion of paradigms which exists towards homosexuality. In 1995 Professor Charles Socarides was invited to speak in London by one of the British analytic organizations (the Association of Psycho-analytic Psychotherapy). Socarides is probably the most famous (or notorious) anti-gay analyst in America, and has preached for many years that homosexuality is a perversion that should be cured. But in addition, Socarides has been one of these analysts whose intemperate language *vis-à-vis* homosexuality bears all the hall-marks of homophobic prejudice (Lewes 1989).

The invitation to Socarides seemed astonishing in itself, but subsequent events rapidly overtook it. A number of psychotherapists wrote an Open Letter, criticizing the invitation to Socarides, and questioning the whole nature of the underground prejudice against homosexuality within the analytic world. The letter states that within the British National Health Service, gay men and lesbians receive less than fair treatment, since so many analysts employed by the Health Service receive their training from homophobic institutes which block gay and lesbian candidates for training. In other words, the Health Service (paid for by heterosexual and homosexual people alike) is employing openly anti-homosexual therapists.[3] But then gay activists took a hand and threatened to attend Socarides' talk and disrupt it. In the end, the invitation was withdrawn.

This small-scale event seemed to bring together many of the major protagonists: the homophobic analyst; the more liberal wing of psychotherapy, writing the 'Open Letter'; gay activists, perhaps rather scornful of the 'liberal' approach; and, sitting in the middle, the therapy organization concerned.

However, this incident seems to have caused a minor snowball effect: a number of analytic organizations have indicated that they will relax their bar on gays and lesbians. None the less, some gay candidates are still being advised to keep their sexual orientation to themselves while undergoing training. This in itself seems an astonishing state of affairs: both the candidate and the institute know that the candidate is gay, but everyone has to pretend he or she is not![4]

One thing is clear from this incident: homosexuality continues to arouse great anxiety, both among heterosexual people and amongst some psychotherapy organizations. In this sense, Freud was unusually non-anxious, but analysis and therapy as a whole betray large amounts of prejudice and unconscious phobia.

THE MORAL/RELIGIOUS PARADIGM

The roots of such prejudice stretch back a very long way. Thus while pagan Greece and Rome tolerated a wide degree of sexual diversity, including homosexual relations between men and boys, the Christianization of the West gradually brought about an increasing stipulation of the evil inherent in sexual desire as a whole. Later, in medieval Europe, what Michel Foucault (1990) describes as the 'centrifugal force' (p. 38) around monogamous heterosexuality began to gather strength, and homosexuality was condemned in increasingly virulent terms.[5]

However, John Boswell, in his influential book *Christianity, Social Tolerance and Homosexuality* (1980) has argued that Christianity was not monolithically hostile to homosexuality, and that there were in fact periods when 'gay sub-cultures' existed, both in civil society and in the Church itself. One might question the possible anachronism of a term such as 'gay sub-culture', but Boswell is probably right to protest against a black and white portrayal of Christianity as 'anti-gay'.

However, a further important issue arises here: Foucault has argued that while obviously the notion of homosexual behaviour was widely known (and condemned) in the Christian West, the notion of 'homosexual identity' did not exist. It is significant that 'sodomy' was a wide-ranging term, referring to any type of non-procreative activity outside marital intercourse; 'buggery' referred to anal sex with man, woman or animal (Boswell 1980; Weeks 1991). I shall return to this argument, as it represents one of the most radical breakthroughs in the contemporary study of sexuality.

The moral/religious arguments against homosexuality may seem rather alien to psychotherapy, but it is quite possible that they have (consciously or not) influenced both the theoretical and practical treatment of homosexuality. Christianity valorized marital hetero-sexuality, and it can be assumed that this ethical system exerts some influence, even if unconsciously, on everyone living in the West.

In this respect it is arguable that Freud, as a Jew, was able to explode the romantic mystification of sex prevalent in Christian cultures and could therefore view homosexuality more dispassion-ately: 'it was this "pariah" Jew who, since he was not bound by Gentile society's rules of discretion and decency, could say aloud what was forbidden by ... the "vice of virtue"' (Roith 1987, pp. 9–10).

Freud was explicitly scornful about Christian ethics, and their internal contradictions and denial of human instincts. One aspect of the Americanization of psychoanalysis that he viewed with some suspicion was its 'ethical' or moralistic stances, which Freud saw as reaction formations to repressed sadism, and as attempts to bring back into psychology notions of 'decency' and morality which he had struggled to remove.[6] It seems significant therefore that it was in Christian, 'ethical' America that the psychoanalytic hostility to homosexuality reached its apogee.

PSYCHIATRIZATION

The eighteenth and nineteenth centuries have been seen by some students of sexuality as a watershed. For example, Foucault (1990) argues that it was at this time that 'sexuality' itself was invented, through the proliferation of discourses about sex – discourses within medicine, psychiatry, criminal justice, biology, pedagogy, to add to the discourses already extant within the Church.

Within this historical view, the nineteenth century has its own particular character: it gave to the study of sex a 'scientific' character. Sexuality was wrung from the grip of the Church and became the property of the sexologist, the psychiatrist and the biologist. It seemed that the moralistic approach to sex, enshrined in the confessional, where sexual secrets could be whispered, exposed and absolved, was overthrown in favour of a positivist approach. This is seen most clearly in the taxonomic approach to sexual 'deviance' and 'perversion'. Much as nineteenth-century collectors constructed taxonomies of insects, birds, mammals and so on, sexologists and psychiatrists such as Krafft-Ebbing constructed vast taxonomies of sexual diversity.

Foucault's wider argument, in his *History of Sexuality* (1990), is that in fact this 'science of sex' was not a value-free, neutral enterprise, but utilized the study of sexuality as a means of exerting power over people. In particular, the creation of a vast taxonomy of sexual deviance tends implicitly to prioritize heterosexuality. The normative undercurrent to studies of sexuality can be seen in the theory of 'degeneracy' or 'degenerence', one of those pseudo-scientific theories which abounded in the nineteenth century and was put forward to account for many 'perversions', and which Freud (1905) criticized fiercely.

Whether or not one agrees with Foucault's more philosophical arguments about the 'construction' of homosexuality in the nineteenth century, it seems clear that the psychiatrization of homosexuality at this time was a momentous event, whose ramifications are still with us. The paradigm of 'sin' was overthrown in favour of the paradigm of 'sickness' and 'cure'. With that omnipotent charisma characteristic of Western science, psychiatry and medicine proclaimed that homosexuality was an illness for which it had the cure. Of course the cures were many and various; many of them exhibiting a sadistic and punitive element which is surely not accidental. And this quasi-torture, especially of gay men, is not some ancient relic of previous centuries – it has continued well into the twentieth century. For example, the South African Truth and Reconciliation Commission has investigated claims that gay men in the South African Army were given electric shock and other forms of 'aversion therapy' in the 1980s.[7] There are also many accounts by gay men of various forms of punitive treatment received in the postwar period in Britain, including electric shock, nausea inducing drugs, and so on (David 1997).

The point I am making is that this paradigm has survived to the present day. It infected psychoanalysis, particularly in the US. It is quite likely that it still pervades popular thinking; no doubt many gay men and lesbians still harbour it in an internalized form. It has sometimes become linked with the traditional religious view; for example, among right-wing Christian groups in the US, who proclaim homosexuality to be both sinful and sick. AIDS added a fearful addendum to this argument, for the right wing could argue that it was a punishment from God for the proliferation of homosexuality. Homosexuality was medicalized all over again in a context of intense 'fear and loathing'.[8] This can be seen in Hollywood productions such as *Philadelphia*, which places male homosexuality within a context of suffering and disease. Granted, in that film, the protagonist is also presented in a heroic light, but he also comes across as a martyr. Homosexuality equals suffering and victimhood.

Surely one of the tasks facing all psychotherapy organizations, particularly training organizations, is to bring such views into consciousness, and not allow them to languish in a state of semi-consciousness or passivity, where they fester. Feminism has demonstrated how dark areas of psychotherapy – in this case, the treatment of women – could be challenged, confronted and changed, for arguably women have themselves been wounded by the psychological disciplines – by psychiatry and psychoanalysis in particular. In the same way, homosexuality has been part of the 'shadow' of the therapy world; thankfully, this shadow is now being exposed to the light.

FREUD AND PSYCHOANALYSIS

Freud had a contradictory attitude to homosexuality. His more positive comments about it are well known: the letter to the mother of a homosexual ('homosexuality is assuredly no advantage but ... it cannot be classified as an illness'), his signing of a statement against the criminalization of homosexuality, his apparent objections to blocking the training of a homosexual candidate.[9]

Theoretically also, Freud made certain assumptions which gave homosexuality a non-pathological status. He separated sexuality from reproduction and argued that 'perverse' components are universal in infantile sexuality, and that such currents are retained in the unconscious. One can cite here his famous comment that 'all human beings are capable of making a homosexual object-choice and have in fact made one in their unconscious', coupled with the comment on heterosexuality: 'the exclusive sexual interest felt by men for women is also a problem that needs elucidating and is not a self-evident fact'. He also supported the notion of bisexuality, which again tended to lift homosexuality out of the realm of pathology. In short, Freud's most radical impulse was to separate the sexual drives from both aim and object; that is, from genitality and heterosexuality.[10]

It is also noticeable that Freud's famous case studies all contain homosexuality as a major theme, as if unconsciously he was drawn to it. One might suggest that in personal terms Freud was less anxious about homosexuality than some post-Freudians – for example, he was able to refer to the homosexual component in his friendship with Wilhelm Fliess and other male figures such as Jung (Gay 1995).

Against this more positive approach, however, one has to set Freud's (1916–17) positing of the heterosexual goal as an ideal against which homosexuality is seen to fail. This attitude is found in his more formal or public statements; for example: 'homosexuals ... are men and women who are often, although not always, irreproachably fashioned in other respects, of high intellectual and ethical development, the victims of *this one fatal deviation*' (p. 345; emphasis added).

The positing of the heterosexual goal or ideal condemns homosexuality as a state of 'arrested development', an avoidance of the conflicts of the Oedipus complex and an obliteration of the parental couple. Thus the gay man wipes out the mother by identifying with her; the lesbian wipes out the father. Another paraphrase of this is that the gay man flees from the female genital and finds an effigy of it in the anus; the lesbian flees from the penis in order to construct a pseudo-penis.

In fact, psychoanalysis has propounded various theories of homosexuality, including the following: for the male homosexual, an identification with mother and desire for father; narcissism – the male partner is an image of oneself; a reaction formation to rage at brothers and father; oral theory (the loss of the breast leading to the substitution of the penis), and so on.[11] The proliferation of different theories is in part a result of Freud's refusal to see homosexuality as a unitary condition (Freud 1905); it can also be seen as an indication of the difficulties which homosexuality presents within the psychoanalytic model. One can also argue that psychoanalysis has been fascinated and obsessed with homosexuality – in other words, very powerful countertransference affects are visible in this debate, often rationalized into a kind of frenzy of theorizing.

If Freud's attitude to homosexuality is therefore a contradictory one, many of his followers began to tilt towards a more negative stance. Eventually psychoanalysis, particularly in the US, acquired a pronounced homophobia, and took over the psychiatric definition of it as a sickness which demanded cure. Furthermore, the antipathy to gay men and lesbians often seems to be as much personal as theoretical. One can cite the gross personal remarks that are frequently made by analysts at public seminars, lectures and so on. One British analyst (Cunningham 1991), for example, remarked on '... the natural disgust we all feel when a homosexual passes in the street' (p. 50). I heard another remark in a supervision group, where, during a discussion of a woman who kept falling in love with gay men, the female supervisor suddenly said: 'She likes damaged goods then.' These remarks are surely strong evidence for unprocessed personal material as much as theoretical analysis.

I should also point out that the first example is taken from an article written in the *British Journal of Psychotherapy* (a largely analytical journal) by a psychotherapist *writing under a pseudonym*. What an amazing comment this is on the fear that still surrounds the discussion of homosexuality in psychoanalysis – that a relatively neutral article has to be written under a false name. I am reminded of Francis Bacon's barbed remark: '"What is Truth?" said jesting Pilate, and would not stay for an answer' (Bacon 1962, p. 3).

This prejudice among analysts has tended to produce huge flaws in analytic research on homosexuality: for example, results from studies of emotionally disturbed homosexuals are commonly extrapolated to the homosexual population at large. To put this rather crudely, the homophobic analyst might study a group of schizophrenic homosexuals, and infer that homosexuals are schizophrenic!

There are much more subtle examples than this: for example, one can cite Joyce McDougall's (1985) influential work on lesbianism. Her article 'Homosexuality in Women' begins by citing her clinical base: 'I have been fortunate enough to have had in analysis four homosexual women and three others who ... were dominated by conscious homosexual wishes' (p. 171). McDougall then states explicitly that many lesbians do not seek therapeutic help. There follows an eloquent description of her seven patients, describing various problems associated with their homosexual desires; for example, feelings of inadequacy, bitterness towards men, excessive masculinity, and so on. But then McDougall begins to talk generally about 'the homosexual woman', not just her seven patients: 'for the homosexual the father is lost as an object' (p. 191). One might think that such research demands the use of a control group – say, of lesbians who have not sought help from psychoanalysis or psychotherapy – but this kind of comparative study is very rare in analytic research.[12]

One also finds a rather naive use of the cause-effect relationship, for example, in the relation of family structure to sexual orientation. Perhaps the most famous example is the triangular relation of a distant father, close mother and gay son. A number of analysts have inferred from such family structures that male homosexuality is 'caused' by 'too much mother, not enough father'. However, one can reverse the causality – it is possible that having a gay son makes many fathers move away, fearful of too intimate a contact (Friedman 1988; Isay 1993).

Another example is the gender/sexuality connection; for example, the link between 'femininity' and male homosexuality, 'masculinity' and lesbianism. Some studies have shown that very feminine boys are likely to become gay – it is therefore tempting (but fallacious) to turn this into a causative relation: all gay men become gay because of excessive femininity. This shows a confusion between correlation and causation (Green 1987).

One might argue that Freud himself was rather casual about using case studies to form massive generalizations: after all, wasn't the Oedipus complex based on one study – of himself? Freud's writing also has a rather nineteenth-century imperious quality to it, as in the following extract:

We have discovered, especially clearly in people whose libidinal development has suffered some disturbance, such as perverts and homosexuals, that in their later choice of love-object, they have taken as a model not their mother but their own selves. They are plainly seeking *themselves* as a love-object, and are exhibiting a type of object-choice which must be termed narcissistic. (Freud 1914, p. 81; original emphasis.)

There is not much doubt here! Freud's language is very assertive – 'we have discovered', 'especially clearly', 'plainly', 'which must be termed' – and seems not to brook much disagreement. This seems to give such passages a hard-edged 'scientific' flavour, but it is open to question whether this is a matter of style rather than research methodology. Certainly much psychoanalytic writing on gender and sexuality has adopted this very assertive style, often based on very meagre clinical evidence.

I will mention one further aspect of analytic attitudes to homo-sexuality: there is a surprising dearth of research into the counter-transference effects of working with homosexual patients. Some of the intemperate language used by homophobic analysts seems to show strong personal bias, but this is generally not taken into account. One might also wonder if projective identification is a factor here: does the gay patient's projected self-hatred find a welcoming bosom in the homophobic analyst? This is a complex issue, since the negative countertransference may also conceal its opposite: say, at the least a *fascination* with homosexuality. I am not suggesting that there is anything wrong with such a fascination – I am sure that all psychotherapists are fascinated with certain areas of human psychol-ogy – but when it is concealed by a pronounced negativity, one might fairly claim that therapists are using their patients to work through their own material. Again, no doubt all therapists do that to an extent, but hopefully they also struggle to become aware of their own biases (O'Connor and Ryan 1993; Frommer 1995).

AETIOLOGY, PATHOLOGY AND CURE

One of the most striking aspects of the analytical approach to homosexu-ality is the hunt for causation. As outlined above, a number of 'causes' have been put forward, particularly for male homosexuality. As far as I know, analysts rarely stop to question their own methodology here – why is it important to discover the origins of homosexuality, whether it be in family structure, internal dynamics, or whatever? The answer to this question seems clear cut – it rests on the assumption that homosexuality is pathological. Then the question becomes: why have gay men and lesbi-ans 'deviated' from the norm? The presumption of pathology leads al-most automatically to the search for causation. This can be clearly dem-onstrated by examining heterosexuality: Freud is unusual in wondering how this arises. Most analysts and therapists assume that heterosexuality is the norm, and therefore one does not need to investigate it. What must be investigated is the 'abnormal'.

This line of argument has an interesting corollary: as homosexuality is depathologized, the quest for origins becomes less compelling; in fact, it becomes irrelevant. Thus, if a therapist is working with a gay or lesbian client who broadly accepts his or her own homosexuality, it seems as pointless to speculate why the client is gay as it is pointless to speculate why the heterosexual client is heterosexual. I am not saying that the issue never comes up, but it will not have the burning urgency that causation has in psychoanalysis.

Aetiology also connects with the issue of 'cure'; that is, if one's therapeutic stance is that therapy aims to 'cure' people of their homosexuality, then causation again becomes very important, for through an understanding of the 'deviation' from 'normal' sexuality, one might hope to put the patient back on the 'right lines'. For example, if one assumes that gay men have identified with their mother rather than their father, then a male therapist might conclude that the gay patient needs to identify with him as a male father-figure, and presumably begin to desire women.

Clearly, the nexus of pathology-causation-cure is a very intimate one in psychoanalytical thinking: conversely, the link is broken once the assumption of pathology is removed.

SHAME AND COLLUSION

A further corollary to these assumptions made in analytical thinking is that practitioners must also rely on collusion by their patients. That is, if a homosexual patient visits a therapist who is convinced that homosexuality is 'sick', perverse, regressive, or whatever, what is such a therapist to do if the homosexual patient has not come to therapy in order to become heterosexual, but to attend to problems much as a heterosexual patient would – depression, emotional problems, and so on? Of course, the therapist has the option of trying to persuade the patient that the root of his or her problems is his or her homosexuality, but that seems both highly risky and unprofessional.

To put this argument more starkly, homophobic therapists must rely on the homosexual's shame and self-hatred. No doubt this is one reason for the growth in gay therapists, whom gay patients are less likely to suspect of a covert agenda to convert them to heterosexuality!

This correspondence between patient shame and therapist blame throws a stark light on those analysts who have taken an uncompromisingly anti-gay line. One must assume that their patients were nearly all full of self-hatred and shame, otherwise how could the therapy make any meaningful progress?

HISTORICIZING PSYCHOANALYSIS

Within the overall history of ideas in Western culture, psychoanalysis has suffered from an inability to historicize its own contribution and the socio-political context in which it has operated. In fact, such speculations are explicitly rejected by Freud and post-Freudians, except for the 'left wing', who attempted to integrate some political theory – for example, Karen Horney, Erich Fromm and Wilhelm Reich.

In particular, a theory of patriarchy (which I shall define loosely as the systematic political domination of women by men) throws a very different light on certain psychoanalytic ideas: for example, the subordination of women, viewed by Freud as an inevitable consequence of biological and instinctual structures, can be seen as part of the patriarchal 'project' – the construction of 'woman' as the mysterious but deeply flawed Other, who is required to service male needs and fantasies.

The same can be said of homosexuality. Once the heterosexual ideal (or 'compulsory heterosexuality') is posited as a linchpin of patriarchal ideology, then it is axiomatic that homosexuality is a 'failure' or a 'fixation'. Thus, Joyce McDougall, in the article mentioned above, discusses the 'sublimation' of homosexuality in women, as against those women who do not sublimate it but express it actively. This is necessarily seen by McDougall as a 'problem' within the psychoanalytic paradigm: 'the overt homosexual ... has met with severe impediments to the harmonious integration of her homosexual drives' (McDougall 1985, p. 173). This strikes me as a perfect tautology, since 'integration' is already defined as 'sublimation'. Thus, the 'integration' of heterosexual desire is defined as *committing* heterosexual acts, but the integration of homosexual desire is its sublimation, and hence, *not committing* homosexual acts; or, to put it crudely, straight people act, gays and lesbians act out.

Thus, socio-historical issues cannot be said to be absent from psychoanalysis, but they are present in a veiled form. In particular, certain characteristics of a patriarchal and capitalist society, such as the dominant position of men and the oppressed condition of women, the abuse meted out to children, the strangulation that is put upon people's sexuality, the punishment meted out to non-heterosexual people – features of particular societies at a particular point in history

– are transformed by Freud into products of inexorable biological or instinctual conflicts.

It has been argued therefore by some therapeutic and sexual radicals, from a socio-political point of view, that the Oedipus complex – the failure to traverse which, Freud claims, produces many pathologies and immature sexualities – can instead be seen as the pathologizing instrument (Brenkman 1993).

In the case of homosexuality, it can be argued, *contra* Freud, that it is not the failure of the homosexual to reach the end-game in the Oedipal snakes and ladders which labels him or her as pathological, but nineteenth-century patriarchal society itself which must pathologize homosexuality in order to preserve that peculiar mix of sexuality, property relations and reproduction which it calls its own, and shrouds in a cloak of mystification, holiness and 'nature', and which Freud reified as an eternal Oedipal conflict. From the standpoint of a radical sexual politics, the homosexual is not damned for getting stuck half-way on the Oedipal ladder, but damned by a patriarchal bourgeois order desperate to prop itself up.

Psychoanalysis biologizes patriarchal social relations, and thereby naturalizes and legitimates the oppression of women and homosexuals, the abuse of children, and the crippling of many heterosexual people by guilt, hate and envy. One can see straight away the gulf between such socio-political argumentation and the psychological criteria used in psychotherapy – for many analysts and therapists the above ideas are simply irrelevant or alien. However, this does not necessarily mean that psychotherapy is intrinsically an apolitical discipline; rather, its political assumptions and alignments are covert.

SCIENCE AND IDEOLOGY

At this point, it seems important to stand back from this historical narrative and consider the overall effect of medicine, psychiatry and psychoanalysis on homosexuality. The net effect is to subject 'the homosexual' to a merciless reification and objectification. Charitably, one might suggest that a kind of 'naive scientism' transformed homosexuality into a 'scientific object', to be scrutinized under the microscope, as so many other phenomena were in the nineteenth and early twentieth centuries. However, that would be to adopt the uncritical attitude of such science towards itself. Against that, one can suggest that such scientific enquiry into human behaviour always has a covert political or ideological bent.

This critique is now familiar from the writings of feminists, radical gay theorists, and others such as Foucault.[13] Science, such thinkers have argued, can be shown to have an unconscious ideological drive – in the case of sexology and psychiatry, arguably to prop up the heterosexual order, which is itself one of the bulwarks of patriarchal society; to justify the criminalization of sexual 'perversions'; to blend an apparent zeal for 'cure' with a more covert but discernible wish to punish. There may be also more subtle nuances involved in the creation of 'sexualities'; for example, a covert fascination with 'perversion', which one can indulge under the guise of 'scientific' research. In effect, this is part of the critique levelled at Freud by Jung (1983): that he had theorized and rationalized a very personal fascination, not to say obsession, with sexuality, and turned it into a quasi-religious enterprise.

Several important socio-political and philosophical issues stand out in relation to the invention of 'sexuality' and 'sexual perversions'. The first is the creation of 'the Other' – a series of outcast figures who embody split-off, projected desires, which can then be safely examined under the fascinated gaze of 'science' and also condemned by a morally outraged public. Foucault has argued in books such as *Madness and Civilization* (1961) and *Discipline and Punish* (1975), that during the modern (post-Enlightenment) era, a number of such 'Others' have been constructed: the mad person, the criminal, the homosexual. To this, one must add the supreme Other within patriarchal society: woman.

Second, the process I have already referred to as 'objectification' is of great importance. 'The homosexual' is not allowed to speak in such scientific enquiries; he or she is subject to an investigation designed to reveal pathological tendencies, but not to reveal subjective states, or self-definitions, or desires and hopes. The object of study is alienated from the study itself and from those carrying out the study.

Third, 'the Other' not only contains aspects of the self which are rejected, but also things which are secretly desired. Thus black people were not only condemned as 'indolent' and 'feckless', but also secretly envied for their 'sensuality', their 'natural athleticism', 'large penises' and so on. Perhaps, then, gay men and lesbians are repositories of forbidden desires which bourgeois society must keep safely at a distance. Thus, there are many common fantasies amongst hetero-sexual people as to the 'promiscuity', 'sexual proclivity', and 'extreme lifestyles' of homosexuals.

The great revolutionary energy of the gay movement has therefore been the transformation of the mute inert object of 'scientific enquiry' into the speaking subject, ablaze with passion and indignation, determined to celebrate the varieties of human sexuality. This transformation surely represents an earthquake, and is similar to that found in feminism. 'The Other' itself begins to define itself, reclaims its own subjectivity and its own identity, and becomes an 'I'.

This revolution makes us look back at the 'science of sex' and suggest that it is bad science, in the sense that such a reifying and alienating procedure does not actually uncover the truth of a phenomenon, but pigeon-holes it into a set of pre-existing categories. This may be one reason why the Kinsey Report (1948) was greeted by psychoanalysts with coolness and hostility: Kinsey did something revolutionary – he asked people about their sexuality and treated their answers with respect (Lewes 1989).

SOCIAL CONSTRUCTION

I have already alluded briefly to the body of ideas known as social constructionism. This argues that human sexualities do not exist 'out there' in nature, simply waiting to be identified by sexologists, much as unknown species of mammal or bird lie hidden in the rainforest. They are constituted, invented, in and by the actual discourses of sexology, medicine, psychiatry, and so on. The 'invert' and the 'pervert' are therefore not objective phenomena, but phenomena brought into being by the actual discursive framework of the 'science of sex'.

This argument can be backed up by various kinds of evidence: first, that homosexual behaviour is found in many societies, but, second, that its social expression and interpretation vary considerably, and third, that attitudes to it vary widely. Anthropologists report cultures where male homosexuality is completely accepted, those where it is heavily stigmatized, and others where there is a degree of ambivalence (Gilmore 1990).

Even more interesting is the social expression of homosexuality. This also varies enormously. One can cite, for example, the Native American Berdache – men who dress as women, have women's occupations and have sex with other men; the Hindu Hijra – castrated men who adopt women's clothes, become devotees of a Hindu goddess and work as prostitutes; the ritualized fellatio of certain pre-industrial cultures (for example, the Sambian), and so on (Horrocks 1997).

Social constructionism also argues that these 'sexualities' do not exist in a context of political neutrality, but are used as a means of political control or ideological manipulation. This can be seen in extreme form in societies such as Nazi Germany, where women were exhorted to become breeding machines, homosexuals were gassed in the death camps, and a bizarre theory of eugenics became the ideology of the state and led to genocide.

This is an extreme example, but the battle over Clause 28 in Britain, and the world-wide struggles over AIDS show how sexuality is not politically neutral, but in fact becomes a fierce battleground between different groups, including the state itself.

A contemporary example concerning homosexuality can be found in Zimbabwe, whose president, Robert Mugabe, made a series of extremely homophobic speeches during the 1980s and 1990s. He has argued that homosexuality is not native to Africa, but is imported by Western imperialism, and that it is highly unnatural.[14] There seems little doubt, whatever Mugabe's personal views on homosexuality, that he is using homophobic utterances to whip up popular support for himself and his government, and to construct scapegoats in Zimbabwean society, presumably to deter criticism of his own government.

Do these socio-political arguments have relevance for psychotherapy? Generally therapy and analysis have remained aloof from such political debates, but there is a great danger in this: that therapy itself will surreptitiously become, or indeed has become, part of an ideological apparatus. The fact that the psychotherapy world is not very good at interrogating its own socio-political role is itself suspicious, for ignorance or neglect in this area often suggests covert complicity. Is therapy part of a punitive or controlling apparatus? Does it covertly support the hegemony of the 'straight white male' and the hegemony of the patriarchal heterosexist state?

Surely today therapists, therapeutic organizations and training institutes are called upon to examine their own position in socio-political terms, particularly *vis-à-vis* those people who were formerly marginalized, and who are now demanding a voice – women, black people, gays and lesbians, children, and so on.

At this point, it is important to mention one of the possible dangers in a zealous adoption of social constructionism – that in its stress on the social relativity of sexual categories such as 'heterosexual' and 'homosexual', it might ignore or diminish the subjective experience of the gay man or lesbian. The same danger can be seen in those radical feminists and others who have argued that the category of 'woman' is itself a creation of patriarchy, and should be rejected (Wittig 1993). But what about those women who want to celebrate their 'womanhood'? Thus the deconstruction of categories and labels might begin to infringe on others' sense of identity, which they may have spent much effort and pain in acquiring. The gay community could object with some cogency that it is they who have created their sense of identity and their lifestyle, and not late capitalism or patriarchal society. A radical social constructionist – or a Marxist – could well argue, however, that this smacks of voluntarism, and ignores the 'spirals of power'[15] in which we are all enmeshed; that to say 'I create my own identity', whether gay or heterosexual, is an inflated fantasy, denying our own subjection to the operations of an alienated social order (Emilio 1993).

REIFICATION

If we bring together ideas from social constructionism together with a radical psychoanalytic model, the results are quite startling. In a brilliant article entitled 'Current Psychoanalytic Discourses on Sexuality', the American psychoanalyst David Schwarz (1995) argues that both anti-gay and pro-gay analysts and therapists tend to reify sexuality into a small number of discrete categories – heterosexuality, homosexuality and bisexuality – thereby obscuring the radicalism of Freud's theory of sexuality as not intrinsically tied to aim or object. As we have seen, Freud also reified sexual categories himself, and prioritized heterosexuality, but then Freud's ideas are often contradictory. But the most radical aspect of Freud lies in the flexibility and fluidity of unconscious desire.

Schwarz can argue therefore that both those therapists who affirm heterosexuality and those who affirm homosexuality are actually accepting concepts derived from popular thinking or 'folk' sexology. To put it more dramatically, they are operating under the aegis of a naive social empiricism which records 'what is' and does not penetrate beneath the surface to the realm of unconscious desire, and which is full of contradictions. One can draw a parallel here with Marx, who protested that most economists and political radicals also accepted whatever existed on the surface of society, and did not strive to grasp the 'deep structure'.

Of course, one can also argue, *contra* Schwarz, that those people seeking psychotherapy often want to conform to such sexual/social stereotypes, and that to suggest to them that their sexuality is much more mysterious and less well defined than they think is not very helpful. Here we find one of the fascinating paradoxes present in psychotherapy: how much does the therapist help the client to find social conformity and acceptability and how much to stress unconventionality? This question is automatically answered within 'patient-directed' forms of therapy: it depends on what the patient/client wants. The therapist ideally has no wants, and certainly does not impose his or her wants on the patient.

One can also refer here to the need for compromise in life. We all have to find ways of finding a middle ground between our deepest desires and the social context we are in. One person wants a stable one-to-one relationship and is prepared to sacrifice other, less conventional, desires; but someone else feels committed to a life of sexual diversity. Perhaps one of the dangers of extreme sexual radicalism is that it ignores many people's wish for safety and conventionality, or, at any rate, some kind of acceptance within a social milieu. In relation to psychotherapy with gay men and lesbians, one might assume that being a 'gay man' or a 'lesbian' is something that many patients would want to celebrate rather than challenge or 'deconstruct'.

What Schwarz's paper does suggest is that the reification of homosexuality is the mirror-image of the reification of heterosexuality, since neither allows for the presence of desires which do not fit into these neat boxes, nor for the simultaneous presence of both desires.

This line of argument suggests therefore that many 'theories of sexuality' are actually theories about the social classifications that have been imposed on sexuality. This is what I mean by 'social empiricism': the acceptance of categories which have been brought into being by the bourgeois/patriarchal order. The revolution wrought by radical social constructionists and some radical therapists is therefore, first, to go back to the most radical impulse in Freud – the notion of polymorphous perversity – and second, to argue, in a completely non-Freudian manner, that all sexualities are socially constructed, or, even more audaciously, are *politically* constructed. But perhaps many gay men and lesbians might accept that point without wishing to see the notions of 'gay man' and 'lesbian' deconstructed in too nihilistic a manner.

THE GAY MOVEMENT

The twentieth century has been a revolutionary one. It has witnessed many political revolutions – by colonial peoples in Africa and Asia, and by oppressed nationalities in Europe and elsewhere. It has also been an era in which marginalized people, those who lacked a voice or an important role in society and culture, began to speak and to assert themselves. The obvious example is feminism in the widest sense. Women have changed their own lives considerably – they have acquired the vote, fought for equality in employment, asserted their right to sexual pleasure, and their right to choose contraception and abortion. Of course, this revolution is not at an end, it is ongoing.

This kind of social revolution, whereby those on the periphery of political power, or who are excluded from power, begin to find their voice and claim power for themselves, is a widespread phenomenon. It can be witnessed in the struggles of black people in white societies; in the advance of working-class people in some societies; perhaps even in children, whose right to be free of abuse is a comparatively recent demand. And of course one must include here the gay movement – the energetic and disruptive self-assertion by gay men and lesbians of their own legitimacy, their right to be homosexual, and to have those relationships and lifestyles which seem right to them. This revolution has been at work throughout the twentieth century, but has really taken off in the last 30 years. It has achieved the decriminalization of homosexuality in some societies such as Britain and the US, and some degree of tolerance by heterosexual people, although this seems to be highly volatile.

One of the extraordinary things about the gay movement is that apparent reverses often seem to have been turned into further advances in self-assertion and confidence. For example, the AIDS epidemic produced a wave of reactionary and punitive propaganda amongst politicians, clergy, the media, and so on (David 1997). One might imagine that the gay community, faced with so many deaths from AIDS, and faced with such hatred and obloquy, would suffer a loss of confidence. But the contrary seems to have happened – the gay community counter-attacked with considerable *élan*, took practical steps to fight AIDS, and came out of the initial crisis in an even greater state of confidence.

Part of this process of 'liberation' has been one of exorcism. Gay men and lesbians have begun to cast out their own shame and self-hatred about being homosexual – after all, homophobia at large, whether practised by governments or 'queer-bashers' in the street, works most powerfully when it meets with an internalized homophobia in the gay person.

TELLING THE STORY

Every oppressed group must find a way to tell its own story – this is part of the revolution. Part of the rise of the gay movement has been to investigate their own history; that is, to uncover both the positive contributions which lesbians and gay men have made to society and culture, and the barbaric punishments they have had to endure. The construction of this historical narrative has different facets. To a degree, it is a question of uncovering the 'hidden history' of homosexuals, just as feminists have begun to dig up from obscurity women artists and writers, women who had political importance, or women who were pioneers in formulating feminist ideas.

There is also theoretical work to be done, since there have been many 'theories of homosexuality' within psychiatry, psychoanalysis, psychotherapy and other psychological disciplines. As we have seen, many of these theories have a negative or punitive slant, since homosexuality has often been used to prioritize and valorize hetero-sexuality. But gay theoreticians have not been content to refute such theories of homosexuality – they have turned the tables by formulating theories of heterosexuality which show it in a less idealized light. For example, feminist lesbians have mounted a ferocious indictment of the misery inflicted on many women in the name of 'compulsory heterosexuality' (Wilkinson and Kitzinger 1993).

Above all, gay liberation, like feminism, changes an *object* into a *subject*. Homosexuals, like women, existed as reified objects of enquiry by psychiatry and medicine and other voices of patriarchal ideology, but began to find their own voice, began to speak of their own condition, and began to tell their own story instead of having their story told for them.

Homosexuality was defined as a problem by patriarchal ideology, of which psychoanalysis has been one of the chief standard bearers, but homosexuals began to announce that although they might be a problem for patriarchy, they did not have a problem. Their solution is no longer to hate themselves, but to declare their autonomy and their right to live a gay life.

FEMINISM

I have already indicated that feminism has made certain theoretical contributions to the study of gender and sexuality which are of great relevance to the study of homosexuality.

First, feminism politicized sexuality, arguing that heterosexuality does not represent a 'natural' or 'biological' principle, but enshrines and mystifies the sexual subordination of women to men. The notion of 'compulsory heterosexuality' has been used graphically to illustrate this point, and has obvious relevance to an analysis of homosexuality (Rich 1993).

Second, the concept of patriarchy is central to the feminist revolution. Patriarchy can be defined as the political domination of women by men, plus the mystification of that domination. But patriarchy does not simply refer to such matters as being able to vote or being able to join professions on an equal footing with men. Feminists have been able to scrutinize the minutiae of 'private life', and have shown that relations between men and women are shot through with patriarchal assumptions and injunctions. Again, it can be argued that it is patriarchy that pathologizes gays and lesbians, and also, paradoxically, sets up the category of 'homosexuality' in order to delimit and police the heterosexual norm.

Third, feminist lesbianism brings together feminism and a militant self-conscious homosexuality. Lesbians have provided a fierce critique of heterosexuality as a form of coercion, and a number of lesbian theorists have made very radical deconstructions of all categories of gender and sexuality, not excluding the category 'woman' itself.

Lesbianism has been of great importance in the revision of theories of homosexuality since feminist lesbianism has politicized homosexuality, and has argued that heterosexuality itself is not a 'natural' state of affairs but is a form of political tyranny. Some feminists have argued therefore that women are able to choose not to be heterosexual. However, this view has been contested by other feminists, both on the grounds that heterosexuality is not *per se* a reactionary position, and that such arguments smack of naive voluntarism (Segal 1994). That is, it is doubtful if one can change one's sexual orientation with ease, if at all. More radical lesbians have objected to the liberalism implicit in the 'lesbianism as choice' argument, arguing that this depoliticizes the lesbian position (Kitzinger 1987).

Lesbianism has also raised many important issues in the fields of gender and sexuality such as the eroticization of power, the use of pornography, sado-masochism, and so on. One of the criticisms that can be made of some lesbian theorizing is that it seems to come dangerously close to a kind of essentialism: lesbianism seems to exist in nature as an original condition. There is also an implicit moralism here: heterosexuality is bad, men are bad, patriarchy is bad, but lesbianism is good. From a psychological point of view, one might want to question the unconscious projections that are being made here. This is ironic, since there is little doubt that lesbianism itself is the target for many projections in contemporary culture – witness the many lesbians who figure in Hollywood films such as *Basic Instinct*, often shown as vampirish, homicidal maniacs (hoogland 1997). However, the solution to being a scapegoat is not necessarily to scapegoat others.

Of course this point can be made about the gay movement in general – it is very tempting to re-project all the sickness and badness and madness that have been imputed to homosexuality back on to heterosexuality. One might paraphrase this as: 'No, I'm not the bad/mad one, you are!'

Clearly, there are many interesting parallels between feminism and the gay movement. Both women and homosexuals have been casualties of psychiatry and psychoanalysis: women by being cast as half-men, a castrated sex forever mourning their lost penis, and forever struggling to find an effigy of it; homosexuals for failing to traverse the Oedipal journey fully, for 'obliterating the parental couple', and so on. It is therefore fascinating to contemplate the rise of feminism and the gay movement in the last 30 years. These forces have risen up not against psychoanalysis or psychiatry in themselves, but rather against the ideological and socio-political barbarism of which they have been part. Feminists have been able to make a formidable retort to their wounding by psychoanalysis. It can be paraphrased as follows: 'we *are* castrated, not by our anatomy, but by the social relations of patriarchy and the institutions of patriarchy, of which psychoanalysis and psychiatry are part. We refute this castration; we claim our right to be autonomous, to seek our own sexual pleasure, our own social and political power.' Another way of putting this is that the famous question put by Freud – 'What do women want?' – is being answered by women themselves, as self-assertive subjects, no longer wishing to be objectified by 'experts' and 'scientists'.

The 'problem' in being homosexual can be similarly expressed: the homosexual 'object of enquiry', presenting such a puzzle to psychiatrists, psychoanalysts and others, begins to speak as a subject, begins to define itself and its aims and needs. Furthermore, the concept of patriarchy – the domination of men over women – proves indispensable in a radical theory of homosexuality, for just as women have complained that their 'inferiority' was not a 'natural' one, but one imposed under patriarchy, so gay men and lesbians can argue that the patriarchal bourgeois order, centred as it is on marital heterosexuality, scorns and castigates homosexuality as 'deviant', 'perverse', 'sick', and so on. In other words, patriarchy has as one of its ideological building blocks 'heterosexism'. The fight against this covert political agenda has transformed the debate over homosexuality – lesbians and gay men no longer feel defensive about their sexual orientation, but can go on the offensive to argue that heterosexuality is neither idyllic nor particularly successful.

GENETICS

Many radical feminists and social constructionists have scorned the use of biological concepts in the examination of gender and sexuality. Biology itself has been shown not to be ideologically or politically neutral, but to contain many covert assumptions about 'masculinity', 'femininity', 'heterosexuality', and so on (Haraway 1989). The concepts of 'nature' and the 'natural' have been shown to be loaded with many unstated political concepts (Weeks 1991).

However, research work in genetics has provided, in the last 15 years, a number of fascinating findings in relation to sexual orientation which have provoked great debate in the gay community. The most interesting areas of research are as follows:

1. Twin and familial studies seem to show that the incidence of homosexuality is high among people who have close relatives who are homosexual. Thus identical twins show a very high 'concordance', more than dissimilar twins and ordinary siblings (Friedman 1988).

2. Research into the 'gay brain' claims that homosexual men have a different brain structure from heterosexual men (Levay 1993).

3. Geneticists have been interested in looking for a 'genetic marker' that is found in homosexuals and not heterosexuals (Hamer et al. 1993).

All of this research must be set against the nature/nurture debates which have raged in relation to other areas; for example, human sexuality as a whole, and language. Most radical theorists of gender and sexuality are sharply opposed to any genetic proposals, since it smacks too much of traditional views; for example, that men are 'naturally' sexually voracious and women are inherently demure. However, to discard any genetic argument seems to be a case of throwing the baby away with the bathwater.

Some gay activists and theorists have welcomed evidence as to the genetic status of homosexuality since this transforms all the moral arguments. One cannot really be accused of moral turpitude if one's sexually is genetically influenced. On the other hand, others have objected to genetic research since it muddies the political analysis of sexual orientation. If being gay or lesbian is seen as a critique of patriarchal society and its values, the 'biologizing' of homosexuality might be seen as an attempt to depoliticize the ferment over gender and sexuality (Sartelle 1994).

PSYCHOTHERAPY AND HOMOSEXUALITY

After considering various paradigms of homosexuality which exist today, one might withdraw in a state of confusion and exhaustion – how can one make sense of such a plethora of theoretical schemes?

The answer, surely, is that no one makes a purely objective or rational assessment of such theories: for example, the homophobic psychoanalyst has not intellectually decided upon his or her stance after a calm and measured examination of the literature on homosexuality. This is the problem: homophobia is evidence of an undigested or unprocessed personal complex. As Rachel Cunningham (1991) remarks about offensive anti-gay remarks made by analysts: 'The force of the impact is not just an indicator of the hypersensitivity of the object – the gay members of the group or audience – it is also an indicator of an unintegrated piece of the speaker's psyche, evacuated at high speed.'

One might feel a certain shock or dismay that psychoanalysis – so proudly fêted by Freud as a discipline which does not shrink from the uncovering of unpalatable unconscious motives and wishes – is capable of such unconscious hatred. However, that would be to idealize psychoanalysis to an alarming degree – why should it be exempt from normal human prejudice and hatreds? Arguably, all social groups, if they are to maintain internal cohesion and integrity, need to hate and scapegoat something (Freud 1921). What is of great historical interest is why psychoanalysts elected to hate homosexuality with such venom and such unconsciousness.

At the other end of the spectrum from homophobia is the position of 'gay affirmation', which mainly represents the stance taken by Humanistic and Existential psychotherapists. For an analytic therapist or a psychoanalyst, gay affirmation smacks too much of special pleading. There are also therapists who are gay who prefer not to be known as 'gay therapists', since they do not have a special identification with the gay movement.

One can imagine in fact that having a therapist who is 'gay affirmative' might prove to be a block for some gay patients/clients, as they might feel too guilty about exploring their own negative feelings about being gay or lesbian. Of course, having a therapist who feels negatively about homosexuality is worse, and one can understand that many gay and lesbian people seeking therapy want to find a therapist who is either gay or actively 'gay affirmative'. To work with an analytic therapist who refused to divulge his or her own feelings about homosexuality might prove rather nerve-racking! On the other hand, it might force one to face one's own underlying attitudes.

Another opposition to 'gay affirmation' can be found in radical feminist theorists, who argue that this 'liberal Humanistic' position still ghettoizes lesbians, and does not permit a political understanding of lesbianism. In her book *The Social Construction of Lesbianism*, Celia Kitzinger (1987) argues that the liberal position privatizes and individualizes sexuality, so that lesbianism becomes a matter of choice and lifestyle. She argues that lesbianism can be a political stance taken against patriarchal sexuality.

One of the merits of this argument is that it deconstructs the liberal attitude towards homosexuality. Liberal humanism tends to assume that it is not itself an ideological position; that somehow it is 'objective' or democratic. Kitzinger, however, argues that liberalism is just as intent on finding a means of social control as more obviously tyrannical forms of control.

This argument is sometimes made about government legislation about homosexuality. Thus the 1967 legislation which decriminalized homosexuality in Britain has two faces: on the one hand, no doubt it was a great relief to gay men, on the other hand, such legislation still assumes that the state has the right to legislate about sexuality. In fact, following the 1967 decriminalization in Britain, prosecutions of gay men actually increased (Haste 1994).

INTRUSIVENESS

One of the most important and interesting issues to come out of a wide-ranging overview of different paradigms of homosexuality is the extent to which they influence psychotherapy, and the extent to which this might be felt as intrusive by patients. To take an extreme example, if one encountered a psychotherapist who militantly argued that human sexuality was a social construction and did not have biological or instinctual roots, one might, as a patient, feel rather diffident about talking about one's own sexuality as a kind of instinct or physical drive, even if this was one's subjective experience. But this would be the case whatever the view put forward militantly by a psychotherapist.

In other words, one normally expects therapists to maintain a kind of tact in these matters, thus permitting the patient to put forward his or her own views.

However, 'tact' does not equal 'vacuum'. In other words, one cannot really argue that therapists should operate without any views on sexuality or any other issue. That is plainly absurd. But it does bring into focus the extent to which the therapist's own ideas are welcome or intrusive in the course of the psychotherapeutic relationship.

In this light, one of the arguments that can be brought against the anti-gay analysts is that they are putting their finger too strongly on one side of the balance. One does not expect one's therapist to disapprove too strongly of one's own lifestyle or actions – that may well reinforce the shame and guilt that many patients/clients feel.

Clearly, there is a delicate balancing act to be carried out here: on the one hand, every therapist does have ideas and feelings about sexuality, and these inform his or her work as a therapist; on the other hand, one does not want them to be too intrusive.

CONCLUSIONS

At present, a large number of competing paradigms or discourses concerning homosexuality co-exist. In this brief sketch I have outlined seven: the moral/religious, the psychiatric, the psychoanalytic, social constructionism, feminism, the gay movement and genetics. There are many overlaps; for example, between the psychiatric and the psychoanalytic, and between feminism, the gay movement and social constructionism. Broadly speaking, one can speak of 'conservative', 'liberal' and 'radical' positions: psychoanalysis has traditionally taken a conservative stance – that homosexuality is pathological and can (even 'should') be 'cured'. Some feminist and 'gay affirmative' therapists take a more liberal position: that sexual orientation is not pathological, and does not need to be 'cured'. There may be a small number of 'radical' therapists who argue that sexual orientation is a socio-political construction and is not simply a matter of personal choice.

Clearly there has been a key shift during the twentieth century: from the reification and pathologization of 'homosexuality', seeing gay men and lesbians as alienated objects, to the subjectivization and positive affirmation of 'gay experience'. This shift has happened in society at large, but has begun to influence psychotherapy, much as feminism has influenced therapy.

One can also point to an opposition, even a gulf, between the socio-political arguments used in feminism and social constructionism, as against the psychological criteria used in psychotherapy. These two approaches often seem quite incompatible, yet one powerful critique of therapy is precisely that it has been politically naive or unconscious, and that it has to wake up to its own hidden political stances, some of which seem quite prejudiced.

Optimistically, one can suggest then that psychotherapy can rid itself of an unconscious and chronic homophobia and a construction of 'the homosexual Other' which is both estranging and projective. The considerable impact of feminism on psychotherapy, and indeed upon all intellectual and artistic disciplines, demonstrates how apparently immovable structures can be dismantled fairly rapidly. Homosexuality remains as a dark corner within the therapy world; a place where prejudice and hatred have flourished. Of course, no one can seriously suggest that the hatreds possessed by all human beings can be abolished, but homophobia represents *an unconscious and denied hatred* – that is the poison which has infected psychoanalysis and other areas of psychotherapy. In the long run, as Freud said, 'one cannot run away from oneself' (Freud 1926, p. 303). Homosexuality has cast long shadows in the world of psychotherapy, but now it is surely time for daylight to replace darkness.

NOTES

1 On clause 28, see Jeffrey Weeks (1991, pp. 134–56); on analysts' support for Clause 28, see Ellis (1997, pp. 369–83).
2 On the erasure of lesbianism, see renée c. hoogland (1997).
3 'Letter of Concern', in *British Journal of Psychotherapy* (1996) 12 (3).
4 Personal communication, Alan Danks.
5 On Greece and Rome, see Rousselle (1993).
6 See the letters between Freud and J. J. Putman cited in Abelove (1993).
7 *Guardian*, 17 June 1997, p. 7.
8 A phrase used by Jeffrey Weeks (1985, p. 44).
9 These texts are collected together in Abelove (1993).
10 The comments on homosexuality and heterosexuality are in S. Freud, *Three Essays on the Theory of Sexuality* (1905, pp. 56–7n); he also discusses bisexuality (ibid., pp. 52–5).
11 Freud summarizes his own theories in 'Some Neurotic Mechanisms in Jealousy, Paranoia and Homosexuality', in Freud (1993), *On Psychopathology* (PFL 10) pp. 197–208. A wider survey of post-Freudian theories can be found in Lewes (1989).
12 A much more extensive critique of McDougall's work can be found in O'Connor and Ryan (1993, pp. 102–3).
13 See the writings of Donna Haraway: for example, *Primate Visions: Gender, Race and Nature in the World of Modern Science* (1989); *Simians, Cyborgs and Women: the Reinvention of Nature* (1991).
14 Reported in the *Herald*, Harare, Zimbabwe, 12 August 1995, p. 1; *Globe and Mail*, Harare, 12 August 1995, p. A8.
15 'Spirals of power' is a phrase used by Foucault (1990, p. 45).

REFERENCES

Note: 'PFL' denotes the Penguin Freud Library.

Abelove, H. (1993) 'Freud, male homosexuality and the Americans', in Abelove, H., Barale, M. A. and Halperin, D. M. (eds) *The Lesbian and Gay Studies Reader*, New York: Routledge.
Bacon, F. (1962) 'Of Truth', in *Essays*, London: Dent.
Boswell, J. (1980) *Christianity, Social Tolerance and Homosexuality*, Chicago, IL: University of Chicago Press.
Brenkman, J. (1993) *Straight Male Modern: A Cultural Critique of Psychoanalysis*, New York: Routledge.

Cunningham, R. (1991) 'When is a Pervert not a Pervert?' *British Journal of Psychotherapy*, 8 (1): 50–1.

Davies, D. and Neal, C. (eds) (1996) *Pink Therapy: A Guide for Counsellors and Therapists Working with Lesbian, Gay and Bisexual Clients*, Buckingham: Open University Press.

David, H. (1997) *On Queer Street: A Social History of British Homosexuality 1895–1995*, London: HarperCollins.

Domenici, T. (1995) 'Exploding the Myth of Sexual Psychopathology: A Deconstruction of Fairbairn's anti-homosexual Theory', in Domenici, T. and Lesser, R. C. (eds) *Disorienting Sexuality: Psychoanalytic Reappraisals of Sexual Identities*, New York: Routledge.

Ellis, M. L. (1997) 'Who Speaks? Who Listens? Different Voices and Different Sexualities', *British Journal of Psychotherapy*, 13 (3): 369–83.

Emilio, J. (1993) 'Capitalism and Gay Identity', in Abelove, H., Barale, M. A. and Halperin, D. M. (eds), *The Lesbian and Gay Studies Reader*, New York: Routledge.

Foucault, M. (1990) *The History of Sexuality: An Introduction*, Harmondsworth: Penguin.

Freud, S. (1905) 'Three Essays on the Theory of Sexuality', in *On Sexuality* (PFL 7) Harmondsworth: Penguin (1979).

Freud, S. (1914) 'On Narcissism', *On Metapsychology* (PFL 11), Harmondsworth: Penguin (1991).

Freud, S. (1916–17) *Introductory Lectures on Psychoanalysis* (PFL 1), Harmondsworth: Penguin (1991).

Freud, S. (1921) 'Group Psychology and the Analysis of the Ego', in *Civilization, Society and Religion* (PFL 12), Harmondsworth: Penguin (1991).

Freud, S. (1926) 'The Question of Lay Analysis', in *Historical and Expository Works in Psychoanalysis* (PFL 15), Harmondsworth: Penguin (1993).

Freud, S. (1993) *On Psychopathology* (PFL 10), Harmondsworth: Penguin.

Friedman, R. C. (1988) *Male Homosexuality: A Contemporary Psychoanalytic Perspective*, New Haven, CT: Yale University Press.

Frommer, M. S. (1995) 'Countertransference Obscurity in the Psychoanalytic Treatment of Homosexual Patients', in Domenici, T. and Lesser, R. C. (eds) *Disorienting Sexuality*, New York: Routledge.

Gay, P. (1995) *Freud: A Life For Our Time*, London: Papermac.

Gilmore, D. (1990) *Manhood in the Making: Cultural Concepts of Masculinity*, New Haven, CT: Yale University Press.

Green, R. (1987) *The 'Sissy Boy Syndrome' and the Development of Homosexuality*, New Haven: Yale University Press.

Hamer, D., Hu, S., Magnuson, V., and Pattatucci, A. (1993) 'A Linkage Between DNA Markers on the X Chromosome and Male Sexual Orientation', *Science*, 261: 321–7.

Haraway, D. (1989) *Primate Visions: Gender, Race and Nature in the World of Modern Science*, New York: Routledge.

Haraway, D. (1991) *Simians, Cyborgs and Women: The Reinvention of Nature*, London: Free Association Books.

Haste, C. (1994) *Rules of Desire: Sex in Britain: World War One to Present*, London: Pimlico.

hoogland, r. c. (1997) *Lesbian Configurations*, Cambridge: Polity Press.

Horrocks, R. (1997) *An Introduction to the Study of Sexuality*, Basingstoke: Macmillan.

Isay, R. (1993) *Being Homosexual: Gay Men and their Development*, Harmondsworth: Penguin.

Jung, C. G. (1983) *Memories, Dreams and Reflections*, London: Flamingo.

Kinsey, A., Pomeroy, W. and Martin C. (1948) *Sexual Behaviour in the Human Male*, Philadelphia, PA: W.B. Saunders.

Kitzinger, C. (1987) *The Social Construction of Lesbianism*, London: Sage.

Levay, S. (1993) *The Sexual Brain*, Cambridge, MA: MIT Press.

Lewes, K. (1989) *The Psychoanalytic Theory of Male Homosexuality*, London: Quartet.

McDougall, J. (1985) 'Homosexuality in Women', in Chasseguet-Smirgel, J., *Female Sexuality: New Psychoanalytic Views*. London: Maresfield.

Mitchell, J. and Rose, J. (eds) (1982) *Feminine Sexuality: Jaques Lacan and the ecole freudienne*, Basingstoke: Macmillan.

O'Connor, N. and Ryan, J. (1993) *Wild Desires and Mistaken Identities: Lesbianism and Psychoanalysis*, London: Virago.

Rich, A. (1993) 'Compulsory Heterosexuality and Lesbian Existence', in Abelove, H., Barloe, M. A., and Halpern, D. M. (eds) *The Lesbian and Gay Studies Reader*, New York: Routledge.

Roith, E. (1987) *The Riddle of Freud: Jewish Influences on His Theory of Female Sexuality*, London: Tavistock.

Rousselle, A. (1993) *Porneia: On Desire and the Body in Antiquity*, Cambridge, MA: Blackwell.

Samuels, A. (1985) *Jung and the Post-Jungians*, London: Routledge and Kegan Paul.

Sartelle, J. (1994) 'Rejecting the Gay Brain and Choosing Homosexuality', *Bad Subjects*, 14.

Schwarz, D. (1995) 'Current Psychoanalytic Discourses on Sexuality: Tripping Over the Body', in Domenici, T. and Lesser, R. C. (eds) *Disorienting Sexuality*, New York: Routledge.

Segal, L. (1994) *Straight Sex: The Politics of Pleasure*, London: Virago.

Weeks, J. (1985) *Sexuality and its Discontents: Meanings, Myths and Modern Sexualities*, London: Routledge.

Weeks, J. (1991) *Against Nature: Essays on History, Sexuality and Identity*, London: Rivers Oram.

Wilkinson, S. and Kitzinger, C. (eds) (1993) *Heterosexuality: A Feminism and Psychology Reader*, London: Sage.

Wittig, M. (1993) 'One is not Born a Woman', in Abelove, H., Barloe, M. A. and Halpern, D. M. (eds) *The Lesbian and Gay Studies Reader*, New York: Routledge.

2   Lesbianism and the Therapist's Subjectivity: A Psychoanalytic View

Joanna Ryan

For the purposes of this chapter I am going to invent a figure – that of the liberally minded practitioner – which, while necessarily fictional in some ways, nonetheless usefully represents a range of attitudes, issues and dilemmas that are likely to be experienced by many practising psychotherapists and psychoanalysts. The context in which it is useful to postulate this figure, with which many readers will probably identify in some way, is that of the historical predominance within psychoanalysis of pathologizing views of homosexuality, and of the concomitant widespread bar on lesbians and gay men being admitted as trainees in psychoanalytic organizations. This long-lasting predominance of orthodox theories, and the many problematic effects of this has been documented in a series of recent writings (for example, Lewes 1989; O'Connor and Ryan 1993; Domenici and Lesser 1995). Amongst these problematic effects has been the sheer difficulty of dissenting or alternative voices gaining any credibility within the psychoanalytic field.

The last ten years have seen considerable and very significant shifts within the psychoanalytic world in relation to homosexuality with regard both to the evolution of different clinical views and practices and also, in many if not all organizations, to the possibility of admission to training. These changes have come about largely through the advent of openly lesbian and gay practitioners, so that lesbian and gay voices have for the first time been able to find expression from within the profession, as therapists, rather than from outside as previously was the case, or as patients in the often problematic clinical writings of mainstream literature (see O'Connor and Ryan 1993, for a critique of much clinical work). The struggles to train and become qualified and to withstand the often homophobic, heterosexist or otherwise prejudiced or ignorant attitudes of many organizations and individuals, are vividly described in *Disorienting Sexualities* (Domenici and Lesser 1995). These efforts to combat discrimination and to forge new ways of working have also been aided by a theoretical broadening out in some parts of the field of psychoanalysis, by influences from feminist and queer theory, from discourse theory, and from the pluralism and deconstructive initiatives that have flowed from postmodernist approaches. Judith Butler's *The Psychic Life of Power* (Butler 1997) describes many of the philosophical moves that have to be made if psychoanalysis is to be brought closer to an understanding of the construction and workings of our categories of gender, sexual orientation and identity. However, such theoretical initiatives are very much in their infancy and have yet to have the impact that is needed in the mainstream of psychoanalytic thought.

These various shifts and upheavals have, however, left something of a theoretical vacuum for many psychotherapists working within a psychoanalytic framework. As I and my co-author argue in *Wild Desires and Mistaken Identities* (O'Connor and Ryan 1993), a more open and inclusive psychoanalytic approach to homosexuality does pose fundamental challenges to many of the bases of orthodox psychoanalytic theory, especially the theorizing of gender, of gender in relation to sexuality, and the nature and status of the Oedipus complex. It is the nature of this fundamental challenge to psychoanalytic theory which may well be the source of much resistance to a less pathologizing approach, as much as, or as well as, prejudice, ignorance and anxiety, which also abound. If much of the classical or orthodox thinking within psychoanalysis about homosexuality no longer holds as the received wisdom, it is perhaps not obvious with what to replace it in thinking psychoanalytically about homosexuality. For the most part this is a question which is not addressed in training. Thus, the many psychotherapists and psychoanalysts who wish to take up a more liberal approach to homosexuality often do not know on what theoretical bases to ground themselves in their attempts to understand their patients or aspects of the therapeutic relationship, where homosexual material is concerned.

One example of this is the question of what is known as 'gender identity'. In the writings of many psychoanalysts both lesbianism and male homosexuality are seen as involving some form of gender identity confusion or disorder. In some versions, such a supposed gender identity disorder is seen as leading to or constitutive of the homosexuality in question, the reason why the individual has not developed a functioning heterosexuality. In this way gender identity and sexual preference or orientation issues are conflated, and tied together theoretically. As a result, in most psychoanalytic theory, there is no theoretical possibility of a woman sexually loving another woman as a woman, but only from the position of some kind of fictive male, or as a baby to a mother. In *Wild Desires and Mistaken Identities* we argue, with examples, that clinical and other experience suggests much greater diversity in these respects than is usually assumed. We also argue that there are many individuals with lesbian desires or relationships for whom gender identity issues do not figure at all significantly in relation to their sexuality. Rather, gender identity issues can be involved in many different kinds of ways in lesbian expressions of sexuality. Some of these may involve serious difficulties in relation to taking up a viable gendered position, but others are not helpfully seen as this kind of a problem at all.

It is not enough, however, simply to dispute this theoretical tie-up as not warranted by clinical experience. It is argued instead that the seemingly close relationship between the two is more a product of the heterosexually gendered discourse in which psychoanalysis, and much of social life, is embedded. Given this, it is almost inevitable that the experiencing of same-sex sexual desire will be associated with anxieties about gender. This is so not because lesbianism is a sign or symptom of conflicted or immature femininity, but because we think, experience and construct ourselves within the terms of the binary gendered discourse – the opposition of male/female, masculine/feminine – available to us, unless we have special reasons for, or support in, not doing so. Psychoanalytic theories are posed in a way which unthinkingly reflect and perpetuate this binary discourse, and the 'deviant' status of those who do not, for whatever reasons, conform. Butler, in an earlier work, describes it thus:

> 'Intelligible' genders are those which in some sense institute and maintain relations of coherence and continuity among sex, gender, sexual practice and desire ... The cultural matrix through which gender identity has become intelligible requires that certain kinds of 'identities' cannot 'exist' – that is, those in which gender does not follow from sex and those in which the practices of desire do not 'follow' from either sex or gender ... (Butler 1990, p. 17)

Another example concerns developmental questions. It is often assumed that a different psychoanalytic approach to lesbianism will provide alternative developmental accounts, answers to the question of why someone has become lesbian, for example. Mainstream psychoanalysis abounds with attempts to show what went wrong developmentally in the histories of lesbian and gay individuals, with the emphasis very much on constellations of supposedly pathogenic parenting. It is often hard for therapists trained in a psychoanalytic tradition not to prioritize in their minds the question, why is this individual lesbian? However, despite extensive efforts psychoanalysis and related disciplines have been notoriously unsuccessful in identifying either causal patterns, aetiologies or personality characteristics associated with homosexuality. The marked imbalance in effort and resources which have gone into these developmental concerns is very striking when compared to the paucity of thought that has been devoted to understanding fears about homosexuality and homophobic prejudice, which are major factors in the lives of most gay men and lesbians, and also in the construction and maintenance of heterosexuality. Furthermore, we do not on the whole ask why someone is heterosexual, although as therapists we may concern ourselves very much with the 'how' of someone's heterosexuality, their various conflicts, inhibitions, idealizations, and so on. To continue, in whatever framework, the effort to 'explain' lesbianism developmentally is to sideline the important 'how' questions concerning someone's homosexuality, including the often vital issue of how they have managed to find the psychic resources to overcome the various difficulties, conflicts and anxieties associated with loving someone of the same gender.

These examples are instances of how practitioners who are concerned to be psychoanalytically liberal about homosexuality also need to be theoretically critical as well. It is not enough simply to maintain, as many do, that it is the quality of the object-relations and not the gender of the love-object that counts. Such an approach is certainly an advance on much that has been written and practised to date, since the gender of the love-object, in relation to that of the subject is a central organizing principle for much of psychoanalysis. However, such an attempt at gender neutrality, well intentioned as it may be, runs the risk of ignoring or being insensitive to the complexity of ways in which the gender of someone's love-object can be the instigator of many different, often highly painful and conflictual experiences, as well as the source of what is most valuable in someone's life. That is, a 'liberal' approach of this kind is inadequate if it cannot take on board the individual consequences of crucial social factors, particularly the various social expressions of the taboo on homosexuality. Homosexuality is lived out within particular contexts that are variously homophobic, heterosexist, indifferent, and so on, so that the experiencing of homosexual sexuality is inseparable from the external and internal constraints and constructions of its social existence. So also our knowledge, psychoanalytic or otherwise, of homosexuality cannot exist as if free of all considerations of homophobia and heterosexism. This seeming freedom, however, is exactly what is presented to us in those clinical reports of homosexual patients which are devoid of any historical or specific context in which the living out of homosexuality can be placed, and in which conflicts could be more productively understood. In the same way, writers and therapists, with their various practices and theories, need also to be situated, rather than figuring in some 'neutral' attempted objectivity.

Most psychoanalytic reports of case material with lesbian and gay patients are also strangely free of any countertransference considerations, which is the main concern of this chapter. This is true even of the more modern writings, where the subject of countertransference could be expected to make an appearance. Despite the various developments in psychoanalytic understandings of this topic, and including authors who, in other works, have shown great sophistication in the use of countertransference, there is a remarkable absence across a wide range of literature. The writer, therapist or analyst in so many clinical reports appears as an exceptionally blank or non-existent figure. Many of these case reports give an impression of a distinct lack of therapeutic engagement or ability to take up and work with transference material, a kind of therapeutic 'hands off' approach. This is often, although not only, in the context of the application of pathologizing, denigrating or heterosexually normative theories. My contention is that the use of such theories can serve to obscure and/or rationalize anxieties about homosexuality, anxieties that should more properly and productively be addressed as countertransferential or other issues for the therapist. The fact that homosexuality of many kinds can and does arouse all kinds of anxieties is rather curiously under-acknowledged within the psychoanalytic arena, and yet psycho-analysis has, *par excellence*, the tools for understanding such phenomena. Unaddressed, such anxieties can lead to all kinds of acting out in a therapeutic context, and to the maintenance of many forms of prejudice.

Frommer (1995), in one of the very few writings on this subject, describes the notable absence of countertransference considerations in relation to homosexual clinical material as 'countertransference obscurity'. He argues, with examples, that this can concern psychotherapists who are not working from an identifiably homophobic position but who are trying to take up a stance of greater neutrality about homosexuality. Such attempts at greater neutrality have not necessarily helped therapists address their own subjectivity in relation to homosexuality; indeed such attempts may even have driven this underground. Frommer describes how such neutrality can mean that homosexuality is more 'tolerated', but that the therapeutic enquiry, exploration and engagement that is often needed is absent. The example he gives concerns the description of sexual activity. The analyst in question interpreted a patient's fear of his analyst's disgust at his (the patient's) sexual activities, in terms of the patient's need to feel only what the analyst felt and his assumption that the analyst could not tolerate any different sexuality from his own. This may well, within the framework of an ongoing therapy, have been an apposite interpretation. But, as Frommer points out, what was neglected here was any exploration of why the patient imagined the analyst would feel sickened. That is, the two issues of the analyst's possible contribution to this state of affairs and also the patient's own internalized homophobia and self-disgust, went unexplored.

Frommer's account corroborates my experience in many discussions, consultations, and so on, with therapists: that it is the announcement, attempted exploration or other expressions of erotic material that often cause particular difficulties for therapists in relation to lesbianism. The signs of such difficulty, with therapists who, with the best of intentions, are trying to work outside of a pathologizing or heterosexist paradigm, are often therapeutic responses of a 'hands off' or somewhat frozen nature. These may take the form of failure to enquire into the precise nature and details of a patient's lesbian desires and experiences, analytic blindspots, defensive displacements of analytic interest, and uneasy silences. In such instances, the patient is left unhelped, and also with fears that the therapist cannot deal helpfully with such material, so that it is perhaps better not to bring it.

One such example is as follows. The patient, a woman whose lesbian sexuality was well established, and who was in a long-established relationship with a partner, brought a series of dreams to her therapist. In different ways these dreams concerned vaginas. In one dream her vagina was being damaged during child-birth (as indeed it had been slightly) and in the dream she was concerned as to whether it was all right. In another dream she was being penetrated vaginally by her partner with both fear and excitement. In a third she was exploring with her mind and in visual images the interior of her partner's vagina, but feeling hesitant to touch the other woman. The patient felt puzzled and also slightly disturbed by these dreams, especially the way in which after each therapy session she had another such dream. Exploration in therapy did not appear to throw much light on these dreams, and the patient did not have many associations, nor did they appear to relate to any difficulties in her actual love-life. There seemed to be something of a therapeutic stalemate; the therapist eventually making an interpretation linking the patient's interest in vaginas to a child's curiosity with her mother's body and with a desire to know. This was a developmental interpretation that the patient experienced as shifting the focus away from the mainly sensuous and erotic nature of her dreams. The interpretation left unaddressed her considerable difficulty in articulating many of the details of her sexual experiences to her therapist, or indeed her sexual curiosity about the therapist. The patient felt angry and unhelped and reinforced in her conviction that she couldn't talk to her therapist about sex, although she did find her helpful in many other ways.

It is significant that this example concerns lesbian eroticism as this is an area in which there have been such marked and significant cultural silences, and a great paucity of language and symbols. From the point of view of the therapeutic relationship, however, we need some more specifically psychoanalytic understandings. I would suggest that a range of fears and anxieties may be involved on the part of therapists who encounter such difficulties. These include: (1) the anxieties attached to being the object of homosexual transferences; (2) fears of his or her own ignorance about homosexual sexuality or lifestyles; and (3) fears of being homophobic, resulting in strenuous attempts not to be, that can stifle thought and creativity. The following are examples of these anxieties and fears.

1. A patient, a young woman, was talking about her difficulties with her boyfriend, including her concern that she did not experience much sexual arousal with him, although she was very fond of him, and planning to get married. The patient also mentioned an intense attachment that she had to a woman at work, including many fantasies of lying in bed with her, touching and stroking each other. These fantasies she did find sexually arousing and became very animated and excited in the telling of them. The therapist explored with her the difficulties with her boyfriend but over a considerable period of time did not respond to or try to explore any of the material relating to the woman friend. Eventually the patient left therapy complaining that nothing seemed to be happening. The therapist's supervisor took up with her why she did not attend to the issues surrounding the woman friend; the therapist eventually admitted that if she were to explore this with the patient, she was afraid the patient might 'come on to her'. In this somewhat crude and raw language are crystallized many fears of rampant, uncontrollable and overwhelming homosexuality that might break loose and that might involve the therapist. The therapist's normal ability to see herself as the object of transferences could not be sustained where the transference in question, in this case not even actual but imagined, was a homosexual erotic one.

In another example (cited in *Wild Desires and Mistaken Identities*), where the patient in question actually did have explicit erotic fantasies about the therapist and also intense feelings of love, the therapist found herself asserting in a most unusual way her heterosexual married status and also her unavailability. The patient experienced this response as both puzzling and rejecting. The therapist was subsequently able to recognize the panic-stricken nature of her response. There are many other instances that we document of ways in which woman therapists have found it hard to allow their lesbian patients to fall in love with them within the therapy and to work with homosexual erotic transferences. This difficulty does undoubtedly represent a deprivation of therapeutic help for many patients and also unwittingly reinforces rather than helps to overcome the taboo nature of homosexuality, and the sense of social and personal rejection and unlovability that many lesbians may have in relation to their sexuality.

It is sometimes said that such difficulties are just instances of the difficulties associated with working with any erotic transference, heterosexual or homosexual, and there may well be some truth in this. But simply to assimilate this very specific difficulty to a general case would lose what is particular to and particularly anxiety-provoking about homosexuality and about being the object of homosexual transferences.

2. It can also happen that when presented with a patient's lesbian experiences, erotic or otherwise, a therapist finds herself falling uncharacteristically dumb, and does not know what to say, or how to help the patient explore what is being presented. Examples of this are reports which concern very particularly lesbian experiences, such as dilemmas about coming out or disclosure; reports about conflicts in lesbian groups, or becoming pregnant and having a baby as a lesbian without heterosexual intercourse. The therapist can feel as if she is in a strange country or alien culture, and could only too easily put a foot wrong, be insensitive or not understand. There are many forms of therapeutic ignorance here, some of which could be addressed by better information on the therapist's part, by reading lesbian and gay literature, and so on. Many lesbian patients do indeed feel it a burden that they have to inform or enlighten their therapists about lesbian culture and social dynamics, or indeed about homophobia.

More fundamentally, however, and more psychoanalytically, this sense of 'ignorance' needs to be understood, and especially the accompanying inhibition of a therapist's normal abilities to explore issues with a patient that are beyond the therapist's direct experience. It would seem that a therapist's imaginative and exploratory capacities become very readily inhibited in the area. One aspect of therapeutic skills is the ability to work with other people's experiences that we have not necessarily had ourselves, and we do so by a special form of sensitivity, clinical knowledge and experience and, sometimes, trial identification. I suggest that this sense of ignorance in relation to homosexuality is driven by a need to remain ignorant or unknowing, which of course raises the question, ignorant of what? The answer that I would give is ignorant of homosexual desire, and that knowing (too much) about someone else's homosexual desires without having recourse to pathologizing, attacking or otherwise distancing and objectifying theory may threaten to stir up desires and feelings which are normally held in some kind of repression. In such cases it is likely that unconsciously or consciously therapists are trying to protect themselves from the arousal of their own homosexual desires, curiosities, longings or memories. In doing so they may be driven to inhibit themselves from the kinds of imaginative identifications that would enable more fruitful therapeutic thought.

In this way the fictive liberally minded practitioner who, with the best of intentions, is trying to forge a better way of working with her lesbian patients, may be more vulnerable to her own conflictual, possibly unconscious feelings about homosexuality than the more orthodox therapist with the protection of theories which firmly locate pathologies in the homosexual patient. Paradoxically, but in accordance with Foucault's (1981) observations about the proliferation of knowledges, such theories may allow the orthodox therapist to investigate, categorize and theorize about her patients with less apparent inhibition than her at present rather inhibited but more accepting colleagues. It is here that attention to countertransference issues as well as to helpful theory is so important.

Freud famously said that psychoanalysis was 'most decidedly' opposed to the 'separating off of homosexuals from the rest of mankind as a group of special character' (Freud 1905, p. 56). He put forward his belief that everyone is capable of making a homosexual object-choice, and in fact has made one in his or her unconscious. It is important to recall Freud's much quoted statement about this, because the history of psychoanalysis has for the most part gone in such a different direction. Furthermore, the intricacies of living out the interrelatedness of homo- and heterosexuality have tended to be obscured by the cultural dominance of heterosexuality, the sheer difficulty of creating and sustaining homosexual lives and loves, and the corresponding need to defend such identities against the many assaults of homophobia and heterosexism. This has produced an often sterile, albeit strategically necessary, polarization and reification of 'identities'. Despite the potential in psychoanalysis to recognise the complex, provisional, conflicted and diverse nature of anyone's sexuality, relatively little attention is paid to ways in which heterosexual and homosexual aspects can co-exist and interrelate, or not. 'Bisexuality' is hardly to be adequate as a concept for what is needed here. This is particularly relevant to the understanding of homophobia and to various countertransferential difficulties that therapists may encounter.

Psychoanalysis could make an enormous contribution to the understanding of homophobia and associated irrational anxieties, but has barely begun to do so. Two recent works, *The Anatomy of Prejudices* (Young-Bruehl 1996) and *The Psychic Life of Power* (Butler 1997), although not clinical or psychoanalytic texts in themselves, make extensive use of psychoanalysis to understand the maintenance of heterosexual primacy, and the taboo on homosexuality. They emphasize respectively repression and foreclosure as potent mechanisms.

Young-Bruehl documents the many forms that homophobic prejudice can take. One of her major categories is that of hysterical homophobia, in which the maintenance of distinctions and difference, 'not one of us' is felt to be necessary. In her view homophobia is primarily a prejudice of categorization. She argues that such homophobia speaks to a very problematically repressed homosexuality, in which homosexual desires can threaten to erupt and have to be energetically kept at bay by various means. The category (of homosexuals) can seem to be all that stands between the individuals in question and some very taboo desires or behaviour. It functions as a repudiation of such acts or desires by ascribing them to another category of people, from whom essential distinction is maintained. The difficulty is that such acts or desires are ones which anyone might, could or actually does engage in or fantasize about doing so; that is, they are shared desires. Psychoanalysis provides us with a very rich understanding about the mechanisms and consequences of psychic repudiations, repressions and attempts at these, and also about the strategies that may be employed to ward off feared and dreaded feelings. It is important in any discussion of homophobia to keep in mind the immense individual diversity that there is likely to be in the extent and form of repression of homosexual desires, and the nature of fears and anxieties associated with this.

Butler's (1997) analysis concerns issues pertaining to the discursive constitution of subjects, and she argues that the formation of the heterosexual subject is dependent on a form of prohibition of homosexual desire that she terms 'foreclosure'. This rigorous barring of desire, she argues, constitutes the heterosexual subject through a certain kind of loss, so that:

the foreclosure of homosexuality appears to be foundational to a certain heterosexual version of the subject. The formula 'I have never loved' someone of a similar gender and 'I have never lost' any such person predicates the 'I' on the 'never-never' of that love and loss. (Butler 1997, p. 23)

Butler goes on to describe what she regards as the 'ontological accomplishment' of such a heterosexual being as being predicated on such constitutive melancholia, 'an emphatic and irreversible loss'. She describes the consequent sociality as one affected by melancholia, in which loss (of homosexual love) cannot be grieved because it cannot be recognized as loss. What this analysis reminds us of is not only the seeming unknowability of homosexual desires for someone constituted heterosexually, but also the depth of longing and grief that can be involved and might be evoked by the arousal of such feelings or their possibility. It is unusual to find such a longing and grief acknowledged within therapy or otherwise. However, it is not hard to see, from a psychoanalytic perspective, the various pathological consequences that could arise from such unrecognized foreclosure of homosexual love.

If we return to our liberally minded therapist, she might well be confronted in her work with aspects of her own homosexuality, unconscious or otherwise. I am not supposing that it is necessarily any easier for a lesbian therapist to work with erotic material that a lesbian patient may bring, but the form of the difficulties that might be encountered may well be different for a therapist who has primarily constituted herself heterosexually. It is not uncommon for lesbians to acknowledge the loss of heterosexuality that they may feel has been involved in becoming lesbian. The therapeutic importance of being able to mourn aspects of heterosexuality in establishing a viable lesbian sexuality and life is well recognized, for example, by Crespi (1995), who argues for a wider therapeutic understanding of this. It is relatively uncommon to find a parallel acknowledgement from heterosexual therapists, and evidence of the mourning of loss in relation to homosexuality is relatively rare in accounts of analyses of women, although lip-service is paid to the idea that this should happen. Many writers – for example, McDougall (1995), who describes her own countertransference 'deafness' in relation to homosexual material with a seemingly heterosexual patient – have indicated shortcomings in this area in their analyses. This disparity is hardly surprising, given the cultural dominance of heterosexuality, but one would hope that in the psychoanalytic domain this could be better addressed than it is.

The kind of therapeutic freezing, distancing or dumbness that I have described thus speaks to unanalysed and perhaps unacknowledged fears, longings and grief about homosexual intimacy. What these might mean for any individual will depend greatly on the nature of repression, repudiation or foreclosure involved, and also on the associated involvement of envy and hostility.

3. Another source of countertransference difficulty for liberally minded practitioners is the very fear of being homophobic or of being felt to be by the patient. Therapists may be afraid that they will say something inadvertently attacking, rejecting or insensitive, or they may anticipate being criticized by the patient, or may feel guilt for the patient's suffering at the hands of a homophobic world that they feel helpless to right.

The therapist's need not to be seen as homophobic can lead to a failure to take up conflicts or difficulties a patient may have in being lesbian. This can sometimes amount to an implicit demand by the therapist to the patient to exempt her from the homophobic world 'out there'. There may be a collusive assumption which may effectively be somewhat of a burden for the patient, much as she might wish it, that the therapist is not and could not be at all homophobic. Well intentioned as some of this may be, it does not give enough chance for necessary projections to be developed and worked with, both in relation to actually damaging experiences the patient may have had, and in relation to the insidiousness of internalized homophobia. It may be necessary, in some cases, for the therapist to be experienced for a time as a source of hateful feelings about the patient's sexuality in order for the dimensions of this to be adequately explored and resolved. The therapist as a transference figure of this kind will only be most useful to the patient if the therapist is not actually homophobic in her conduct of the therapy and in the understandings she conveys to the patient. But she will also only be useful if she does not attempt to deal with what may be a distorted perception of herself by reassurance or correction, from her own anxiety at being seen in this way. The anxiety that a liberally minded practitioner may feel about being homophobic may be aroused because some of the patient's concerns about this can have the effect of stimulating her own hostility and her fear of this hostility. The therapist is vulnerable to finding herself being pushed into an identification with the aggressor, which may be a greatly feared position.

Another ingredient in this constellation can also be therapist guilt – guilt at the oppressive nature of the world; guilt perhaps that the patient has suffered in a way that the therapist has not, guilt at the therapist's limited ability to make the world a better place; guilt that she might indeed have some hostile feelings towards some aspects of homosexuality. What is involved here is fear of the patient's aggression and a too-ready identification with a helpless victim status, as a reaction to other feared feelings.

To focus on possible countertransference difficulties that therapists may encounter is not to ignore the possible and important part that patients may contribute to these difficulties. Nor is it to ignore what an acknowledgement of countertransferential difficulties can indicate about patients' conflicts and projections. It is rather to attempt to rectify what has been an enormous imbalance in psychoanalytic concerns and to suggest some lines along which countertransference may be discussed. However, many of the issues outlined above do relate to conflicts that patients may feel about themselves; for example, shame and self-hatred in relation to lesbian desires, fears of rejection and exposure, anxieties about femininity and masculinity. The 'silence' of so many lesbians about their sexuality and erotic experiences – something that has often been complained about by clinicians – and the falling into silence by their therapists (or other defensive reactions) when homoerotic material is at issue, do not necessarily mean the same for either party. However, the one is often a useful clue to the other. The extent, depth and resilience of feelings of shame and self-hatred – the hallmarks of internalized homophobia – are sometimes not sufficiently appreciated in the understandable desire to provide more affirmative therapy than has hitherto been available for lesbians and gay men.

In conclusion, it is argued that psychoanalytic therapy with lesbians can best be advanced through a careful attention to often obscured or resistant countertransference experiences. This is a more fruitful path, rather than attempting to produce more developmental 'explanations' or accounts of lesbianism. Through the exploration of therapist countertransference issues, considerable insight of a psycho-analytic nature is likely to be gained about the complexities of the interrelatedness of homo- and heterosexualities, and also the modes of operation of homophobia.

REFERENCES

Butler, J. (1990) *Gender Trouble: Feminism and the Subversion of Identity*, London: Routledge.

Butler, J. (1997) *The Psychic Life of Power: Theories in Subjection*, Stanford, CA: Stanford University Press.

Crespi, L. (1995) 'Some thoughts on the Role of Mourning in the Development of a Positive Lesbian Identity', in Domenici, T. and Lesser, R. (eds) *Disorienting Sexuality: Psychoanalytic Reappraisals of Sexual Identities*, London: Routledge.

Domenici, T. and Lesser, R. (eds) (1995) *Disorienting Sexualities: Psychoanalytic Reappraisals of Sexual Identities*, London: Routledge.

Foucault, M. (1981) *The History of Sexuality, Vol. 1*, Harmondsworth: Penguin.

Frommer, M. (1995) 'Countertransference Obscurity in the Psychoanalytic Treatment of Male Homosexual Patients', in Domenici, T. and Lesser, R. (eds) *Disorienting Sexualities: Psychoanalytic Reappraisals of Sexual Identities*, London: Routledge.

Freud, S. (1905) 'Three Essays on the Theory of Sexuality', in *On Sexuality*, Penguin Freud Library, no. 7, Harmondsworth: Penguin, 1979.

Lewes, K. (1989), *The Psychoanalytic Theory of Male Homosexuality*, London: Quartet.

McDougall, J. (1995) *The Many Faces of Eros*, London: Free Association Books.

O'Connor, N. and Ryan, J. (1993) *Wild Desires and Mistaken Identities: Lesbianism and Psychoanalysis*, London: Virago.

Young-Bruehl, E. (1996) *The Anatomy of Prejudices*, Cambridge, MA: Harvard University Press.

3 Psychoanalysis and Male Homosexuality: Queer Bedfellows?

Bernard Ratigan

This chapter is about gay men who are more-or-less easy with their sexual orientation even though they may have had major mental health problems. It considers the relationship between gay men and psychoanalysis and psychoanalytic psychotherapy. It is written by a psychoanalytic psychotherapist who is also a gay man.[1]

The visit to Britain of the American psychoanalyst Charles Socarides in the spring of 1995 may prove to have been a turning point in the relationship between gay men and psychoanalysis in Britain. For about two decades before Socarides' visit in 1995 the situation in the US had been changing. The bitter historic debates over the inclusion of homosexuality in the second edition of the *Diagnostic and Statistical Manual of Mental Disorders* (DSM-II)[2] in 1973 was but the eruption of earlier, largely underground and unreported, dissatisfactions with the value-laden, unscientific and frankly prejudiced work of some, but by no means all, American and British analysts. In these accounts homosexuality had been portrayed in a very negative light and from which patients should be cured, rescued or saved (Herman 1995). The British analytic establishment seemed genuinely, if rather naively, surprised that what was planned as a series of private, behind closed doors, so-called 'scientific' meetings became the subject of considerable interest in the broadsheet newspapers and even loud verbal demonstrations. Socarides' views were branded as homophobic and dangerous. Those who called for freedom of his speech feared that the suppression of debate could do nothing to further the cause of scientific debate of homosexualities. The difficulty seems to be that the status of homosexuality is so problematic in the analytic establishment that open debate (including that with non-analysts) has, so far, been very difficult. Those who wanted Socarides silenced argued that his views provided a cloak of intellectual and clinical pseudo-respectability which fuelled the culture of homophobia in which gay men are sometimes subject to murderous attacks.

There are interesting cultural parallels between the debate about homosexuality and psychoanalysis and that between homosexuality and religion – especially the monotheistic and Semitic religions of Judaism, Christianity and Islam. For all three of these major influences on social, legal and moral spheres, (especially) male homosexual identity and behaviour are highly problematic categories.[3] Indeed, it may be argued that the monotheistic religions and psychoanalysis are the two major intellectual roots for considering homosexuality as abnormal and requiring condemnation or treatment.

It is of interest that for non-analytic psychotherapies homosexuality is usually much less of a problem. This may go some way to explain the popularity of such approaches with gay men. Why should any sane person undertake a form of therapy which has a history of seeing a core aspect of the human person as deviant, perverted or sick? This chapter seeks not to excuse or deny the homophobic culs-de-sac into which psychoanalysis has at times wandered, rather it seeks to ask a question of psychoanalysis: has it anything useful to say to gay men – especially gay men with mental health problems – without making things worse? The evidence in the gay community, albeit largely anecdotal, about the attitudes of psychoanalytic clinicians towards homosexuality makes gay men wary. The suspicion among many gay men is that psychoanalysis is part of a repressive homophobic culture which does nothing to liberate and much to oppress. Being gay and involved in psychoanalysis risks accusations of trading with the enemy. Freud saw a link between male homosexuality and paranoia (Freud 1911), but the way psychoanalysis has been used, or allowed itself to be used, to oppress gay men must raise serious doubts about any claims made for it to be a neutral scientific enterprise. Psychoanalysis and homosexuality then are strange bedfellows indeed.

There have been many academic debates in the last decade or so that have considered the status of homosexuality (Seidman 1996). These collapse broadly into two camps: the essentialists, seeing both hetero- and homosexualities as biologically based, and the constructivist thinkers, seeing them as socially constructed. The general aspects of these important debates can be seen in Bristow (1997) and more specifically with regard to male homosexuality in Greenberg (1988). Although psychoanalysis stands largely in the essentialist camp it does not seem that all the evidence is in with regard to the question of the aetiology of either hetero- or homosexualities.

BERLIN AND VIENNA: WHERE IT ALL STARTED

By the end of the nineteenth century there had been important developments in the human sciences in the cities of Berlin and Vienna. When Magnus Hirshfeld helped set up the *Wissenschaftlich-humanitäre Komitee* (WhK) (Institute for Sexual Science) in Berlin on 15 May 1897 it was in some ways the beginning of the modern gay movement: when homosexuals began a self-conscious journey on which they are still travelling.[4] At the same time in Vienna, Sigmund Freud, another radical thinker and scientist, was at work on his project which was to become known as psychoanalysis.

Neither homosexuality nor psychoanalysis actually 'began' in the last decade of the nineteenth century, but the coining of the two terms dates from that time. As men have probably had sex with each other since the beginning of time, so, I think, human beings have probably listened to each other's dreams since the emergence of language. What is characteristic of psychoanalysis and homosexuality is that they are both transgressive activities in which the construction of meaning by the actors is a central aspect of the activity and project. Both psychoanalysis and homosexuality, in addition, inspire or attract degrees of opprobrium because they challenge established orthodoxies.

Radical as Freud was, and believed himself to be, he was certainly influenced by the intellectual climate of his time. There had been, both in Germany and in Britain, much interest among the Victorians in the varieties of human sexual activities. Kraft-Ebbing in Germany and Havelock Ellis in Britain were among a number of sexual topologists who were busy mapping the further reaches of what was seen variously as exotic, disordered or mad. The area between medicine, morality, religion and sex has always been characterized by tension. What was important about these quasi-anthropological projects was that they pushed back contemporary notions of what was possible sexually even if it was not considered normal or moral. In this project, the work of the late nineteenth- and early twentieth-century sexologists is helpful in understanding Freud's work and the reaction to it.

There was a shift from the work of the sexologists, with their attempts to catalogue the varieties of human sexuality, to Freud's work in which he saw the human being as containing a much wider variety of human sexual possibility or potential, if not experience, that had been recognized officially heretofore. When, in the 1890s Freud was writing the classic case histories of women patients, he was still writing about patients – the other. The turning point in his development of a new theory of the mind and of the complexity of human sexual experience was perhaps his own self-analysis (Anzieu 1986). It led to two ground-breaking volumes that not only set a course for psychoanalysis but also had a much wider impact: *The Interpretation of Dreams* in 1901 and the 'Three Essays on the Theory of Sexuality' in 1905. For the purposes of this chapter the most relevant areas, in a vast list of ideas, which have done much not only to shape the clinical activity of psychoanalysis but also to shape much of twentieth-century culture are those concerning infant and therefore adult sexuality (Parker 1997). Freud, although not having much direct experience of the human infant, saw it as polymorphously perverse. By this he meant that the infant has a capacity to be physically and sexually excited by a whole range of sensations in its body and its local environment. As a biological determinist Freud saw the human being as another animal which needed to move into adulthood and biological maturity to reproduce for the safeguarding of the species. He struggled because he already knew that there is more to human sexual activity than the begetting of offspring. His developing models of the mind and sexuality had somehow to take into account the gap between his Darwinian inheritance, which argued that sexual activity was a prelude to reproduction and a way of preserving the species, and what might be called the emergent facts of actual sexual diversity brought home by the contemporary sexologists. Freud's concept of perversion was therefore necessary to partially explain the gap between the dominant view of human beings – heterosexual, missionary position, to produce babies – and the much wider emerging map, which was rather more colourful and florid. In the decades since Freud first wrote about perversion the term has changed its meaning (Neu 1991). It has never been used without its pejorative aspects or tone. It is not really possible to argue that Freud himself used it in a neutral value-free way; he was no more free of the conventional, bourgeois morality of his day than we are of ours. He, like the sexologists, was struggling to research a difficult area that was very definitely not respectable to bourgeois society and he risked professional disapprobation and stigmatization. Worse for Freud, he was a Jew, albeit neither a believing nor a practising one, in a profoundly anti-Semitic culture trying to make a reputation and a living for his growing family. When in the 'Three Essays on the Theory of Sexuality' he wrote of a constitutional and universal bisexuality, an idea which he took from Wilhelm Fleiss, it could be argued that there was a major shift in mental and sexual topography of the human being. Freud was as much a prisoner of his time as we are but his work on the mind and on human sexuality took the work of the sexologists a significant step forward in that it opened up the link between behaviour, including sexual behaviour, and mind. The sexologists had been very concerned to list and to categorize the varieties of human sexual activity (Weeks 1985). Freud took it a step further by opening up each human infant and positing a radically new view of what constitutes normality. With this shift, the possibility of non-pathological homosexual identity and behaviour have their origins.

Freud offers a model of the human infant (and by extension child, adolescent and adult) struggling towards a more-or-less secure sexual identity as if there is a constant psychic battle going on, full of what he was to call 'vicissitudes', standing in the way of the development of a fully functioning heterosexuality. Reading Freud, and even more so reading Klein,[5] I never fail to be amazed at the struggle which leads any human infant to emerge as anything so well defined as having a functioning hetero- or homosexual identity: there are just so many vicissitudes along the way. In my clinical work, albeit with a moderate-to-severely disturbed patient population, I meet many people who are best described as confused as to their sexuality and sexual orientation. One of the most convincing accounts of the sheer complexity of human sexual development can be found in Meltzer (1973). As with Freud, Meltzer has to be read carefully. There is material useful to the understanding of gay male sexuality but it is easy to read it as heterocentric.

There is no doubt that Freud used, if not needed, homosexuality in developing his theories of mind. One very important example in the Freudian canon is his work with and theorizing about 'The Wolf Man' in the *History of an Infantile Neurosis* (Freud 1918). In Freud's analysis of Serge Pankejeff, 'latent' homosexuality plays a nodal position in explaining the patient's psychopathology and psychodynamics. Davis (1995), an art historian, has written persuasively about the use Freud made of homosexual subjectivity in explaining his patients' dynamics. While it is not possible to argue that Freud approved, or disapproved, of homosexuals, I think he did see homosexuality as part of the range of human sexual experience. Although some of his later followers (for example, Bergler 1947) were to take a much more stern and condemnatory stance towards gay people, a claim can be made that Freud, like the early sexologists, was a pioneer who both brought in from the cold a range of sexualities, male and female, and formed later notions of what it was/is to be human and sexual. It was not surprising that when the Nazis started burning books in Berlin and other German cities in the 1930s both the works and the ideas of Freud and the sexologists went up in flames. It was not long, of course, before the flames were not just consuming the books but also the people about whom the books were written – in the context of this chapter, notably homosexuals; male and female.[6] Whilst the books may have been burned in the Nazis' attack on thought, fortunately the ideas the books contained proved more durable.

Somehow it proved impossible for the radicality of Freud's ideas about human sexuality to be assimilated by the wider culture and retain their integrity or force. The American gay psychoanalyst Kenneth Lewes (1988) has tracked the shifts that took place from the time of Freud's original work, with all its revisions, to what I want to call a much tamer and domesticated psychoanalysis that began to emerge with the development of ego-psychology, especially in the US during the 1930s and 1940s (Lewes 1988). It was here that a dangerous position began to be taken by psychoanalysts with regard to homosexuality. Freud could write the famous 'Letter to an American Mother' in 1922 with its liberal message (for its time) (cited in Lewes 1988). By the time many of the European refugee analysts had set up in practice in the big cities of the US, the equivalent of the 'witchfinders general' of the sixteenth century could be seen at work hunting out homosexuals and attempting to 'treat them into hetero-sexual normality'. The new, tamed, domesticated psychoanalysis allowed itself to be used to 'cure' homosexual 'perverts'. Psychoanaly-sis itself had been perverted by US-based ego-psychologists and became part of an anti-homosexual crusade. It was ironic that psychoanalysis, an activity which grew out of a (secular) Judaism should itself become part of an oppressive clinical and cultural apparatus. As the homosexual writer, E. M. Forster, wrote in his novel *Howard's End*, 'Only connect!' (Forster 1941).

The biological determinism leading to 'normal' heterosexuality and abnormal, 'perverted' homosexuality has been charted in many volumes explaining human growth and development from a psycho-analytic perspective (Rayner 1986). There can be little doubt, notwith-standing all that I have written so far in this chapter, that psychoa-nalysis *per se* has developed a rather dim view of homosexuality – both male and female. Although there have been attempts to resite homosexuality in women which have led to some outstanding revisions (O'Connor and Ryan 1993), the work on psychoanalysis and gay men is at a less developed stage. The legacy of feminism has provided a rich source of theory and clinical work on which to build for the current project.

In recent years there have been a number of contributions from gay or gay-friendly psychoanalysts and theorists. Lewes' (1988) work has al-ready been noted. As a contemporary Freudian, clinically and theoretically an heir to Freud's biological determinism, he places considerable emphasis on drive theory. To object-relations and interpersonal clinicians his work has a rather deterministic feel. Isay (1989) has taken the traditional psychoanalytic idea that the aetiological psychogenesis of male homosexuality is overinvolved mothers and emotionally absent fathers, and creatively suggests that an alternative reading of the same clinical facts might be that fathers sense at some pre- or unconscious level that their male child is in fact homosexual and emotionally withdraw from the child. The mother becomes more (not necessarily over-) emotionally involved with the male child in an unconscious attempt to fill the gap left by the withdrawing father. Cornett (1995) has attempted to marry Kohut's 'self psychology' and Sullivan's 'interpersonal therapy' with clinical ideas derived from existentialism in a persuasive argument which further strengthens the diversity of clinical work with and by gay men. The problems faced by the 'out' gay male psychoanalytic psychotherapist, and his patients, are addressed by Cornett in a realistic way which respects the importance of both issues such as the transference and the fact that gay therapists and their patients do live in the same social world. An example of this is when he invites his readers to consider the impact of a psychotherapy patients meeting their psychotherapist in a gay bath house. There are clearly a number of possible responses to this kind of dilemma but Cornett's courage in confronting such issues is respectful to psychoanalytic practice and the realities of gay men's lives – both patients and psychotherapists.

THE PSYCHOANALYTIC FRAMEWORK

When Freud began to abandon hypnotherapy and develop what is now understood as the 'psychoanalytic attitude', he was attempting to create a structure and an epistemological space in which patient and analyst could engage to the benefit of the patient (Etchegoyen 1991). Psychoanalysis and psychoanalytic psychotherapy are attempts to construct a bounded mental structure in which the analyst or therapist is neutral (or as neutral as can be achieved), emotionally available or attuned to what the patient is consciously and unconsciously attempting to do with him or her within the structure of the therapy. There is a stability of person, place and time. Sessions begin and end on time. There is no physical contact between the patient and therapist – what goes on between them is a mental activity and a verbal exchange. There is no reassurance and there is no affirmation. The austerity of the analytic framework is intentional and designed to elicit the unconscious processes at work in the patient's mind. The suspicious, frightening, criminal, loving and erotic aspects of all human beings' minds can be vented and exposed in the safety of the structure. What the stability of framework and neutrality of the analytic therapist also does is to allow the patient to construct his or her pattern of relating to others to emerge in the transference. Within the structure of the analytic frame there is therefore considerable plasticity. Psychoanalytic psychotherapy, especially from a Kleinian perspective (Hinshelwood 1994), pays particular attention to the aggressive, murderous, envious feelings human beings have towards other people in their lives and to themselves as well as the loving, grateful and generous aspects. It looks at the less and least acceptable aspects of the human condition. In this, psychoanalytic psychotherapy is distinctively different from many of the other forms of psychotherapy represented in this book. As an epistemology it also stands in contradistinction to many contemporary and taken-for-granted models of the human condition. The mental life of the adult is placed in the context of the human infant's earliest psychic experiences – replete as that is with alternate bliss and terror between the presence of the 'good' and the absence of the 'bad' breast. The search for the other object (or person as I would rather have it) is central to Klein and to other object-relations theorists. The shifts between the paranoid-schizoid and depressive positions are useful clinical and heuristic devices for understanding shifts in mental life. It stresses the a- and irrational over the rational; the murderous over the benign; it looks to the internal psychic world over external reality, at least in the clinical setting.[7] After much searching I find it the most clinically effective and intellectually satisfying mode of thinking and working; especially with the more disturbed patient populations – heterosexual, bisexual, homosexual, transgendered and those who seem to be hard to pin down.

There are clearly tensions here for gay men involved in psychoanalytic psychotherapy. If the analytic attitude of epistemological and emotional neutrality is striven towards then it should not matter, in my view, if the patient or the psychoanalyst or psychoanalytic psychotherapist is homosexual or heterosexual, or male or female. In the analytic situation, the therapist is what the patient makes him or her – in the transference at least. The therapist is also in both the maternal and the paternal transference at different times and is loved and hated. Bion (1970) has written controversially of the analyst entering every session without memory, desire or will. The difficulty is that even the most well analysed psychoanalyst or analytic psychotherapist lives in a psychological space and an intellectual and political climate in which heterosexuality is seen as having the biological if not moral superiority and imperative over homosexuality.

Later in the chapter there is an examination of the notion of the possibility and utility of the concept of 'affirmative therapy'. Before getting to that there needs to be a discussion of the notion that what is important is the provision for the patient of a mental space (Young 1994) in which to think free from pressure from the psychotherapist implicit in both the homosexuality-as-pathology model (Socarides 1978) and in the 'gay affirmative' model. Of course, in the aftermath of postmodernism and deconstructionism, the possibility of there being any value-neutral human science or therapy is seen by the avant-garde as mythic, but it can be argued that this is a useful myth which is respectful of human beings and attempts to avoid the implicit patronization in the therapist 'affirming' the patient. The psychoanalytic position is clearly a threat to the current gay hegemony of political correctness.

Space does not permit the key psychoanalytic concepts of the dynamic unconscious, transference, counter-transference, projection, introjection, projective identification, unconscious phantasy and the mechanisms of ego-defence to be explained in this chapter (see Laplanche and Pontalis 1983; Hinshelwood 1991) but some of them are illustrated through made-up clinical vignettes of psychoanalytic psychotherapy with gay men. Throughout, the clinical emphasis will be on work with male patients for whom their homosexuality is largely ego-syntonic. It will be noted, though, that in such a deeply homophobic society as contemporary Britain the idea that any gay man can be entirely without aspects of internalized homophobia is not entirely believable.

'GAY AFFIRMATIVE' THERAPY?

There has been a growth in recent years of what is claimed to be 'gay affirmative' therapy. Maylon (1982) has argued for a form of meta-therapy independent of school which sees homophobia rather than homosexuality as pathological and in need of challenge. Davies, writing out of a person-centred approach, has also cogently argued for a what he calls 'the core condition of respect' (Davies 1996). Davies cites Clark who provided a non-analytic but persuasive and influential manifesto of gay therapy.

The role of the therapist in psychoanalytic psychotherapy with gay men has, and continues to be, the subject of debate. This section considers the role of therapist in psychoanalytically informed gay psychotherapy with gay men. The debate in psychoanalysis, recently reported in the *International Journal of Psycho-Analysis*[8] about distortions in the analytic frame caused by therapist-related (over-) identification with the patient is relevant to work with gay men (Jacobs 1993). Similarly, the debate about 'the aims of psychoanalysis' (Steiner 1996) raises important questions for gay men and lesbians involved in psychoanalytic psychotherapy. These debates lead back to the radical difference between the psychoanalytic attempt to be a neutral space for thinking and other models which attempt, for whatever reason, to take sides. It is a return to the tension between psychoanalysis as science and as therapy.

What follows is a brief account of some recent UK papers on homosexuality as illustrative of the current point reached in the debate with reference to work by Krikler (1988), Hildebrand (1992), Grosz (1993), Burgner (1994) and Limentani (1994), and to add to the critique of the recent thinking in the US so thoroughly undertaken by Lewes (1988 and 1995). Lewes catalogues examples from the writings of the work of such analysts as Beiber et al. (1962) which present a sad picture of the views held by psychoanalysts of male homosexuals from the 1930s to the 1960s. Both Lewes' examples from the American context and those writing in Britain (Rosen 1996) reveal a range of theoretical and clinical attitudes which include those who do not appear to recognize how they unconsciously or unknowingly problematize or pathologize homosexuality. It is of note that, since the advent of HIV and its spread among gay men in North America, Western Europe and Australasia, psychoanalytic theorizing about male homosexuality has tended to assume that HIV is predominantly linked to homosexuality (Hildebrand 1992). Of course, taking a world-wide perspective, HIV is a disease that affects heterosexuals more than homosexuals. It is perhaps a comment on the Western-centric nature of psychoanalysis that it assumes that what happens in North America and Europe is what happens everywhere. So it is mainly in the literature on psychoanalysis and HIV that we can find where psychoanalysis currently stands in relation to homosexuality.

One of the fullest contemporary statements of psychoanalysis on homosexuality is that by the late Adam Limentani. His views about psychoanalysis and homosexuality got mixed up with his political and personal views – as, for example, when he wrote of 'the homosexual lobby' and of '... protests by gay groups and public displays of their propensities, which may not in the long run further their cause' (Limentani 1994, p. 50).

Another example of recent British psychoanalytic theorizing about male homosexuality can be found in a paper by Hildebrand in which he writes of some clinical work he undertook with a gay man with an advanced HIV illness. The paper is written out of a metropolitan

British experience and implies that HIV is a disease that mainly, or even only, affects gay men. Hildebrand writes,

> one cannot deny that aspects of the homosexual lifestyle are profoundly unacceptable to non-homosexuals and that this is particularly true in the field of sexual behaviour ... (Hildebrand 1992, p. 457)

It is as if any idea of striving towards clinical neutrality or objectivity has been abandoned. He asserts that 'many' homosexuals

> tend to disregard the person and interact with the bodies, sexual organs and orifices of their often casual sexual partners in a way which diminishes or even tries to destroy the identity of that person ... (ibid.)

Hildebrand goes on to give an often enunciated explanation of gay male sexuality:

> The numbers of sexual partners and generalised promiscuity of those who 'cottage'[9] ... can be accounted for ... [as] a manic denial of the values and behaviour of the heterosexual community dispensed through culture and secondly because the sexual excitement which is engendered by such behaviour must involve hostility – the often hidden desire to harm the other person which is central to all forms of sexual perversion whether sado-masochistic, fetishistic, or homosexual ... (ibid., p. 458)

He then goes on to acknowledge his debt to the psychoanalyst Stoller.

Hildebrand describes the psychoanalytic psychotherapy of gay men with HIV undertaken by clinicians associated with the Tavistock Clinic, a specialist government-funded psychoanalytic psychotherapy clinical, teaching and research centre in London. He mentions the work of Kenneth Lewes, which he describes as coming from a 'markedly pro-homosexual point of view' before going on to assert that in 'all' the cases treated by the group there has been an

> early psychological catastrophe in the relationship to the patients' mothers which has not been dealt with in the oedipal phase by a sufficiently strong identification with their fathers so that their homosexuality has been a major part of a life-long defence against primitive oedipal and pre-oedipal elements. (ibid., p. 459)

There follows an account of the psychoanalytic psychotherapy of a gay male patient with advanced HIV infection. What is noticeable is the somewhat unrecognized homophobia of the therapist (Hildebrand) evident in much of the preliminary theorizing and the contrast with the actual clinical work with the patient.

Another member of Hildebrand's group, Marion Burgner, has written of her impressions of her gay male patients who transmute their feelings into

> a familiar paranoid stance against the heterosexual, in their eyes homophobic, analyst who is intolerant of their sexuality ... the Russian roulette flavour of their sexuality which preceded the infection may become intensified and their desperate attempts to defend against anxieties of annihilation, disintegration and madness are clearly visible in their perverse sexual enactments ... (Burgner 1994, p. 211)

Burgner recognizes that she is dealing with the 'very disturbed end of the spectrum' when she writes:

> their relationships – or perhaps it is more apposite to say contacts are, in the main, shallow ephemeral and perverse. (ibid., p. 212)

Lewes has recorded the unrecognized or unconscious hostility in many of the post-Freud generation of American psychoanalysts' accounts of their work with male homosexual patients. Hildebrand and Burgner also display similar unrecognized countertransference distortions with their gay patients.

In light of the frank prejudice exhibited by psychoanalysts towards gay men, it is no wonder that psychoanalysis as a whole is itself seen by many gay men as oppressive and having nothing to offer. It is in this context that demands for a gay affirmative therapy thrive.

Finally, in this brief survey of current psychoanalytic approaches to male homosexuality, I would like to turn to a paper by Grosz (1993) on his work with a gay man with HIV. Here we see an example of how psychoanalysis can be used in the treatment of a gay man without a whole constellation of negative conscious and unconscious counter-transference distortions being present. Perhaps this marks a shift, reflecting changes in the wider society, in which homosexuality is less problematic to younger people. An example of Grosz taking the patient's homosexuality seriously but not seemingly getting swamped by it is illustrated when he writes:

My own understanding is that Mr A is NOT turning from his poisoning maternal object to a strong paternal object for safety or protection. From the point of view of his object relations: Mr A turns to a man to re-find his mother with a penis. Mr A's homosexual partner is a re-finding of the maternal object he has lost. He acts to escape the catastrophe of separation; he acts to replenish and restore his unconscious phantasy as a secure relation to his maternal object. (Grosz 1993, p. 971)

'THERE'S NOWT SO QUEER AS FOLK'[10]

The relationship between sexual orientation and the rest of the personality is complex. Some have argued that as homosexuality *per se* is a perversion, it is a form of erotic hatred (Limentani 1994). I do not take this view, though I do think some homosexuals, as well as some heterosexuals, suffer from perverse character organizations. Working in a National Health Service specialist psychotherapy service both the theorizing and the clinical work on which this chapter is built reflects work with more psychologically disturbed male homosexual patient populations. The work described by the new American school of gay psychoanalysts and psychoanalytic psychotherapists is based upon individual psychoanalytic psychotherapy with patient populations who, for the most part, appear to be functioning. The currently dominant model of gay affirmative therapy (Davies and Neal 1996) also gives the impression of being directed at a similar level of client problem. This is not to diminish or deny the pain and suffering such patients endure but a question is left unanswered about the possibility of psychotherapeutic work with the more severely disturbed populations of gay men, including those with, or recovering from mental illnesses and those with personality disorders. This chapter is based upon a premise that there are some psychologically disturbed gay male patients, whose homosexuality is nevertheless ego-syntonic, who can be helped by the depth of work possible in psychoanalytic psychotherapy. However, unrecognized, countertransference-driven hostility as well as internalized homophobia on the part of the therapist constitutes a frame violation and will tend to vitiate the psychoanalytic ideal of therapeutic space neutrality, thus making real therapeutic work very difficult, if not impossible. When attempting to treat any patient with more severe levels of disorder, the problem of unrecognized countertransference hostility on the part of the therapist is present. An understanding of projective identificatory mechanisms is essential in psychoanalysis, especially in clinical work with difficult patients, but it is not a substitute for therapists grasping their own problems with either the homosexuality of their patients or themselves. Like therapy where therapist and patient come from very different ethnic/cultural backgrounds, work with gay men undertaken by heterosexual therapists needs special training and supervision. It is for future theoretical and clinical research for gay psychoanalytic psychotherapists to think about the treatment of ego-dystonic male homosexuals and patients who developmentally have yet to arrive at some settled sexual orientation.

ON AND BEYOND THE COUCH:
TO WHOM DOES PSYCHOANALYSIS BELONG?

For many years the discussion of the relationship between psychoanalysis and homosexuality was almost entirely one-sided: psychoanalysis discussed homosexuality and homosexuals. It is only in recent years with the emergence of a sense of a gay consciousness, that the possibility of a critique from what might be called 'the other side' began to develop. Gay men are now using psychoanalytic theory and practice to better understand the powerful forces and prejudices ranged against them. As Franz Fanon was able to use psychoanalysis to understand racism in the colonial French setting of the 1940s (Fanon 1968) so what we are seeing now, in the context of (male) homosexuality, is use being made of what was previously seen as 'the enemy's' ideas; is this a case of trading with the enemy or not letting the devil have all the good tunes?

Psychoanalysis, as a body of theory and practice, has been one of the two major ideological well-springs of homophobia – the other can be located in the monotheistic religions of Judaism, Christianity and Islam. The growing sense of self-confidence in the gay community enables a psychoanalytically informed critique to develop. A question that arises is: to whom does psychoanalysis belong? At first, historically, it was clear that psychoanalysis belonged to Freud and his circle in Vienna. These were all, or mainly, clinicians. Like the Talmud before it, the Freudian urtext and the (epi-) phenomena of psychoanalysis became the subject of academic rather than purely clinical interest. Psychoanalysis has become one of the major intellectual and cultural ways of describing and understanding psychosocial phenomena (Parker 1997). Homosexuality, although nominally first coined in the last days of the nineteenth century, is also a defining concept/ activity in the twentieth century. If we think of the examples from literature, film and the arts generally it is valid to argue that a preoccupation with (especially male) homosexuality has been a growing theme throughout the century. The arrival of HIV and AIDS has accelerated this process.

Psychoanalysis can now be utilized to understand and support gay men. The 1980s and 1990s have seen a movement that claims allegiance to psychoanalysis, but in a cautious manner. Writers such as the Americans Lewes (1988), Friedman (1990) and Cornett (1995) have begun the process of challenging the psychoanalytic hegemony which has for so long problematized male and female homosexuality. It is of interest that so far a non-problematic psychoanalytic approach to homosexuality has come from the US. Ryan's chapter in this volume (Chapter 2), on psychoanalysis and lesbianism, has been written out of the British experience. The ground-breaking work of the British psychoanalytic psychotherapists O'Connor and Ryan (1993), writing from a lesbian perspective, grows out of a well established feminist critique stemming back to the work of Mitchell (1974). For gay men interested in psychoanalysis, especially in Britain, it has taken a much longer time. Hopefully, this chapter will play its part in rectifying the position. It is not as if gay men are not interested in therapy; many non-analytic schools have their gay adherents. My sense is that the seemingly anti-gay attitude in psychoanalysis makes gay men despair of finding anything useful. There have always been homosexual people in psychoanalysis, both as practitioners and as patients.

As far as practitioners, analysts and therapists are concerned, it has been easier to keep one's head down and use the excuse of therapist/ analyst transparency as justification for staying in the 'therapeutic closet'. I have always found this a difficult position to understand psychoanalysts and psychoanalytic psychotherapists taking as it seems to contradict a much more fundamental psychoanalytic notion: that of the dynamic unconscious. Many gay men can give willing testimony of what is sometimes called colloquially a 'gaydar' (gay radar) by which they know or suspect, unconsciously, who is gay and who is not. I believe that if the patient on the couch does sense the sexual orientation of his or her analyst or therapist it will be distorted by transference. We are beyond words here and deep into the unconscious and into unconscious communication.

The split between Freud and Jung deprived psychoanalysis of the creative, and probably libidinal, tension that characterized their friendship. The divorce has deprived Freudian psychoanalysis not only of an understanding of the spiritual dimension in human existence but also of a vision of same-sex relationships leading to wholeness. Hopcke et al. (1993) have assembled a collection of Jungian perspectives on gay and lesbian psychological development. Currently, we are a long way from a parallel Freudian or Kleinian volume. What Freud and Klein left us, I believe, is a rather more astringent body of theory and practice which may be of use to gay men.

It is to Klein that this chapter now turns to see if there is anything of use in both clinical settings and in social/cultural analysis. She struggled in her work to remain faithful to Freud's ideas but she developed them considerably. She had a radical view of human nature and human destructiveness which is not immediately appealing and stands in marked contradistinction to ego-psychology, to Humanistic psychologies and to the wholeness of Jungian analytical psychology.

Kleinian therapy does not set out to affirm or educate. It is austere, challenging and does not have floppy boundaries. Klein, being a woman and a mother, had, I believe, a significant impact in extending our understanding of the importance of the mental life of the human infant and its crucial relationship to the physical body and mind of the mother (or primary care giver – the biological sex of the care giver does not matter as long as he or she is in the maternal role). Klein's categorization of the paranoid-schizoid and later depressive positions and the relationship of the infant to the parental couple are, I would argue, relevant for gay men in psychotherapy. Bion has done much to extend Klein's original theorizing on the importance of symbol formation on the origins of thought. His rather arcane psychological epistemology eventually reduced thought to an algebraic grid. One useful idea from Bion (1962) is that of attacks on thinking which can be illustrated in a rather mundane example: gay men can often feel that they do not exist when the heterosexual imperative ('Everyone is or must be heterosexual') is operating as it is usually.

GROWING UP GAY

Growing up gay in a heterosexual family and world is a strange and usually estranging experience. Most psychoanalytic accounts of human growth and development which purport to 'explain' homosexuality make little sense to me. The orthodox Freudian and Kleinian accounts of early human psychosexual development allow for a universal bisexuality and see all human beings being made up of heterosexual as well as homosexual drives, impulses and affections. While it is clear that the heterosexual direction is the most commonly followed by the majority of children, it is nevertheless clear that for a minority, and for whatever reasons, it is not the path taken by those who will later be gay. Detailed psychosexual histories, taken by a non-homophobic clinician, of adult gay men usually reveal a very early sense of 'difference', often before the so-called latency phase. This sense of difference can manifest itself in a number of forms and attempts have been made to understand it. What seems to happen is a growing awareness in the child that he is different but that the difference does not yet have a name. Knowing but yet not-knowing. As attempts are made to socialize, and often cajole the child into the norms of being a boy in a heterosexual world, an internal split can open up in the child's mind, the outcome of which can be that he learns to repress his emotions. There is a whole genre of gay accounts which track the often painful process of growing up gay.[11]

Psychoanalytically, what is interesting is the strength of the drive over/against the psychosocial forces in the family, school, peer group and media, pushing the child towards conformity with the heterosexual norm. Even growing up within a well functioning, loving family, the gay child will at least experience considerable internal tension. One solution attempted by some boys is to adopt feminine patterns of behaviour; another is to shift to a 'hyper-masculinity'. They have been characterized as 'sissy boy' versus 'jock' identifications (Green 1987). Psychodynamically, I would see them both as attempts to resolve an internal crisis caused by the mismatch between what the child feels and is supposed to feel towards the same and other genders.

The pre-gay child does not have available in his mental world a language that fits his growing experience of reality and he can therefore learn not to trust his experience. It is often difficult for heterosexual people to see the heterosexual imperative that surrounds both boys and girls. Perhaps a close analogy is growing up black in a predominantly white society, but even this breaks down because usually the black child will have access to black culture, possibly through parents, siblings or family. For the gay child there is usually none of this and what images that do exist of homosexuality are heavily prejudicial. It can lead to a profound sense of isolation and, in later life, possible difficulties in making and sustaining adult, emotionally nourishing, relationships. In most societies there seems a great anxiety that if children and young people are given anything other than strongly negative images of homosexuality as just another way of being human they will be seduced into it and flee heterosexuality. From a psychodynamic viewpoint the attacks on the pre-gay child can be seen as narcissistic wounds which can sometimes lead the adult gay person to psychotherapy. A simple example comes to mind of ordinary displays of affection like hand-holding, in which heterosexual young people can engage, but which are denied to young gay people without there being an issue made of it – at least in Britain and

North America. Without wishing to overload the action of hand-holding as an activity when added to all the other symbols denoting affection, possession, belonging and status that make up our lives as human beings, the alienation of the gay child growing up without such tangible signs is, I think, cumulative and ultimately psychologically corrosive and therefore damaging. It may also go some way in helping to understand the exuberance among many gay men when they meet other gay people. The 'in your face'-ness of much gay scene culture has many of the marks of other minority groups when they meet up, glad, for once or for a little time, to be free of the powerfully deadening demands of living in an oppressive culture. It may be a form of social reaction formation. The psychoanalytic psychotherapist working with gay men will be much more in touch with the deadening impact of growing up gay in a world in which the child thinks and believes himself the only one of his kind. There is a need for psychoanalytically informed research on the early, pre-pubertal life of gay men.

QUEER TALES?

The presentation of psychoanalytic case material has been the major method by which theory and practice has been advanced over the last 100 years. The practice is now under critical scrutiny on a number of fronts; both methodologically and ethically (Tuckett 1993; Goldberg 1997; Ward 1997). To ensure patient confidentiality is preserved, in what follows I have made up clinical vignettes which aim to catch the essence of what I want to illustrate by disguise, amalgamation and condensation. I acknowledge the problem of distortion. There is an example taken from group therapy and two from individual psycho-therapy. In the group example I have interpolated into the history of a real slow open group a series of illustrative fictions.

'You Remind Me of that Julian Clary[12] Chappie': Gay Men in Groups

It is a therapeutic truism that as people are born and live in groups, so they should be treated in groups. Yet, in Western society, the predominant model remains that of individual therapy and I have no doubt that this reflects much deeper individualistic cultural values in the West. I always encourage my colleagues to 'think group' when making assessments of patients for psychotherapy. We often sit in assessment meetings, hearing assessments being presented, all thinking, almost willing, the 'group' outcome, yet are disappointed when patients say that whatever form of therapy they will entertain, it must not be a group. My sense with many gay male patients is that the rough-and-tumble of a well run psychotherapy group is often the treatment of choice as it can enable the gay group member to work through many of the narcissistic wounds acquired in growing up gay and move beyond defining themselves only in terms of their sexual orientation.

Tracing comments on gay men and groups in the literature is a revealing activity. There can be a danger that gay men in psycho-therapy groups will be used for the benefit of the group process. Yalom, one of the originators of interpersonal group psychotherapy, wrote in the mid-1970s:

> Patients do not seek therapy because they are 'homosexuals'; they request help instead because of profound problems in relating to others, reflected, in part, by problems in their sexual orientation. As therapy proceeds and the group and the patient lay aside the appellate of 'homosexual', the patient's manifold problems of dependency, self-contempt, and fear of competition become evident and accessible for therapy. The same type of schematization operates as other members ruminate at length about whether or not they are homosexuals; as they realise the universality of so-called perverse behaviour, they begin to understand that labels are irrelevant and dehumanising. Thus, in this way the patient with a homosexual orientation often adds breadth and depth to the group. (Yalom 1973, p. 413)

By the time Yalom's fourth edition was published in 1975, almost all references in the text to homosexuality had disappeared.

The London-based group analyst Roberts has written:

> Overall this category of patient adds a valuable extra dimension to our groups, and I particularly like to have an overt homosexual in all my groups when I can. (Roberts 1991, p. 106)

My 'Julian Clary' reference leads me to consider the importance of epistemology in our work; how knowing and not knowing are important. The 'Julian Clary' in question was a young man in his early twenties who joined a well established once-weekly psychotherapy group. He was very tongue-tied and the group soon passed through the honeymoon period with him and began to tackle him about his lack of clarity (and his strangulated upper-class accent) when he spoke. Some months into his time in the group a woman in her fifties, not well known for saying anything about herself or any other group member, uttered the memorable phrase about the man reminding her of 'that Julian Clary'. There was a frisson in the group as she said the words but the moment passed. Some months later, the young man came out to the group as 'bisexual'. As is often the case in such situations the group heaved a sigh of relief and gave out a collective, 'Well of course we all know that.'

Another man in the group had disclosed the following in his assessment for psychotherapy: when he was a teenager he had got drunk one night and ended up in bed with a man for whom he was doing some car repair work and they had sex. It had been a traumatic incident in his life and the cause of shame. After the Julian Clary character had 'come out' this man became agitated and started defending 'people's' right to define themselves in terms of sexual orientation how they wanted. It was their 'choice'. Some weeks later he became very upset in the group and disclosed the drunken gay sex incident, but was terrified that it be read as an attack on the Julian Clary group member.

I am interested in how people, patients and non-patients, come to see, define and experience themselves as homosexual. Group therapy can provide a rare opportunity to discuss these questions in a relatively controlled environment. It is usual for the whole range of attitudes to homosexuality (positive and negative) to be represented in most therapy groups. The presence of a gay person can be the stimulus for the subject to come up; the main danger being that the gay man or lesbian may be pushed into 'representing' homosexuality rather than using their group for their own purposes.

Our Julian Clary character had been thoroughly prepared for the group. He had discussed his problems with his sexuality at length and had been advised that it was not necessary for him to 'come out' immediately upon joining the group. What happened was, I think, that his difficulties in communicating with other people became very apparent to the group. He thought it was to do with his sexuality. The group's view was that the problem he needed to work on in the group was not his sexual orientation but rather how he 'interrelated' (as he put it, in the rather tortured language he had acquired from his mother's attempts to make a gentleman of him and by elocution lessons to remove his strong regional accent). A year later he was able to speak to other people in the group in a much more natural manner and to 'mix' rather than 'interrelate' better with people in his larger, social world. He also stopped calling himself bisexual and said instead that he was gay.

The woman who had made the perhaps rather hurtful Julian Clary remark shortly after he entered the group was voicing what I want to call unconscious knowledge of the dispossessed parts of the man's sexuality. That is, the group were much more aware of the man's sexuality and his confusion over it than he seemed to be. Questions of gender and sexuality have always had a strong voice in the group. There have been gay men in the group before and they have done well, as has the group in dealing with them. Having a gay therapist has also had an impact in shaping the culture of the group in that, I suppose, I always have at least one ear to homosexual material and transferences.

A year after the Julian Clary character joined the group another man, 'P', started. After a few weeks he started telling a story. It was clear that the group was being kind to him and let him tell the story even though it was clearly 'out-of-the-group' and effectively stopped the group from working. The story centred on a male work colleague of P's becoming infatuated with him and giving him a lot of 'grief'. P clearly felt relived to be able to tell his tale. Immediately after he had finished speaking, 'Julian', who had been looking increasingly agitated as the tale unfolded, jumped in to 'invite' P to consider the role he had played in 'inviting' the interest of the other man. The rest of the group remained attentive but quiet. I made a comment about 'Julian' feeling responsible for tackling 'the homosexual question'. The woman who had made the Julian Clary remark responded by saying that we should try and forget about the gender of P's work colleague. It was a nice try and demonstrated just how far this lady had come in her 20 months in the group. Of course, it did not work as a suggestion because, I think, sophisticated as the group is, the homosexual element is dangerous. Within minutes of P ending his tale another male member of the group was talking about 'benders' in a clearly hurtful (and possibly hurt) way. P came the next week and said he was leaving and did so after about 30 minutes. In an individual exit interview he said he was gay 'really' but had never found the guts to face up to it. This was a salutary warning to the therapist who had assessed him for the group and not tuned into the man's homosexuality.

Individual Psychoanalytic Psychotherapy With Gay Men

'Mr Z', a 40-year-old male homosexual, was referred for psychoanalytic psychotherapy after spending over a year in a psychiatric hospital as a result of becoming suicidally depressed when his business collapsed. As part of his inpatient treatment he was seen by a female clinician who encouraged him to talk about his history. The youngest of a large, and much older sibling group, he had memories of being sexually abused by a number of adults from the age of eight until he was about thirteen years of age. At assessment, he said he was aware from before the abuse started of being 'different' from other boys that he knew and that he had feelings of attraction to another boy which he later believed to be sexual. He had come to realize that the other boy was also involved in the sexual abuse and had later disappeared, in his phantasy, annihilated by the abusers.

From the time he left school he was sexually active with other young men. Living in small towns, he gradually gravitated to cities with more thriving gay communities. He began a career in the building trade and was moderately successful over the years in setting up his own business. His difficulties in making and sustaining relationships did not improve and, as his business career became more successful, he used his money to cover up his inadequacies with other gay men of his own age. Having money stopped him facing up to his difficulties and his pattern strengthened of buying sex when he felt the need. His sexual partners had to have reached puberty and be able to have sex, but he only wanted young men with smooth bodies. While having sex, Mr Z made certain that he never took off his clothes because he felt badly about his own body.

This pattern of Mr Z having a career which provided him with enough spare cash to pay for sex when he wanted it seemed to provide some kind of psychic equilibrium for him until an economic downturn cast his business on to the financial rocks. With his source of ready cash gone, the psychic glue which had held him together began to dissolve and he soon became engulfed by acute and severe depression. It was as if the sexual contact he had been able to purchase was functioning in a protective manner, acting as a regulator of his self-esteem and profoundly despairing internal material.

Mr Z experienced psychotherapy as persecutory. One of the most noticeable features of his presentation in sessions was his profuse sweating. He gradually began to see that there was link between his sweating and the abuse he had suffered as a child. Memories began to surface of the smells of abuse; especially those of semen and of unwashed genitalia. When two of his friends attempted to get another man to have sex with them while he was present, Mr Z started to hyperventilate. When he came to his next session he painfully traced back to how he had been present when men tried to get him and another boy to have sex with them. Gradually, as the treatment unfolded, he became somewhat less paralysed by his night fears, had less severe headaches and sweated less in sessions. He remained a frightened man but one who felt less trapped by his past.

Towards the end of the therapy, he reflected on the treatment, and his view of what made the work possible was the 'certainty' of the sessions. He said he had a sense that the therapist 'knew' what he was talking about and that he could talk about his homosexuality without having to explain it.

The following material illustrates the concepts of unconscious and persecutory guilt, reparation and the shift to the depressive position in the treatment of a gay man with an HIV+ diagnosis.

'Mr C', a 30-year-old gay man, was diagnosed as HIV+ at the age of 25. He complained to his physician of an inability to keep an erection with his partner. Mr C initially discussed with the physician having a course of injections into his penis to enable him to have a firm erection during sex. After some discussion he told the physician that he wondered if it was 'something in my mind' that was stopping the erections as he had no difficulty in masturbating himself to orgasm when alone. Mr C was assessed and offered a course of focal psychodynamic psychotherapy (Aveline 1995; Malan 1995) to which he adjusted quickly and easily, regularly and punctually attending all sessions. In the assessment, when a full history had been volunteered, he had been able to say to the psychotherapist that he wondered if guilt was a factor in his erectile problem, but said he felt confused because the idea of his feeling guilt did not fit in with the way he thought about himself. In the therapy, which he and the therapist agreed would last for 26 sessions, a formulation was agreed which focused on helping the patient to see that he was a rather more complex character than he had allowed himself to think he was, and that his penis was a very delicate indicator of the conflicts he experienced mentally.

In the treatment, he was able to allow to consciousness what were very frightening thoughts. All the gay men close to him had the virus. Some had already died; others had been very ill, and he himself had a bout of pneumo-cystis pneumonia (PCP) just before he was referred. Although he had not been hospitalized, one of his ex-lovers had also been ill and had been hospitalized. Mr C had organized the care of the ex-lover and visited him frequently while he himself was unwell. In the therapy he was able to speak of the hurt he felt, that all the attention was going on the other man in hospital while he felt ignored by their friendship network. This led on to the emergence of themes revealing layers of envy and finally to thinking about the role of guilt and reparation.

Always something of what he called a 'quiet activist', he often sported T-shirts which proclaimed that he was proud to be HIV+, and similar sentiments. Mr C used the focal therapy to start exploring the link between himself and his current partner and the previously unconscious guilt. He was unsure if he had infected his partner or not, but what came to light in the therapy was, in his words, 'May I have killed him?' Mr C struggled in the therapy with the phantasy that he had 'killed' the partner because he had to fight through many layers of what he felt he 'ought', or perhaps more correctly 'ought not' to feel.

In one session towards the end of the treatment, Mr C said to the therapist that he wondered how the therapy 'worked'. Without waiting for an answer he spoke of feeling relieved that what used to cause him concern at the outset, 'just talking' as he put it, he now valued because he could not allow himself to think things he knew were there to be thought anyway but could not be though about before (Bion 1962; Symington and Symington 1996). He was able to explore his conflicts of feeling a hypocrite, that he was an activist who was also very frightened, learning that motives are always mixed and this is a freeing basis for moral action, not the opposite. In terms of the original reason for the referral he was able to make the unconscious link between the hard penis and the phantasy of killing which, of course, was not easy to think about.

GAY MEN AND THEIR PSYCHOTHERAPISTS

Searles (1972) has written about the complex relationship between the unconscious of the patient and that of the therapist in psychoanalytic psychotherapy. Through the relative austerity of the model it is as if as much as possible is being cleared away for this two-way communication to be exposed. Of course, psychotherapists often turn a blind eye to one side of the communication, preferring to explore transference phantasies. For gay men, a process of scanning may be going on, both in and out of the consulting room (Isay 1996) which I have called the 'gaydar'. Writing from a self-object position influenced both by Kohut (1971) and existential ideas (Yalom 1980), we have already noted how Cornett (1995) has documented the process well by which the gay man, when a child, suffers many narcissistic wounds, such that they become part of the taken for granted reality of life. My view is that the emergence of the 'gaydar' is the consequence of these wounds and serves a highly functional and defensive purpose. Confronted with a possible psychotherapist, the gay patient may choose to question the therapist about his credentials and he will doubtless get some information on which to base a decision about starting treatment. From a psychoanalytic psychotherapy point of view, I would suggest that the gay man will want not just to listen to the words of the therapist, but also to be with him and explore his own countertransference to the therapist. Here we move rather rapidly out of the realm of conscious knowledge to a much more difficult area. By what I have come to understand as a form of projective identification, the gay man (un)consciously scans the unconscious of his therapist to see if there is any threat there. As in all cases of projective identification, the prototype communication is that between the infant, struggling to get rid of terrifying internal material, and the more-or-less good-enough maternal container who can receive the projections and process them in a way which makes them less toxic and so return them to the infant. It is not necessary that, what has been named the 'maternal container' (Segal 1975), is biologically female – or, indeed, a mother. In psychoanalytic psychotherapy with gay men it is likely, I believe, that the most effective therapists will be women or other gay men and the least effective will be male heterosexuals. Indeed, if my hypothesis is correct, heterosexual male therapists will often pose a considerable threat to gay men as they will evoke early experiences, from when the gay man was a child, of the oppressive culture gay children tend to grow up in.

CONCLUSION: TOWARDS A QUEER PSYCHOANALYSIS?

The use of the word 'queer' by homosexuals in the 1990s is, in part, a shift away from the liberal pressure that many gay men have felt to conform to dominant heterosexual norms in order to be accepted. Psychoanalysis, I have argued, has been perverted into attempting to push male homosexuals into heterosexuality. In response, queer theory has little to say that is good about psychoanalysis (Seidman 1996).

Part of Freud's original project for psychoanalysis was to help patients to love and to work. The author Iris Murdoch has one of her characters, 'Axel' in *A Fairly Honourable Defeat* (1970) comment that being homosexual is just another way of being human. The current chapter is not a defensive or proselytizing polemic in which converts to the author's point of view are sought. Its aim is more modest in that it is an attempt to ask: can we use anything from psychoanalytic praxis to help in understanding gay men in psychotherapy? More specifically, is it possible to salvage anything from the specifically Kleinian account of psychoanalysis to help in the treatment of gay men with mental health problems – most notably those with more serious emotional problems and personality disorders? Has the Freudian or Kleinian baby to be thrown out with the bathwater because it is fatally compromised, or does it have something to offer gay men?

NOTES

1 The editor of this volume was unable to get a British psychoanalyst, as distinct from a psychoanalytic psychotherapist, to write this chapter as, at the moment, there do not appear to be any 'out' gay British male psychotherapists.

2 The first editon of what has been called psychiatry's diagnostic 'Bible' was published in 1952. The third edition, produced in 1980, had a category covering ego-dystonic homosexuality but otherwise omitted ego-syntonic homosexuality. The fourth edition was published in 1995.

3 For example, the revised 1997 Latin text of the Catechism of the Catholic Church, first issued in 1992, changes homosexuality from being 'objectively' to 'intrinsically' disordered. This semantic shift in the Vatican may well reflect intra-mural psychoanalytic discussions currently in progress. As a shift it seems a very long way from the experience of most gay men living, post-Stonewall, in North America, Western Europe and Australasia.

4 The first 100 years of homosexuality was celebrated in Berlin by a large exhibition, the catalogue for which is itself a landmark document: *Goodbye to Berlin: 100 Jahre Schwulenbewung*, Berlin: Schwules Museum/Akademie Der Kunste, 1997.

5 As with Freud, there is no substitute for reading Klein's own words (see Klein 1992–96). However, useful background work can be found in Hinshelwood (1991; 1994). To see how Klein's work was developed by some of her followers, see Spillius (1988).

6 A first-hand account of the life and death of homosexual prisoners in the Nazi concentration camps can be found in Heger (1980).

7 There is also a significant and, in the subject of this volume, perhaps relevant interest in the British Kleinian school of engagement with extra-clinical phenomena such as politics, culture and the arts (Rustin 1991). From another perspective, Shepherd and Wallis (1989) edited a collection on gay politics and culture which includes an important paper by Fletcher (1989) which takes forward Freud's thinking about homosexuality in the context of the revision by Lacan, Laplanche and the French theorists. The French seem to have escaped the worst aspects of psychoanalytic homophobia.

8 Jacobs (1993), a Jewish psychoanalyst working in New York City, has written about the process of how the inner experiences of the analyst operate in the analytic situation. He shows how the thoughts, fantasies, memories of bodily movements and autonomic responses that are experienced in the analytic hour affect interventions, the kinds of transference-–countertransference interactions which develop. For how the debate in the *International Journal of Psycho-Analysis* developed, see Green (1993).

See also Tuckett (1993). One day soon perhaps we will have the equivalent discussion by 'out' gay British psychoanalysts. Domenici and Lesser (1995) report on the situation in the US.
9 'Cottaging' is British male argot for seeking and having sex in public lavatories.
10 This is a popular expression commonly used in regions of northern England.
11 The locus classicus of the genre being Edmund White's (1988) semi-autobiographical novel *The Beautiful Room is Empty*.
12 Julian Clary is a British, camp, totally 'out', gay stand-up comedian who blatantly mocks the conventions of (especially male) heterosexuality.

REFERENCES

Anzieu, D. (1986) *Freud's Self Analysis*, London: Hogarth.
Aveline, M. (1995) 'How I Assess for Focal Therapy', in Mace, C. (ed.) *The Art and Science of Assessment in Psychotherapy*, London: Routledge.
Beiber, I. et al. (1962) *Homosexuality: A Psychoanalytic Study of Male Homosexuals*, New York: Basic Books.
Bergler, E. (1947) 'Differential Diagnosis Between Spurious Homosexuality and Perversion Homosexuality', *Psychiatric Quarterly*, 31: 399–409.
Bion, W. (1962) 'A Theory Of Thinking', *International Journal of Psycho-Analysis*, 43: 306–10.
Bion, W. (1970) *Attention and Interpretation*, London: Tavistock.
Bristow, J. (1977) *Sexuality*, London: Routledge.
Burgner, M. (1994) 'Working With The HIV Patient: A Psychoanalytic Approach', *Psychoanalytic Psychotherapy*, 8: 201–13.
Cornett, C. (1995) *Reclaiming the Authentic Self: Dynamic Psychotherapy with Gay Men*, Northvale, NJ: Jason Aronson.
Davies, D. (1996) 'Towards a Model of Gay Affirmative Therapy', in Davies, D. and Neal, C. (eds) *Pink Therapy*, Buckingham: Open University Press.
Davies, D. and Neal, C. (1996) *Pink Therapy: A Guide for Counsellors and Therapists Working with Lesbian, Gay and Bisexual Clients*, Buckingham: Open University Press.
Davis, W. (1995) *Drawing the Dream of the Wolves: Homosexuality, Interpretation, and Freud's 'Wolf Man'*, Bloomington and Indianapolis: Indiana University Press.
Domenici, T. and Lesser, R. (1995) *Disorienting Sexuality: Psychoanalytic Reappraisals of Sexual Identities*, New York: Routledge.
Etchegoyen, R. H. (1991) *The Fundamentals of Psychoanalytic Technique*, London: Karnac.
Fanon, F. (1968) *Black Skin, White Masks*, London: Macgibbon & Kee.
Fletcher, J. (1989) 'Freud And His Uses: Psychoanalysis And Gay Theory', in Shepherd, S. and Wallis, M. (eds) *Coming On Strong: Gay Politics and Culture*, London: Unwin Hyman.
Forster, E. M. (1941) *Howard's End*, London: Edward Arnold.
Freud, S. (1901) 'The Interpretation of Dreams', in Strachey, J. (ed.) *The Standard Edition of the Complete Psychological Works of Sigmund Freud* 24 vols, London: Hogarth, 1953–73, volumes 4 and 5.
Freud, S. (1905) 'Three Essays on the Theory of Sexuality', *S.E.* 7: 130–243.

Freud, S. (1911) 'Psycho-Analytic Notes On An Autobiographical Account Of A Case of Paranoia (dementia paranoides)', *S.E.* 12, 9–82.

Freud, S. (1918) 'From the History of Infantile Neurosis', *S.E.* 17: 3–22.

Friedman, R. (1988) *Male Homosexuality: A Contemporary Psychoanalytic Perspective*, New Haven, CT: Yale University Press.

Goldberg, A. (1997) 'Writing Case Histories', *International Journal of Psycho-Analysis*, 78: 435–8.

Green, A. (1993) 'Two Discussions Of "The Inner Experiences Of The Analyst" And A Response From Theodore Jacobs', *International Journal of Psycho-Analysis*, 74: 1131–45.

Green, R. (1987) *The 'Sissy Boy Syndrome' and the Development of Homosexuality*, New Haven, CT: Yale University Press.

Greenberg, D. (1988) *The Construction of Homosexuality*, Chicago: University of Chicago Press.

Grosz, S. (1993) 'A Phantasy Of Infection', *International Journal of Psycho-Analysis*, 74: 965–74.

Heger, H. (1980) *The Men with the Pink Triangles*, trans. Ferbach, D., London: Gay Men's Press.

Herman, E. (1995) *Psychiatry, Psychology and Homosexuality: Issues in Lesbian and Gay Life*, New York: Chelsea House.

Hildebrand, H. P. (1992) 'A patient dying with AIDS', *International Review of Psycho-Analysis*, 19: 457–69.

Hinshelwood, R. (1991) *A Dictionary of Kleinian Thought*, revised edition, London: Free Association Books.

Hinshelwood, R. (1994) *Clinical Klein*, London: Free Association Books.

Hopcke, R. H., Carrington, K. L. and Wirth S. (eds) (1993) *Same-Sex Love and the Path to Wholeness: Perspectives on Gay and Lesbian Psychological Development*, Boston, MA: Shambhala.

Isay, R. (1989) *Being Homosexual: Gay Men and their Development*, New York: Farrar Straus Giroux.

Isay, R. (1996) *Becoming Gay: The Journey to Self-Acceptance*, New York: Pantheon.

Jacobs, J. J. (1993) 'The Inner Experiences Of The Analyst: Their Contribution To The Analytic Process', *International Journal of Psycho-Analysis*, 74: 7–14.

Krikler, Bernice (1988) 'Homosexuality in the Eighties', *Journal of The British Association of Psychotherapists*, July: 23–42.

Klein, M. (1992–96) *The Writings of Melanie Klein* (4 vols), London: Karnac.

Kohut, H. (1971) *The Analysis of the Self*, New York: International Universities Press.

Laplanche, J. and Pontalis, J. B. (1983) *The Language of Psycho-Analysis*, London: Hogarth.

Lewes, K. (1988) *The Psychoanalytic Theory of Male Homosexuality*, New York: Simon and Schuster, (reprinted as *Psychoanalysis and Male Homosexuality*, 1995).

Limentani, A. (1994) 'On The Treatment Of Homosexuality', *Psychoanalytic Psychotherapy*, 8: 49–62.

Malan, D. (1995) *Individual Psychotherapy and the Science of Psychodynamics*, second edition, London: Butterworth Heinemann.

Maylon, A. (1982) 'Psychotherapeutic Implications of Internalised Homophobia in Gay Men', in Gonsiorek, J. (ed.) *Homosexulaity and Psychotherapy*, New York: Haworth.

Meltzer, D. (1973) *Sexual States of Mind*, Perth, Scotland: Clunie.

Mitchell, J. (1974) *Psychoanalysis and Feminism*, Harmondsworth: Penguin.

Murdoch, I. (1970) *A Fairly Honourable Defeat*, London: Chatto.

Neu, J. (1991) 'Freud and Perversion', in Neu, J. (ed.) *The Cambridge Companion to Freud*, Cambridge: Cambridge University Press.

Parker, I. (1997) *Psychoanalytic Culture: Psychoanalytic Discourse in Western Society*, London: Sage.

O'Connor, N. and Ryan, J. (1993) *Wild Desires and Mistaken Identities: Lesbianism and Psychoanalysis*, London: Virago.

Rayner, E. (1986) *Human Development: An Introduction to the Psychodynamics of Growth, Maturity and Ageing* (third edition), London: Allen and Unwin.

Roberts, J. (1991) 'The Patient With Gender Problems And Other Sexual Difficulties in Groups', in Roberts, J. and Pines, M. (eds) *The Practice of Group Analysis*, London: Routledge.

Rosen, I. (1996) *Sexual Deviation* (third edition), Oxford: Oxford University Press.

Rustin, M. (1991) *The Good Society and the Inner World: Psychoanalysis, Politics and Culture*, London: Verso.

Searles, H. (1972) 'The Patient As Therapist To His Analyst', in Giovacchini, P. (ed.) *Tactics and Techniques in Psychoanalysis* vol. 2: *Countertransference*, New York: Jason Aronson.

Segal, H. (1975) 'A Psycho-Analytic Approach To The Treatment Of Schizophrenia', in Lader, M. (ed.) *Studies in Schizophrenia*, Ashford: Headley Bros.

Seidman, S. (1996) *Queer Theory/Sociology*, Oxford: Blackwell.

Shepherd, S. and Wallis, M. (eds) (1989) *Coming on Strong: Gay Politics and Culture*, London: Unwin Hyman.

Socarides, C. (1978) *Homosexuality*, New York: Jason Aronson.

Spillius, E. B. (1988) *Melanie Klein Today: Developments in Theory and Practice*, Volumes One and Two, London: Routledge.

Steiner, J. (1996) 'The Aims Of Psychoanalysis In Theory And In Practice', *International Journal of Psycho-Analysis*, 77: 1073–83.

Symington, J. and Symington, N. (1996) *The Clinical Thinking of Wilfred Bion*, London: Routledge.

Tuckett, D. (1993) 'Some Thoughts On The Presentation And Discussion Of The Clinical Material Of Psychoanalysis', *International Journal of Psycho-Analysis*, 74: 1175–89.

Ward, I. (1997) *The Presentation of Case Material in Clinical Discourse*, London: Freud Museum.

Weeks, J. (1985) *Sexuality and its Discontents*, London: Routledge.

White, E. (1988) *The Beautiful Room is Empty*, London: Picador.

Yalom, I. (1975) *The Theory and Practice of Group Psychotherapy* (second edition), New York: Basic Books.

Yalom, I. (1980) *Existential Psychotherapy*, New York: Basic Books.

Yalom, I. (1995) *The Theory and Practice of Group Psychotherapy* (fourth edition), New York: Basic Books.

Young, R. (1994) *Mental Space*, London: Process Press.

4   Radicalizing Jungian Theory[1]

Claudette Kulkarni

WHAT MAKES A JUNGIAN?

Jung was the only one among us who could claim the luxury of saying he was glad he was *not* 'a Jungian'.[2] The rest of us have had to find ways to explain what it means to call ourselves 'Jungians'. When asked about this, I usually offer some sort of simplified answer involving references to the unconscious and some mention of dreams, archetypes and myths. I do this all the while knowing that this is really a very difficult question to answer in a nutshell of any size and that almost any description I give will be inadequate. Yet, here I am faced with addressing that same question in order to set the stage for the radicalizing of Jungian theory that I will propose, one that I hope will help create a more hospitable climate among Jungian practitioners for lesbian and gay clients.

A certain elitism prevails in Jungian circles, one that results in a distinct gulf between the official Jungian community of 'insiders' (that is, analysts) and the broader but unofficial Jungian community of 'outsiders' (that is, non-analysts). Since I am not an analyst, my views are technically those of an outsider, someone standing at the margins of the Jungian world looking in. In some ways, that is my preferred location since I generally experience the margin as a chosen 'site of resistance' from which to work for change (hooks 1990, p. 153). It is in the margins that 'revolution is best practised' (Stanley and Wise 1990, p. 44) because outsiders are usually less vulnerable to being pressured into going along with established dogma or official interpretations. For an insider, 'the temptations of assimilation, of keeping one's head down and "getting on", are so much greater' (ibid.).

For me, being a Jungian does not mean that I must defend or try to salvage Jung in any personal sense. I look to Jung for inspiration and grounding, and I consider him to have been a truly remarkable thinker and psychologist. But I also readily accept that he was a human being with faults, prejudices and misconceptions, and that he was quite capable of making mistakes, of misinterpreting what he observed, and even of making things fit his preconceptions. Yet, in spite of all this, I still find Jung's psychology to be the one which best expresses my sense of psyche as soul. So, when I say 'I'm a Jungian', I simply mean that Jung's understanding of the psyche is at the core of my own.

I must confess that my sense of being a Jungian is informed and shaped by two other frames of reference, both of which I appropriate from a relatively postmodern perspective: feminism and hermeneutics. From feminism, I bring a desire to transform society so that all people can flourish unhampered by cultural constructs and stereotypes, especially but not limited to those involving sex and gender. From hermeneutics – 'the art of (text) interpretation' – I bring a disposition rooted in philosophical reflection and reflexivity and a concern with the question of how understanding is at all possible. My source of inspiration here is the philosophical hermeneutics of Hans-Georg Gadamer which shares much common ground with Jungian practice.[3] From postmodernism, I bring a general scepticism about the possibility or advisability of trying to establish knowledge which is 'certain', a profound doubt about fixed identities, and a desire to deconstruct virtually everything.

WHAT IS THE PROBLEM WITH JUNGIAN THEORY?

In the context of this enquiry, the problem in Jungian psychology today is more one of heterosexism than homophobia. The vast majority of Jungian practitioners do *not* have an irrational fear or hatred of homosexuals (that is, they are not 'homophobic'). Nevertheless, the structure of Jungian theory, as we shall see, clearly privileges heterosexuality (that is, it is 'heterosexist'). So, while individual Jungian practitioners might find ways to avoid the most extreme pitfalls of heterosexism in their work with clients, the fact is that heterosexist prejudices permeate Jungian theory and inevitably shape a heterosexist practice. In order to expose the underpinnings of Jungian heterosexism, we will need to review some basic Jungian concepts.

SIMPLIFIED FUNDAMENTALS OF JUNGIAN THEORY

Basic Structure of the Psyche

As one of the depth psychologies, Jung's 'analytical psychology' is built upon a belief in the power and presence of the unconscious in our everyday lives. In contrast to some of the other depth psychologies,

Jung's work exhibits a kind of reverence for the unconscious and the mysteries of its ultimately unknowable forces. For Jung, the unconscious is the reservoir of everything which is not conscious, that is, everything which has been repressed or forgotten or is not yet known. Therefore, it is also the well-spring of all creative and destructive potentials, the *prima materia*[4] and matrix out of which consciousness arises. This very rich unconscious finds expression both in the personal unconscious of every individual and in the various layers of a shared or 'collective' unconscious (that is, that vast portion of the unconscious whose images we 'inherit' through family, tribe, ethnic group, and so on).

The collective unconscious is populated essentially by an indeterminate number of 'archetypes'. These primordial psychic entities function somewhat like instincts. They are part of our collective 'genetic' inheritance (not to be taken too literally) and give us access to the entire range of human patterns of experience and behaviour. An archetypal pattern is like a paradigm or story within which we give meaning to our experiences and try to understand them. Over the course of one's lifetime, psychic energy[5] related to various experiences, relationships, environmental influences, received cultural values, religious beliefs, family stories, and so on, gathers around particular, relevant archetypes (metaphorically, much the way metal filings are attracted to a passing magnet). Each of these accumulations of psychic energy develops into what Jung called a 'complex': an emotionally charged and largely unconscious pocket of associated experiences, ideas, feelings, and images, all clustered around a central core or archetype. The personal unconscious consists essentially of such complexes. Despite the negative connotation attached to the term 'complex' in popular usage, a complex for Jung is not necessarily 'good' or 'bad' – it simply *is*. However, because it contains more or less unassimilated or unintegrated material, it can seem to take on a life of its own when it gets triggered into action: it can overwhelm the ego, act in its place, and appear to be autonomous, especially if the contents of that complex are particularly unresolved. This can be troublesome at times (as, for example, in a violent outburst of rage) or helpful at other times (as, for example, in a crisis when a complex leads the ego to discover previously unknown capacities). In either case, the complex must be 'unpacked' and its contents resolved and/or integrated into the ego's sense of itself. For a Jungian, complexes form the matrix of our everyday lived experience, essentially allowing us to navigate through life and interact with others.

The complexes most often associated with individual consciousness are: the ego (the centre of consciousness and gatekeeper to the unconscious), the persona (the 'mask' by which we adapt to the demands of others and the world), and our sex (male or female). While there are potentially an unlimited number of archetypes in the personal unconscious, the most prominent and generic of these are: the shadow (those parts of ourselves which we disown because they conflict with our established sense of self), which is represented symbolically by people of our own gender; the anima (the contrasexual or 'feminine' qualities within a man) or the animus (the contrasexual or 'masculine' qualities within a woman), both of which are represented symbolically by people of the 'opposite' sex; and the Self (the centring and organizing principle which makes possible 'individuation' and its goal of 'wholeness'[6]).

BASIC DYNAMICS OF THE PSYCHE

With this basic topography in place, let us now review Jung's perceptions of the dynamics which operate within the psyche so that we can come to understand how he was led inescapably to his particular conclusions about homosexuality. We will look at four interrelated concepts: compensation, oppositions, complementarity and contrasexuality.

Compensation

Jung had observed that it was in the nature of consciousness to be 'one-sided,' that is, to develop (or, really, to overdevelop) in one particular direction at the exclusion of all other possibilities.[7] But he also had observed that the psyche seemed engaged in a ceaseless process of individuation or movement towards wholeness, as if it were following a call to fulfil the individual's highest potential. Jung reasoned that if the tendency towards one-sidedness went unchecked, the achievement of 'wholeness' would be precluded. So he came to the conclusion that the psyche must have some kind of self-correcting or self-regulating mechanism. Accordingly, Jung posited a compensatory relationship between consciousness and the unconscious, one by which the unconscious supplies the individual with whatever is missing from the conscious attitude, and vice versa.

Oppositions and Complementarity

It was also Jung's observation (preconception?) that psychic energy is always expressed as a pair of opposites: light–dark, male–female, good–bad, active–passive, and so on. Given his understanding of compensation, Jung then took the next logical step and declared that each pole of any pair of opposites must be characterized by qualities which supplement, or are 'complementary' to, the elements associated with the 'opposite' pole. That is, if we were to draw up a list of characteristics for each pole of a pair of opposites, the two lists would necessarily complement one another and, together, would create a 'whole'. The inescapable implication, of course, is that one *needs* the opposite list of qualities in order to complete oneself and in order to achieve 'wholeness'.[8]

Contrasexuality

For Jung, 'wholeness' is invariably associated with consummating a 'marriage of opposites'. The epitome of this 'coniunctio' (another term borrowed from alchemy) is the marriage between the 'masculine' and 'feminine' principles, as this is personified in the sexual encounters of males with females, since, in spite of repeated disclaimers to the contrary, Jung often wrote as if he believed that men embody the 'masculine' principle and women the 'feminine' principle. Like all other pairs of opposites, these two opposing principles complement one another. Therefore, the individual needs both of them in order to become 'whole'. But how does one gain access to the 'opposite' qualities? Relying on his own experiences of an internal voice which he visualized as his female 'soul image', Jung proposed the construct of 'contrasexuality', that is, the idea that men have an inner or *unconscious* 'feminine' aspect (the anima) and women have an inner or *unconscious* 'masculine' aspect (the animus). The goal ultimately is to become 'whole' by achieving a marriage between one's outer sexual identity and one's inner 'contrasexual' aspect. But how?

In order to answer this question, we need to recognize that from a Jungian perspective there are three somewhat interconnected avenues available to an individual for relating to unconscious material: (1) identification, whereby one identifies with the unconscious material and believes 'this is really me' (whether momentarily or permanently); (2) projection, whereby one projects the unconscious material on to someone else so that it looks as if it belongs to that Other; and (3) the invoking of the transcendent function, whereby one allows or even invites the unconscious to supply images (through dreams, active imagination, artwork, and so on) which give one relatively direct access to the unconscious material.

Of these possibilities, Jung believed projection to be the most immediate and useful in accessing the inner 'Other'. The individual projects his or her 'contrasexual' aspect on to an Other of the 'opposite' gender/sex (because only a person of that 'opposite' sex is 'best fitted to be the real bearer of' a soul image which contains those 'Other' qualities associated with the 'opposite' sex (Jung 1953–79, *Collected Works* [hereafter CW], vol. 6, para. 809). If the individual can 'hold the tension' between these opposites, then 'the transcendent function' will be constellated and it will produce symbols (for example, through dreams, drawings, and so on) that point towards the meaning of the situation and allow the individual to identify, withdraw, and integrate the projected material, thus enabling a process of transformation that will lead towards 'wholeness'. For Jung, all of this can happen only if one is sexually involved (either literally or symbolically) with a member of the 'opposite' gender/sex, or, at the very least, if one interprets one's dream images, and so on, using this framework of heterosexuality.

By this point, it probably is becoming clear that heterosexism is actually woven into the very fabric – and quite literally institutionalized in the structure – of classical Jungian theory through its reliance on oppositions, its insistence on complementarity as the path to 'wholeness', and its valorizing of contrasexuality. Nor would it require much of a leap to realize that all of this is also pointing us inevitably towards the construction of only one 'normal' sexuality (that is, heterosexuality) so that any other expression of sexuality (for example, homosexuality) will become theoretically and necessarily problematic. All of this will become more obvious, however, as we survey some of Jung's stated views on the topic of homosexuality.

JUNG'S VIEWS ON HOMOSEXUALITY[9]

We will now turn to some of the statements Jung made about the phenomenon of homosexuality. While this may further complicate our task of trying to find a way to better understand homosexuality without giving up a Jungian perspective, it will also give us some additional insight into Jungian formulations about this subject.

Jung's Dilemma

Jung's attitude towards same-sex love evolved and changed over the course of his long life,[10] but, throughout, he seemed hounded by a profound and almost palpable ambivalence towards this subject matter. This, it seems to me, was the result of the play and conflict among the following factors.

Interpretation of psychic phenomena as symbolic and metaphorical. For Jung, interpretations of psychic phenomena must never be taken literally or as objectively accurate descriptions of some absolute reality. Instead, they are explanatory and amplificatory statements in which the metaphorical 'as if' is always implied. So, for example, when Jung points to heterosexuality as a symbolic expression of 'the union of opposites', he is interpreting the sex act symbolically: the sexual union between a man and a woman represents symbolically the union of the 'masculine' and 'feminine' principles. It is 'as if' these two principles come together in the sex act – partly because this is a union between 'opposite' sexes, but also because, in projecting one's inner 'opposite' or 'contrasexual' (anima/animus) on to the Other, one is thereby able to achieve one's own intrapsychic union or *coniunctio* between the outer/conscious personality and the inner/unconscious personality, and thus become 'whole' (if only momentarily).

Every psychic phenomenon is meaningful. For Jung, every psychic phenomenon, by definition, must be meaningful and any search for the meaning of a phenomenon can never be satisfied by merely uncovering the 'causes' of that phenomenon ('causality'). Rather, it must discover that particular phenomenon's 'prospective' or purposeful role in achieving the goal of individuation ('finality').[11]

'Normality' is overrated. Jung's views on 'normality' often seem rather postmodern. Rix Weaver quotes Jung as saying: 'What I fear greatly and suspect greatly is normality. That is something people are trained to. It is like a tight lid' (Weaver 1982, p. 93). In a 1929/1933 essay, Jung acknowledges that although the initial aim of psychotherapy is to become 'a normal and adapted social being' (that is, to feel that one fits into and can cope with the world) (CW16, para. 161). He goes on to insist, however, that this cannot be the ultimate aim of psychotherapy since 'the very notion of a "normal human being" implies' a kind of 'levelling down' to 'the average ... To be "normal" is the ideal aim for the unsuccessful, for all those who are still below the general level of adaptation.' Therefore, 'normality' can be a 'desirable improvement only to the man who already has some difficulty in coming to terms with the everyday world'. For those who have 'more than average ability', the idea of being 'nothing but normal' is one of 'deadly and insupportable boredom, a hell of sterility and hopelessness' (ibid.).

In spite of these passionate denunciations of 'normality', Jung was never able to sanction adult homosexuality because he could never see it as anything more than, to use Hopcke's description, 'a manifestation of psychological immaturity, a fixation or arrest in psychosexual development, and, for this reason, disturbed' (Hopcke 1989, p. 18).[12] In other words, homosexuality in adults could not be 'normal'.

Views of sex/gender. Jung was certainly a prisoner of the sex and gender stereotypes of his time and seemed never able to see beyond them, at least not theoretically. Several authors have noted the ironic fact that Jung was surrounded throughout his life by many accomplished women, all of whom defied prevailing stereotypes and yet seemed devoted to supporting and defending his theories in spite of the fact that their own lives provided ample evidence to disprove many of them.[13] In addition, Jung tended to conflate sex and gender in ways that obliterated the distinction between identity and behavior and denied the role of culture in the formation of gender identity.[14]

Reluctance to discuss sex in depth. Jung generally tended to interpret sexual issues as misunderstood spiritual strivings. While he was willing to acknowledge sex as a powerful form of psychic energy, he was not willing to give it the kind of primacy Freud had accorded it and he generally avoided discussing the topic in any embodied detail, especially after his final break from Freud in 1914.[15]

We might summarize by noting that while Jung was committed to relativizing sex (as an alternative to Freudian pansexualism), he also was committed to the idea that every phenomenon must play some kind of meaningful role in the individuation process. He could not in good conscience simply dispose of homosexuality by undertaking a search for its 'causes'. He would have to find some meaning for it in the context of the psyche's drive towards 'wholeness'. But this created a dilemma for Jung: how could he find a way to see homosexuality as meaningful if he believed it was not 'normal'?

Jung's 'Solutions'

At first, Jung proposed various ideas which might let him conceptualize homosexuality as meaningful without reducing it to the level of a sexual perversion, but also without allowing it ever to achieve a status equal to heterosexual sex as a vehicle for individuation. For example, in a 1910 letter to Freud, Jung argued that there should be no moral stigma attached to homosexuality because it is, after all, 'a method of contraception' (cited in Hopcke 1989, p. 44) and, in a 1928 essay, he referred to female homosexuality's historical role 'as a stimulus to the social and political organization of women, just as male homosexuality was an important factor in the rise of the Greek *polis*' (cited in ibid., p. 26).

By the mid-1930s, however, Jung had consolidated his own thinking, formulated a theory of homosexuality that relied on the constructs outlined above, and posited a 'normal' process of sexual development (heterosexuality) that had individuation as its aim and hypothesized homosexuality as an aberration. Homosexuality thereby became something that had to be explained in terms of 'what went wrong' and, so, in spite of his reluctance to speak in causal terms, Jung in effect opened a kind of back door into the pseudo-question of what 'causes' homosexuality.

Yet, if we look at certain of Jung's writings, we can find some nearly redeeming features in his theorizing about homosexuality. I will cite just one example here, from an essay in which Jung discusses the dangers of identifying with the anima and argues that a man's psychological well-being depends on his projecting his anima on to a woman. However, Jung then allows an exception for men who have not yet reached mid-life. All that is required in the first half of life, he declares, 'is for a man to be a man' by 'free[ing] himself from the anima fascination of his mother' (CW9i, para. 146). Therefore, identification with the anima is an acceptable, though temporary, strategy – as, for example, in the case of 'artists' and 'homosexuality'. Jung then goes on to say something quite remarkable:

> In view of the recognized frequency of this phenomenon [identification with the anima], its interpretation as a pathological perversion is very dubious. The psychological findings show that it is rather a matter of the incomplete detachment from the hermaphroditic archetype, coupled with a distinct resistance to identify with the role of a one-sided sexual being. Such a disposition should not be adjudged negative in all circumstances, in so far as it preserves the archetype of the Original Man, which a one-sided sexual being has, up to a point, lost. (ibid.)[16]

In other words, since the phenomenon of identification with the anima occurs frequently and since every phenomenon must be meaningful and interpreted symbolically, then we cannot interpret an example of this phenomenon (that is, homosexuality) as perverse.

Rather, it must be an expression of individuation gone awry ('incomplete detachment from the hermaphroditic archetype') which occurs when the homosexual, in an attempt to be more 'whole', tries to disidentify from 'the role of a one-sided sexual being' (that is, from the role of a sexual being who insists on being only and all 'male') and ends up in love with another man.

One might argue from this that Jung is conceptualizing homosexuality as an unconscious though misdirected corrective to heterosexuality. I believe, however, that this would be a serious misinterpretation of Jung's actual views – and a questionable strategy since it basically endorses the privileging of heterosexuality by leaving heterosexuality as its reference point. What I think Jung really means to insinuate here is only that homosexuality is a kind of reaction formation to a fear of one-sidedness. For Jung, the image of the hermaphrodite is the image of a primordial and, therefore, *unconscious* and undifferentiated mixture of 'masculine' and 'feminine' energies, a being with both male and female genitalia. In the *Rosarium Philosophorum*,[17] the hermaphrodite is pictured at an early stage in the process and represents a 'lesser *coniunctio*'. It thus points *towards* the goal of individuation and, therefore, cannot represent that goal. The gendered image which does illustrate the goal of individuation for Jung is the androgyne, the final image in the *Rosarium*. The androgyne, unlike the hermaphrodite, is the product of a union between the *differentiated* 'masculine' and 'feminine' principles. It symbolizes the 'greater *coniunctio*', which is achieved symbolically in the sexual union between a man and a woman.

I agree with Christine Downing that Jung saw homosexuality as 'a misguided attempt to actualize psychical androgyny' (Downing 1989, p. 115). In Jung's view, heterosexual males are the norm because they identify with 'the masculine'[18] and project 'the feminine', while homosexual men, in their desire to not be one-sided, are misguided into identifying with 'the feminine' and projecting 'the masculine'. That is, homosexuals misinterpret the symbolic nature of their sexual urges and, as a result, can never achieve the *coniunctio* because the union between two bodies of the same sex cannot reflect the union of 'opposites'. Of course, we might also point out here, using similar logic, that heterosexuals can also fail to achieve the *coniunctio* since the projection of the anima/animus on to a person of the 'opposite' sex may also miss the symbolic nature of the inner 'Other' and instead get stuck at the literal level of a physical act and never result in any kind of *coniunctio*, inner or outer. In other words, heterosexuality can also be understood as a failure to completely detach from the image of the hermaphrodite.

In any case, what I find most intriguing in all of this is Jung's provocative remark about homosexuality's purpose in relation to the preservation of the archetype of 'the Original Man'. To understand what Jung is getting at here, we must first consider what this archetype represented to him. Since Jung's references to this image are mostly found in his work on alchemy and gnosticism, they are not easily explained outside of those contexts. However, from my reading of Jung, it seems to me that he conceptualized 'the Original Man', first as symbolic of the original human condition, that is, 'spirit trapped in matter' and thus 'in need of salvation' (CW11, para. 420) and, second, as 'bisexual' (CW12, para. 210).[19]

So, what is Jung saying when he notes that the 'one-sided sexual being' (heterosexual male) has lost contact 'up to a point' with this archetype? The embedded implication is that heterosexuals are more 'one-sided' than homosexuals. This is extremely interesting because it suggests that although heterosexuality is the only 'normal' path, it is also a 'one-sided' one and, therefore, presumably somehow problematic in terms of individuation, and that while homosexuals may be misguided and not 'normal', they are at least attempting to address this problem of one-sidedness. I believe this is where Jung opens the door to viewing homosexuality as being meaningful in its own right and not just as a symbolic corrective to heterosexual one-sidedness. In this post-Jungian reconstruction of Jung's statement, homosexuality is not derived from heterosexuality. It is really an alternative to it, a different-but-equal path towards individuation.

So, while Jung does not find homosexuality to be perverse, and while he does struggle to attribute to it some kind of meaning, his own interpretations of homosexuality never really get beyond his assumption that there is something deficient about same-sex sexuality. If we are to find our way out of this heterosexist quagmire, we must step outside the conversation that Jung was constrained within, a conversation whose terms are set by the filters of a heterosexist belief system. That means we must abandon explanatory appeals to gendered images (like the hermaphrodite or the androgyne) because these genderized images are rooted in socially constructed and stereotypical abstractions. Resorting to them simply keeps us stuck in a framework that requires, and thus assumes, the concept of gender. If we stay within the language and constructs of this conversation, we simply give it legitimacy, and thus, in effect, allow heterosexism to continue dictating the terms and language of our discussion and thereby to continue limiting our understanding.

WHERE ARE WE TODAY?

Delineating a World After Jung

Andrew Samuels' landmark book *Jung and the Post-Jungians* (1985) signalled the beginning of a new era in Jungian thought, a time for questioning what Jung had taught us. While Samuels does not define this term 'post-Jungian' that he coined, he does describe it as denoting 'both connectedness to Jung and distance from him' (p. 19). This suggests that a post-Jungian is someone who acknowledges a debt to Jung, but refuses to be bound by Jung's particular and limited vision.

Post-Jungian Views on Same-Sex Love

How have Jungians tried to rectify heterosexist theory? Or have they? While Roger Payne finds it surprising that there is so little Jungian litera-ture on a phenomenon as 'extremely common' as homosexuality (Payne 1990, p. 155), I find this lack of interest to be indicative of how inherently heterosexist much Jungian theory is and of how the question of same-sex love must be 'at the nexus of some unthinkable anxieties' (O'Connor and Ryan 1993, p. 14). To date, there has been only one book by an analyst that was devoted entirely to the topic of homosexuality, namely, Gra-ham Jackson's 1991 book on homoerotic relationships entitled *The Se-cret Lore of Gardening*. While Jackson is highly critical of some aspects of Jungian theory, he abandons a promising start by proposing yet another fourfold typology made up of two pairs of opposites. While his opposites are ungendered in any overt sense (for example, 'the green man' is oppo-site 'the yellow man'), his analysis remains traditional in that it contin-ues to prize the union of 'opposites' over all other possibilities.

Among Jungians who are not analysts, there was very little in-depth writing about same-sex love before 1989. In that year, two remarkable books suddenly appeared: Christine Downing's *Myths and Mysteries of Same-Sex Love* and Robert Hopcke's *Jung, Jungians, and Homosexual-ity*. These were followed in 1993 by a collection of essays, edited by Hopcke, Carrington and Wirth, entitled *Same-Sex Love and the Path to Wholeness*. Finally, the most recent contribution to this effort has been my own post-Jungian perspective on *Lesbians and Lesbianisms* pub-lished in 1997.

Since the topic of homosexuality has received so little serious attention from Jungians, it might be useful briefly to categorize the range of Jungian views on this topic.[20]

The Conservators

The Conservators occupy the orthodox end of the spectrum. They follow Jung's views very closely with the intent of 'systematically elaborating, deepening, and widening' his work (Douglas 1990, p. 112). Most of these Jungians believe that there is generally nothing inherently wrong with Jungian theory. We might say that these Jungians, technically, are not really post-Jungian at all because there is virtually no distance between them and Jung. They rarely deviate from his views. The Conservators tend to view homosexuality as Jung did. In other words, their interpretations are homophobic at worst and heterosexist at best. Hopcke has remarked that such theorists miss 'the genius of some of Jung's most important insights and attitudes' and thus fail to 'advance Jung's own thinking' in any meaningful or creative way (Hopcke 1989, p. 102). As a result, the Conservators really have nothing to offer us in terms of our task.

The Reformulators

The Reformulators generally offer arguments that run something like: 'Let's admit that Jung was "a product of his times", acknowledge and discard his most offensive blunders, and then update and use what's left.' Their intent is mainly to salvage Jung's ideas by modifying them rather than deconstructing them and they frame the problem as one which will disappear if we simply admit Jung's cultural/historical contexts and biases. They tend, therefore, to dismiss or explain away Jung's 'incorrect' views without considering how those views permeate his theory as a whole and how that might be problematic. I find this approach to be unconvincing and inadequate. The issue here is not simply whether Jung should be held accountable for his views, but, more importantly, whether analytical psychology can continue to ignore the harm inflicted on people by its heterosexist bias. While most Reformulators accept the legitimacy of lesbian/gay relationships, they also persist in promoting views of gender that are rooted in heterosexual norms (for example, by arguing that both men and women have an anima *and* an animus) or that attempt to rescue Jung's theory by complicating it (for example, by using concepts such as 'the anima of the animus'). Such strategies remain stuck within heterosexist language and overlook the many questionable assumptions which lay at the foundation of Jungian thought on sex/gender.

The Radicals

The Radicals want to engage in a rigorous critique of Jung without sacrificing his independent spirit (or their own) and without simply dismissing Jung's ideas or concealing them behind obscuring reinterpretations. In borrowing freely from postmodern ways of thinking, they argue for dramatic and fundamental shifts in Jungian theorizing. Their aim is first to deconstruct and then to reapply Jung's original insights in ways that he himself could or would not. The Radicals are iconoclasts who believe that it is time for Jungians to stop trying to redeem 'Jung the man' and instead to commit ourselves to 'a program of renewal from within' (Samuels, 1989). This requires that we mourn Jung and his 'flaws'. Then maybe we can really learn from him and follow up on some of the truly subversive possibilities that he opened up for us. The Radicals tend to challenge Jungian ideas in order to make room for the experiences of those who simply do not fit into traditional Jungian categories, theories, or constructs. They are vocal in pointing the way towards new theoretical avenues for theorizing on gender and sexual orientation. Their focus is on deconstructing concepts typically considered sacred by Jungians: for example; gender, 'wholeness', 'contrasexuality', 'the opposites', and the 'feminine' and 'masculine' principles.[21] This urge to deconstruct is not necessarily fuelled by a desire to entirely undo or discard all of these concepts, but rather to unravel and expose their underlying heterosexist assumptions and preconceptions.

APPLYING RADICALIZED JUNGIAN THEORY

A science's level of development is determined by the extent to which it is capable of a crisis in its basic concepts. (Heidegger 1953, p. 8)

It might seem ironic to some and even heretical to others that I quote Heidegger in support of a radical post-Jungian position. However, in spite of Jung's vitriolic attacks on Heidegger, I believe that they had more in common than not and I think Jung would have agreed with the spirit of Heidegger's remark: knowledge and understanding must be useful and practical to survive. Applying this to the context of psychological theory, we might say that a psychology which is not useful is a psychology without purpose and that a theory (and its practice) which do not liberate their subject matter from the forces which conspire to hide or distort it, which does not help us better understand the phenomena before us, and which cannot tolerate scrutiny is a theory not worth having.

I believe that those who care deeply about Jungian thought must take the risk of pushing it into a crisis. I trust that Jungian theory will survive this test, not because it has already achieved some 'high' level of development, but because it is capable of re-imagining itself. I do not think that I could call myself a Jungian if I did not believe this.

How I Apply What is Left of Jungian Theory to my Clinical Practice

There are a lot of Jungian ideas which will continue to be useful even after Jungian theory has been submitted to radical post-Jungian analyses and critiques. This remaining and revitalized theory can be applied in the same ways that Jungian theory is usually applied: namely, from the perspective of helping the client deepen the work of individuation by crafting more meaningful interpretations.

CLINICAL VIGNETTES

I come to my work with clients holding firmly to the belief that to be gay or lesbian is to be on a legitimate path towards individuation. This is not to argue that everyone who lives as a lesbian or as a gay man has made a choice to individuate (I would not make such a claim for those who live as heterosexuals either). The following vignettes demonstrate how I use some of the radicalized Jungian theory I have been discussing. These are not case studies, just stories about certain clients whose experiences help illustrate both the unusefulness of conventional Jungian theory and the usefulness of a radical revisioning of that theory. I have taken precautions to disguise identities, including the use of fictitious names and the alteration of various details. Also, in recognition of Jung's belief that the first stage of therapy is confession – the goal of which is to cleanse the individual of secrets that act 'like a psychic poison' alienating us from others (CW16, para. 124) – each vignette includes my version of the client's initial confession. There is very little in any of this material that could be called 'objective'. This is in accordance with my belief that 'objectivity' is an unachievable and even undesirable fantasy which only attempts to make invisible the investigator's biases. I have preferred instead to use the hermeneutic method of 'foregrounding' my biases.[22]

Looking in the Mirror: A *Coniunctio* of 'Likes'

> Women are becoming individuated through mirroring themselves increasingly accurately and fully, and through finding more comprehensive mirrors. (Douglas 1990, p. 149)

Although Claire Douglas is talking here strictly in asexual terms about women in general, I believe her point has relevance for both lesbians and gay men because she is challenging the Jungian obsession with complementarity. Douglas argues that a psychology of women constructed as 'opposite to and complementary to man's fails to mirror woman herself' (ibid., p. 291). So, when women look into that mirror, they often see an image constructed mainly by male others. While Douglas does not take her insight to its logical conclusion, namely, that a same-sex relationship might be a 'more comprehensive mirror', I would like to do so here.

Jung, of course, saw this kind of intense mirroring as a problem of identification and, therefore, as inherently suspect. But, with some theoretical reconstructing, we could arrive at a very different interpretation: namely, that the experience of intense mirroring which can occur between people of the same sex might exemplify an alchemical *coniunctio* of 'likes' rather than one of 'opposites'. Lyn Cowan, who is currently President of the Inter-Regional Society of Jungian Analysts (USA), has pointed out, in fact, that alchemical conjunctions are 'inherently sexual image[s] in Jungian thought' which 'may happen between sames as well as between opposites' (Cowan 1994, p. 75). Christine Downing, a scholar noted for her work in both Jungian and psychoanalytic studies, makes a similar point when she describes homosexuals as people 'who have become who we are primarily through relationships based on analogy rather than contrast, on mirroring rather than the complementation of opposites' (Downing 1989, p. xvii).

The following story of 'Shelley' offers us an opportunity to explore what can happen when a woman looks into the mirror and sees herself.

Shelley's Confession

Shelley walked in the door agonizing over how to resolve an enormous inner conflict: She was married to a man she believed to be good and decent. They had two adolescent children whom she adored. She had taken marriage vows which she regarded as promises never to be broken. But she could not reconcile all of this with her growing feelings of discontent and a dawning sense of being a lesbian. She felt torn apart and did not know what to do. She had 'met' another woman online and found herself becoming excited at the prospect of getting involved with this other woman (even though they had not yet even met since Jane lived hundreds of miles away).

The idea of making a decision according to what was best for her, and in spite of how it might affect others, was 'a novel thought' for Shelley when it surfaced, and it caused her great amazement and consternation. Shelley's husband, Mike, was very dependent on her for just about everything. Shelley was the ultimate caretaker, both at home and as the major breadwinner. She performed the tasks of both mother and father to her children – and, in many ways, to Mike. Over time, she began to describe Mike in terms that revealed her sense of him as inadequate, fragile and incapable of fulfilling his responsibilities. She could not imagine that he could function without her. Like their children, he needed her care and protection. How could she leave him? Shelley's childhood was showing through here: she had grown up with an alcoholic father who was physically abusive and a mother who was typically both unavailable and ineffectual in protecting her against her father. Shelley had learned to be very self-sufficient, to discount at a conscious level any feelings of abandonment or disappointment and to sacrifice herself for others.

From a Jungian perspective, Shelley was doing it all. There were not really two people in the relationship, just Shelley doing everything, including the more 'masculine' things like having a hugely successful career. Where Shelley was feeling inadequate was in the area of interpersonal skills, the traditional domain of 'the feminine'. By the time Shelley came into therapy, she was facing a daunting and, to her, impossible choice: her own individuation and happiness versus the pain such a decision would inevitably cause others.

Course of Therapy

Shelley eventually accepted the challenge to individuate. Within a few weeks of starting therapy, she left her husband and began to explore the possibility of living and identifying as a lesbian. At that point, Shelley felt free to pursue her interest in Jane and made several trips to visit her. As Shelley's feelings for Jane blossomed, she came to see Jane as her first 'real' love and became determined not to let this opportunity pass her by. From the beginning, their relationship has been intense and sometimes volatile, but with every crisis Shelley has discovered a little more about herself. And even though Jane is very much like Mike in some important ways, it is clear that Shelley is daily becoming more and more her own person. However, even after she became involved with Jane, it took Shelley many months before she could even begin really to let go of Mike and leave him to his own fate. Her sense of responsibility for him (along with her concern for her children) prompted her to shoulder more than her fair share of their joint liabilities.

Shelley wants desperately to live with Jane and would do almost anything to make that happen. But Jane's life is in nearly continuous crisis and Shelley is not willing to take care of Jane the way she fell into taking care of Mike. She acknowledges a deep longing to 'fix' things for Jane, but seems convinced that this is neither possible nor advisable. She has come to realize that she can devote her resources to working on herself instead.

Theoretical Considerations

Shelley looked into the mirror (metaphorically represented by her computer screen) and fell in love with the woman she 'saw', Jane, even before she had ever actually seen Jane. Did Shelley fall in love with Jane because Jane was a woman? Before they had met in person, there was no way to know for sure that Jane was really a woman, and so it could be argued that Jane's actual gender was irrelevant to Shelley except through Shelley's inner images and experiences of 'woman'. When Shelley looked into the mirror, she projected something from deep within herself on to it. She then fell in love with this 'other' person whom she imagined to be 'a woman' like her. That is, when Shelley looked into the mirror, she saw herself and fell in love. She does not realize this, of course. She is still too overwhelmed by the idea that someone as 'special' and 'wonderful' as Jane could be interested in her. I believe that Shelley sees in Jane both her own achievements and her own undeveloped potentials. In Jane, all these unrecognized qualities look 'special' and Jane seems 'wonderful'. Shelley cannot yet see all of this, but it may not matter since, in Jane, Shelley has found a 'more comprehensive mirror'. Looking into this mirror has allowed Shelley to see an image of herself, disguised as Jane, rather than an image of the expectations of others that she saw in the mirror that Mike held up for her. Through her unconscious 'identification' with Jane she has opened up a door into herself that she could not even see before.

Jung assumed that an idealized transference on to someone of the same gender was problematic because it indicated an 'identification' with that other person via one's 'conscious,' or supposedly already 'known' external (male/female) self rather than a projection of one's unconscious inner 'opposite'. However, while Shelley does identify with her image of Jane's gender, it was this identification which allowed Shelley to experience more parts of herself than she had ever before imagined were even there. Simultaneously, Shelley also projects a lot on to Jane – all of it unconscious, but not necessarily 'masculine' by anyone's standards. In fact, Shelley's frustrations with Jane are much like her frustrations with Mike: Jane seems unable to manage her financial and business affairs. Shelley does not need others (male or female) to 'carry' such projections for her because these are activities at which Shelley herself is quite competent. Shelley projects what she most needs to have mirrored back to her, the qualities she cannot otherwise get access to, the qualities required to form a deep relationship, the qualities many Jungians call 'feminine'. Of course, these qualities that traditional Jungians might call 'feminine' seem to me to be simply qualities that were unavailable to Shelley given her history. She had tried to project these on to Mike originally, but he could not carry them, not because they are inherently 'feminine' but because men are not socialized to develop these qualities, and so Mike did not have them either. In many ways, Jane also cannot carry these projections for Shelley, but what is different between Mike and Jane from Shelley's perspective is that while Mike did not know what to do with these projections, Jane is more than willing to reflect them back to Shelley, however imperfectly. This, I believe, is in keeping with the dynamics of a *coniunctio* of likes. This is not to claim that such a result can happen *only* in a *coniunctio* of likes, merely that it *can* happen. Interestingly enough, Shelley and Jane are quite opposite in certain ways. For example, Shelley is essentially an introverted thinking type while Jane would best be described (at least through Shelley's reports of her) as an extroverted feeling type.

Classical interpretations might reduce Shelley's experience to narcissism (by associating Shelley's sighting of herself in the mirror with Narcissus' reflection in the pool), or to a shadow projection (by referring to Jung's insistence that the shadow is personified by someone of the same gender), or to an unresolved mother complex (by pointing to the lack of adequate mirroring received from her mother during childhood). However, such reductive explanations would only cover over and make us lose sight of the reality of Shelley's lived experience. For example, pointing to narcissism would only emphasize the tragedy of Narcissus' inability truly to love himself without appreciating Shelley's creative solution to this for herself. Or attributing the relationship to a shadow projection would merely uphold the arbitrary hierarchy under which

Jung claimed that the contrasexual operates at a 'deeper' level of the unconscious than the shadow, thus implying that same-sex relationships are less valuable than heterosexual ones. As for the issue of her mother complex, Shelley's relationship with her mother certainly did provide a template for her later relationships and Shelley certainly is struggling to find the mirroring she never got. But, so what? Should we discount heterosexual relationships in which a person is grappling with unmet needs? Would it not be equally disingenuous to depreciate Shelley's relationship on that basis? In the end, I would argue that genderizing the unconscious in these ways seems unnecessary, unproductive and uninspired.

It also seems to me that Shelley's story provides us with evidence which refutes Jung's claim that homosexuality involves a failure to detach from the archetype of the hermaphrodite. Jung had a culture-bound (mis)understanding of this image which we are in a better position today to deconstruct and thereby to realize that its split into male and female is a reconstruction of prevailing cultural norms by which human beings have been divided into two genders according to their most visible indicators of sex: their genitalia. When Shelley and Mike tried to put their two halves together, it created only an undifferentiated 'whole'. For Shelley, this was eventually stifling to her own individuation, so she detached herself from 'the archetype of the hermaphrodite' by leaving her marriage. That is, Shelley's detachment from the hermaphrodite was expressed as her separation from her husband and heterosexuality. As long as Shelley felt bound to Mike, she could not begin a meaningful individuation process or explore the parts of herself that were not being mirrored in her relationship with Mike. Was Shelley ever in love with Mike? Or was she attracted to his inadequacies because they allowed her freedom to play roles typically assigned to men? Leaving Mike would mean she would have to face questions about herself in terms of her sexual identity and gender roles. In the end, it was breaking her commitment to Mike and making a decision to follow her heart that allowed her to free herself of the image of the hermaphrodite and strike out on a course towards something more fulfilling.

WHAT HAS GENDER GOT TO DO WITH IT?

As we have seen, Jung was convinced that a person's sex (which Jung conflated with gender) is a basic and instrumental factor in achieving the goal of individuation: 'wholeness'. So, while Jung was astute at avoiding the topic of sex as such, he tended instead to genderize everything. For Jung, consciousness was 'masculine' and the unconscious 'feminine,' any behaviours or feelings which did not fit his preconceived and rigid notions of 'masculine' or 'feminine' were explained by attributing them to the 'contrasexual' aspects of the personality, and 'wholeness' could be achieved only through hetero-sexuality and via a relationship with one's anima/animus complex.

This next story is about 'Marty', a gay man whose individuation process calls into question all of these genderized assumptions and preconceptions.

Marty's Confession

Marty was catapulted into therapy when his lover of ten years ended their relationship. Lou had been Marty's first and only male lover. They had met in a professional context and Lou had soon become a kind of mentor to Marty, someone whom Marty could admire and emulate. Theirs was in many ways the story of Pygmalion, although with a few twists. Ini-tially, Marty very much idealized this relationship, but it soon became clear that the relationship had had many problems, not the least of which was that there was a marked lack of intimacy between Marty and Lou, as if each was using the other to evade himself. In addition, the relationship provided Marty with various excuses for ignoring his own career (while Lou's flourished) and for staying very, very deep in the closet since, as long as they were together, Marty had no reason to confront his own sexuality. Marty had internalized a host of homophobic beliefs and had developed many 'avoidance' defences, including a profound disdain for 'the gay community' and for the idea of 'labelling' himself 'gay'. Marty came into therapy feeling traumatized by how Lou had ended the rela-tionship and intent on doing whatever it would take to restore the relationship and his old 'comfortable' life. Marty's individuation process had been on hold for many years and he wanted to keep it that way.

Course of Therapy

Initially, Marty blamed himself for the break-up and spent months trying to understand what had happened and what he had done 'wrong'. He felt compelled to 'understand why' Lou had done this to him. He analysed and dissected himself and everything that had happened. Marty was basically re-enacting old patterns here. He had been abandoned before birth by a father whom his mother refused to talk about and his mother had alternated between neglecting and abusing Marty (and his many siblings) in her scramble to find ways to support her children and manage Marty's alcoholic stepfather. Marty got lost in the shuffle and adopted the role of family mediator to help him cope and feel more in control.

Marty was in therapy for well over a year before he realized that he must be in it for himself. This was a revelation to him. He began to make tentative but definite forays into exploring both his sexual identity and the gay community that he had avoided for so many years. Marty cycled through the various 'coming out' stages fairly quickly: encounter, immersion, re-emergence, internalization and synthesis, and he will undoubtedly revisit any or all of these stages again. At present, however, he has come to accept and even to prize his sexuality in a way that he could not have imagined previously. Marty has been involved with several men; one rather seriously. James was just 'coming out' when Marty met him and, in a twist of fate, Marty became a kind of mentor to James in this process. While the relationship did not last very long, they remain good friends and, in fact, Marty now has a small circle of close gay friends. In other words, Marty has proceeded, with bumps and starts, along an individuation path that was blocked before Lou 'dumped' him. It was the break with Lou which served as the catalyst for change.

Theoretical Considerations

Lou and Marty were not 'opposites'. Nor did either of them identify with or play out the role of being 'feminine' to the other. Physically, Marty is a handsome, well-built man; tall, muscular and 'masculine' in appearance. It might be argued that Marty 'identified' with Lou who was the successful man that Marty wanted to be, or that Lou served as a father-figure for Marty (as many heterosexual men do for hetero-sexual women), or that Marty's life provides more examples of the mirroring that can occur in same-sex relationships. What piqued my curiosity more, however, was a different question: how was Marty's individuation process 'broken open' by the rupture with Lou? What really happened there? How did the end of that relationship 'jump start', so to speak, Marty's individuation process?

I am reminded here of Gadamer's remarks about 'the priority of the question'. Space constraints do not allow me to explicate this fully, so I will only mention that Gadamer links the capacity to experience life with the ability to form questions: 'We cannot have experiences without asking questions' because 'the openness essential to experi-ence ... has the structure of a question' (Gadamer 1960, p. 362). That is, without questions we cannot reflect on what is happening to us.

However, we usually do not ask such questions unless our understanding of a situation is somehow 'disrupted', revealing 'breaches' that force us to ask the (unconscious) questions which we had been avoiding or which we could not yet have formed. This is certainly what happened to Marty. He had been going along for years in a relationship that was 'comfortable' and 'familiar' to him. It was only when his understanding of the relationship was 'disrupted' that he could begin to ask the questions which would bring him eventually face-to-face with himself. It seems to me that none of this hung on gender.

LIFE WITHOUT ANIMUS

Jung pointed out occasionally that, linguistically and psychologically, there is a connection between the terms anima/animus and 'animosity'. That is, a relationship which involves the anima/animus 'is always full of "animosity"' because these complexes are so emotionally loaded (CW9ii, para. 31). When they are triggered, they 'lower the level of the relationship' bringing it closer to its 'instinctual basis'. The relationship takes on a life of its own and 'its human performers' find themselves surrounded by a 'cloud of 'animosity' and, when it is over, they 'do not know what happened to them' (ibid.). A woman 'possessed' by the animus will be 'argumentative' (ibid., para. 48) and she will let loose a torrent 'of opinionated views, interpretations, insinuations, and misconstructions' (CW9ii, para. 32). On very rare occasions, Jung refers to the 'positive aspect' of the animus, claiming that it 'gives to woman's consciousness a capacity for reflection, deliberation, and self-knowledge' she would not otherwise have (ibid., para. 33).

I am not the first one to point out that while Jung's concept of the animus may have served a purpose historically by giving women 'legitimate' access to traditionally 'masculine' qualities, it is today a no-win construct for women. For example, a competent woman can be dismissed as 'animus possessed' or her sense of self can be minimized when she is expected 'to give credit to the "positive animus" for her own self-directed accomplishment' (Cowan 1994, p. 61).

The next story about 'Maggie' challenges Jung's ideas about the animus and exposes the genderism which underlies it.

Maggie's Confession

Maggie came into therapy a few years ago on the threshold of retirement and just as her 20-year relationship with Carol was coming to an end.

She knew something was wrong with her life, but only after much gentle prodding was she willing to engage in a process of uncovering the layers of her life. Maggie had been adopted into a loving but traditional family in which girls were expected to marry. Soon after high school, she met and married Chuck, a man who proved to be both alcoholic and abusive. She thought things could be OK if she could just figure out how to play the role of a woman 'right', that is, if she could just be a 'better' wife and mother. But nothing satisfied Chuck. Maggie blamed herself for that. What little self-esteem she had had eroded quickly and she lived for many years in fear and frustration. Then Emily came along and swept Maggie off her feet. Although this relationship did not weather the many crises it spawned, Maggie did eventually leave her husband. She entered into a series of lesbian relationships in which she found herself playing the role of the 'butch', the 'masculine' partner in a lesbian relationship. In those days, Maggie explained, that was how things were: 'you had to be either butch or femme'. From Maggie's perspective, the choice was clear. She had already done all those 'feminine' things in her marriage and by now she wanted more. Then came the relationship with Carol who was controlling and domineering. It was confusing and painful for Maggie who came to see herself as defective and to be convinced that everything she did was wrong. She survived by doing 'anything to avoid conflict'. By the time Maggie came into therapy she was tired of trying to be what others wanted, but she was at a loss to understand how just to be herself.

Course of Therapy

Once Maggie settled down to work, she was able to face many of the buried memories she had brushed aside, though she resisted confronting the residual affects of those experiences. She even 'dropped out' of therapy for a while. When she came back, she could not understand why she was feeling so 'depressed' every time someone died – which was happening frequently because Maggie had several friends who were HIV+ and she was reaching an age at which family members and childhood friends begin to die. She was also still struggling to come to terms with the loss of her relationship with Carol. It seemed like all of the losses of her life were getting tangled together. Eventually, Maggie became willing to feel the sadness of so many losses, but she generally continued to elude my attempts to uncover her deeply buried emotional life. Then she met Linda, the woman with whom she expects to live out the rest of her life. Since then, Maggie has been more willing to take risks and to dig deeper.

Theoretical Considerations

Maggie's relationship life can be divided into three phases: her marriage to Chuck, her relationship with Carol, and her current 'marriage' to Linda. According to Jungian theory, Maggie was projecting her animus on to her husband during her married years. Otherwise, she would have had to identify with it – which would have made her 'argumentative' and 'opinionated' – and there was no room for that with a violent husband. There certainly was plenty of animosity in the relationship, but it was all coming at Maggie. (Actually, one might wonder who was really 'animus possessed' in that relationship.) Later, with Carol, Maggie had a chance to do something different. A Jungian might say that she identified with her animus by taking on the 'butch' role. But there is really no indication that Maggie played this role out of any internally driven sense of wanting to be 'male'. Rather, she was just following the rules – rules established in imitation of the prevailing model of heterosexual relationships. Only after meeting Linda did Maggie's sense of role-playing change, probably because her fear of self-reflection was offset by the sense of safety she experienced with Linda, who was the first person in Maggie's life to accept her just as she is, without pigeon-holing her into any kind of 'feminine' or 'masculine' roles. Has Maggie learned to 'integrate' her animus, as a traditional Jungian might claim? I doubt it. To ascribe Maggie's various talents to her 'animus' would be to fall into the point-less trap described earlier of giving credit to the 'masculine' animus for qualities that truly and simply belong to Maggie.

Jungians have for too long tried to explain lesbianism by resorting to the idea that it represents some form of identification with the 'masculine' and rejection of 'the feminine'. Maggie might even be a good example of this *if* we were looking at her only through the preconceptions of traditional theory and then hypothesized, as Jung did, that she must have wanted to 'be' a man. However, all this only conflates gender with sexual orientation and ignores how Maggie's story exemplifies something that most heterosexuals never have to face: namely, the need to make choices about gender roles and to deal with questions of sexual identity. Gays and lesbians do this every day without much social support and without being able to take refuge in culturally sanctioned models. This takes a lot of courage, especially for someone like Maggie who 'came out' long before the advent of a gay rights movement.

It seems to me that what may be showing through here is the Jungian fear of gender ambivalence. Jungian theory, in its andro-centrism, simply has no room for the idea that men and 'the masculine' are irrelevant to lesbians (as is 'the feminine' for that matter). Lesbians are women who love other women and who may, or may not, hate or reject the company of men – just as they may, or may not, hate and reject the company of fish. In other words, lesbian relationships fly in the face of a heterosexist theory which insists that women 'need' men to complete themselves.

PROPOSAL FOR A PROGRAMME OF RENEWAL
TO END JUNGIAN HETEROSEXISM

> [One] can really defend the evidence one has accumulated only when all efforts to doubt it have failed. (Gadamer 1989, p. 120)

In *Wild Desires and Mistaken Identities* (1993), Noreen O'Connor and Joanna Ryan make clear that the removal of problematic theory from a body of literature and its practice cannot be accomplished as if this were simply a surgical procedure by which the offending material can simply be removed while leaving everything else intact. They insist that such an undertaking also requires the creation of a 'theoretical and conceptual space ... for non-pathological possibilities in relation to homosexuality' (p. 10). In other words, while theoretical culprits must be identified and exorcised, there also must be a conscious effort on the part of theoreticians and practitioners to rework the existing official body of knowledge rather than to simply tack on new theory. O'Connor and Ryan identify three areas of concern in relation to psychoanalysis: theory, language, and matters related to clinical practice. They insist, first of all, that heterosexuality be removed from its position as the standard for what is 'normal' sexuality; second, that new terms and concepts be developed that recognize the diversity and actuality of gay/lesbian experience; and, third, that clinicians come to realize that their claims to knowledge, even those which seem based 'objectively' in clinical work, are in effect shaped and coloured by their theoretical stance and countertransferential reactions.

I believe that analytical psychology would benefit from a similar revamping. The minimum requirements which follow would apply to all Jungians (insiders and outsiders) and their training programmes. This programme of renewal from within, it seems to me, is the mandate of a radicalized post-Jungian theory.

Heterosexuality must be removed from its position of presumed superiority.

> Imagine how many Lesbians there would be in the world if we got the kind of airtime and publicity that heterosexuality gets. (Penelope 1992, p. 40)

Jungians must renounce the idea that heterosexuality is the only 'normal' sexuality and/or that it is superior to any other sexuality, and we must begin to formulate theories which recognize and accommodate (and thus 'legitimate') a diversity of individuation processes. Corollaries to this would be that clinicians not assume that a client is heterosexual or presume that a gay/lesbian client's sexuality is the problem, that theoreticians include the experiences of gays and lesbians matter-of-factly when discussing cases or providing examples intended to demonstrate or prove theoretical points, and that both clinicians and theoreticians be on the lookout for and attentive to any evidence of genderism or heterosexism, in themselves or in their clients or in their theories.

New/revised theories/concepts/language must be developed which are inclusive of a range of alternative sexualities.

> Any serious check to individuality ... is an artificial stunting. ... only a society that can preserve its internal cohesion and collective values, while at the same time granting the individual the greatest possible freedom, has any prospect of enduring vitality. (CW6, para. 758)

Jungians must be willing to submit Jungian theory to intense and rigorous re-examination. Most notable among the ideas in need of this are: the traditional reliance on oppositions and complementarity as universal explanatory principles; the linking of compensation with complementarity; the pervasive use of socially-constructed categories like 'the masculine' and 'the feminine' as if they are self-evident and genetically-based; the notion of contrasexuality; and various assumptions about sex, sexuality, sexual orientation and gender (for example, that there are only two sexes and that they are 'opposite', not just different from each other; that one's sex automatically defines one's gender, that the qualities of sex and gender are innate, and so on).

Some might ask 'What will be left?' if we deconstruct, revise, and/or discard so much.

I believe that there will be a lot of Jungian theory remaining even after we do all of this because I believe that the radicalized approach I am advocating will actually enrich and expand upon other possibilities latent in Jungian theory, as I hope was demonstrated in the previous section.

Claims to knowledge derived from clinical practice must be inter-rogated and contextualized.

> One of the reasons why science succeeds in convincing us that it reveals the truth about nature is that the social contexts in which knowledge claims are transformed into scientific facts and artefacts are made invisible. (Nellie Oudshoorn, cited in Shulman 1997, p. 81)

Clinicians who call themselves Jungians need to consider how their theoretical preconceptions inform and construct their interpretations and how this in turn affects their claims to knowledge. This is an area that has been long ignored or underrated by most Jungians. However, in a new and outstanding book, Helene Shulman, Jungian analyst and philosopher, initiates a conversation into these questions with great integrity and insight (Shulman 1997). Hopefully, this signals the beginning of a new wave of Jungian self-analysis.

NOTES

1 I am grateful to Jan Marlan for taking time to read this chapter and to offer some invaluable suggestions.
2 From an often-repeated story about how Jung once proclaimed in frustra-tion (maybe in the context of political wrangling over establishing a training institute in Zurich) that he was glad he was 'Jung', and so did not have to be a 'Jungian'.
3 For more about this, see Kulkarni (1997).
4 A term Jung borrowed from alchemy which refers to the original state of a substance to be transformed.
5 Jung's term for a broadly conceived libido not limited to sexuality.
6 The notion of 'wholeness' (a kind of ego-fantasy of achieving total control) is extremely problematic, but beyond our scope here.
7 Jung noticed this initially in relation to personality development, where his observations led him to conclude that every individual develops a style of consciousness dominated by one or two modes of consciousness (introver-sion or extroversion) and one or four functions (thinking, feeling, sensation or intuition).
8 The idea of 'opposites' is not without merit, but it was widely overused by Jung in ways that are often mechanistic and rigid.
9 I am indebted here to Hopcke (1989) and Downing (1989) for their analyses of Jung's complicated views on homosexuality.
10 *b.* 26 July 1875; *d.* 6 June 1961.
11 Note here the teleological bent in Jung's theory. Jung often criticized Freud's method as reductionistic because it focused on finding the causes of phenomena.
12 For actual citations, refer to Hopcke (1989).
13 See, for example, Hall (1980) and Douglas (1990). For a sustained discussion of a particular example, refer to my analysis of Esther Harding's work in Kulkarni (1997, pp. 39–51).

14 Of course, even when we distinguish sex from gender, we are still left with many questions about the meaning of biological 'sex', as Judith Butler (1993) has so powerfully elucidated.

15 I can only speculate about possible reasons for this. Perhaps it reflects the impact on Jung of his intense and seemingly sexually loaded attachment to Freud, or his childhood experience of sexual molestation, or his extra-marital sexual liaisons. Of course, to focus on these 'reasons' is reductive and casual. A more prospective investigation would search for the things that 'called' to Jung, like his fascinations with spirituality and 'wholeness'.

16 Of course, in the very next sentence, Jung emphasizes that an anima identification which continues past mid-life leads to 'a diminuation of vitality, of flexibility, and of human kindness' and to a number of other questionable traits (CW9i, para. 147).

17 The medieval alchemical text often quoted by Jung and which includes a series of images Jung considered to be symbolic of the individuation process.

18 O'Connor and Ryan (1993) note in the context of lesbian experience that such explanations fail to account for 'the "other" woman, the supposedly feminine one, who desires another woman' (p. 174).

19 Jung used the term 'bisexual' (much as Freud did) to indicate the existence of both 'male' and 'female' qualities in an individual and not to suggest attraction to both sexes.

20 I am borrowing here from Douglas (1990) who, in surveying Jungian attitudes towards 'the feminine', identifies two categories of Jungians: Conservators and Reformulators. For a more extensive discussion of these categories, refer to Kulkarni (1997).

21 While my focus is on heterosexism, a similar critique needs to be done in terms of the racist and classist implications of Jungian theory.

22 A method I have discussed in detail in Kulkarni (1997).

REFERENCES

Butler, J. (1993) *Bodies That Matter: On the Discursive Limits of 'Sex'*, New York: Routledge.

Cowan, L. (1994) 'Dismantling the Animus'. Unpublished paper.

Douglas, C. (1990) *The Woman in the Mirror: Analytical Psychology and the Feminine*, Boston, MA: Sigo.

Downing, C. (1989) *Myths and Mysteries of Same-Sex Love*, New York: Continuum.

Gadamer, H.-G. (1960) *Truth and Method*, rans. J. Weinsheimer and D. Marshall, New York: Continuum, 1993.

Gadamer, H.-G. (1989) 'Hermeneutics and Logocentrism', trans. R. Palmer and D. Michelfelder, in D. Michelfelder and R. Palmer (eds), *Dialogue and Deconstruction*, Albany: State University of New York, pp. 114–25.

Hall, N. (1980) *The Moon and the Virgin: Reflections of the Archetypal Feminine*, New York: Harper and Row.

Heidegger, M. (1953) *Being and Time*, trans. J. Stambaugh, Albany: State University of New York, 1996.

hooks, bell (1990) 'Choosing the Margin as a Space of Radical Openness', in *Yearning: Race, Gender, and Cultural Politics*, Boston, MA: South End Press, pp. 145–53.

Hopcke, R. (1989) *Jung, Jungians, and Homosexuality.* Boston, MA: Shambhala.

Hopcke, R., Carrington, K. L. and Wirth, S. (eds) (1993) *Same-Sex Love and the Path to Wholeness: Perspectives on Gay and Lesbian Psychological Development,* Boston, MA: Shambhala.

Jackson, G. (1991) *The Secret Lore of Gardening: Patterns of Male Intimacy,* Toronto: Inner City.

Jung, C. G. (1953–79) *The Collected Works of C. G. Jung* (Vols 1–20), Princeton, NJ: Princeton University Press.

Kulkarni, C. (1997) *Lesbians and Lesbianisms: A Post-Jungian Perspective,* London: Routledge.

O'Connor, N. and Ryan, J. (1993) *Wild Desires and Mistaken Identities: Lesbianism and Psychoanalysis,* New York: Columbia University Press.

Payne, R. (1990), 'Some Reflections on Homosexuality', *Harvest* 36: 155–63.

Penelope, J. (1992) *Call Me Lesbian: Lesbian Lives, Lesbian Theory,* Freedom, CA: Crossing.

Samuels, A. (1985) *Jung and the Post-Jungians,* London: Routledge and Kegan Paul.

Samuels, A. (1989) 'Jung, Anti-Semitism, and the Fuehrerprinzip' (Recording). Pittsburgh, PA: Pittsburgh Jung Society.

Shulman, H. (1997) *Living at the Edge of Chaos: Complex Systems in Culture and Psyche,* Einsiedeln: Daimon.

Stanley, L. and Wise, S. (1990). 'Method, Methodology and Epistemology in Feminist Research Processes', in L. Stanley (ed.), *Feminist Praxis: Research, Theory and Epistemology in Feminist Sociology,* London: Routledge, pp. 20–60.

Weaver, M. I. R. (1982) 'An Interview with C. G. Jung: 1955', in F. Jensen and S. Mullen (eds), *C. G. Jung, Emma Jung and Toni Wolff: A Collection of Remembrances,* San Francisco, CA: Analytical Psychology Club, pp. 90–5.

5 A Feeling of Community? Individual Psychology and Homosexualities

Christopher Shelley

> Our idea of social feeling as the final form of humanity – of an imagined state in which all the problems of life are solved and all our relations to the external world rightly adjusted – is a regulative ideal, a goal that gives us our direction. This goal of perfection must bear within it the goal of an ideal community, because all that we value in life, all that endures and continues to endure, is eternally the product of this social feeling. (Adler 1938)

In this chapter it will be argued that within Individual Psychology, practitioners have theorized homosexualities[1] in such a way as to make available to discursive exposure the conformist[2] aspects of the Adlerian approach, particularly in regard to gender. Indeed, traditional Adlerians have posited gender conformity as an aspect of healthy mental functioning. I will argue that the compulsory heterosexuality that rests at the core of gender conformity is directly related to the disdain for homosexual relations that many traditional Adlerians have expressed. By undercutting this conformism and the universalizing theories which sustain conformist assumptions (a critique based on my own subscription to postmodernism[3]), I seek to point the way forward for a system of psychology which, from its radical inception, sought to bridge the gap between an understanding of mental distress and the social and political institutions which support and provide the impetus for this distress. I firmly believe that Adlerians can reclaim this idealism but only after a painful examination of why this process first requires radical revision. That the Adlerian discourse is ultimately a dialectical one, as argued by Ansbacher and Ansbacher (cited in Adler 1978), allows for occasional and even radical reformulation. Here, I see no need to redefine my approach as neo-Adlerian. Rather, I seek to reform within the system, as much as it is possible to do so. In this sense, I wish to 'move towards' rather than create divisions by 'moving against' – that Adlerians can agree to disagree and continue to work together is an assumption I have taken within my critique.

THE SOCIALLY BOUND INDIVIDUAL

Individual Psychology was founded by the socialist-leaning physician Alfred Adler (b.1870, d.1937) and later organized and extended by theorists such as Ansbacher and Ansbacher (1956), Dreikurs (1967, 1971), Shulman (1973), Mosak (1977), Powers and Griffith (1987), Stein (1991), Kopp (1995) and Slavik and Croake (1998).[4] It is a socially focused system which explicitly stresses *context*, but Individual Psychology (IP) can also be somewhat confounded with the political construct of *individualism* (Jacoby 1975), a criticism that is justified for most practitioners of psychology (regardless of school) inasmuch as we focus on the individual as the site of intervention rather than on social and political institutions. However, the Adlerian system does not simply or neatly fold into such a criticism; we also hold a therapeutic goal of an increase in a person's social feeling and community values above and beyond any other facet in therapy, inclusive of the pursuit of individual goals. By exploring an individual's striving for meaningfulness, Adlerians aim not only to encourage a sense of coherence in living but also to explore, as Sloan describes it, '... that relatively unthought space between sociality and individuality' (Sloan 1996, p. 13).

Indivisible[5] is what Adler had intended with his representation of *Individual*, in reference to the Latin root *Individuus*, meaning 'indivisibility'. Here, Adler was creating his own theory centring not just on the social bases of neurosis but also the *holistic* nature of the mind, within a social context. That *uniqueness* is intertwined within this definition cannot be denied, but rather is celebrated; each of us is unique. However, the individual cannot be conceived of as separate from the social forces, context and institutions with which he or she is inseparably bound. Just as the internal parts are regulated by the whole, so too are the social dimensions holistically bound with the interior dimensions of the psyche. These convictions were further deepened by Adler's reading of the South African philosopher and political leader Smuts' *Holism and Evolution* (1926). Adler was also strongly influenced by the German philosopher Vaihinger (1911), who offered a Nietzschian and neo-Kantian reading of 'As-If' and who spoke of purposeful and goal-directed (teleological) mental structures as *fictions*. These fictions may operate as fantasies and as quasi-hypotheses to orient oneself to the world on the basis of as-if. Fictions differ from hypotheses in as much as they generally remain untested and, for that matter, do not have to be proven in order to be operable. That there is a striving to what Adler referred to as a *fictional final goal* or *guiding fiction* (for example, perfection) shows us Vaihinger's influence on Adler's thinking. Fictional finalism also complements Adler's phenomenology (a standpoint he shared with Jung) and an existential concern with the meaning(s) of life within the individual subject's phenomenal field. Combined with a social emphasis, a person creates these (usually non-conscious) fictions that guide the individual through life while setting the perspective of his or her biased apperceptions, facilitating selective inattentions. The theory also retains a psychodynamic element with interest in unconscious[6] aspects to overall movement patterns and schema of life (view of self, others and the world) which Adler referred to as *Style of Life* or *lifestyle*. Adlerians use various means by which to understand and share subjective apperceptions through methods garnered from imaged and metaphorical material (for example, dreams, parapraxes, early recollections, metaphors). A certain recognition of the transference and countertransference[7] is utilized within IP, but differences with psychoanalytic theorizing on repression (and the related meta-psychology), the so-called determinism of a sexualized libido, rejection of the psychoanalytic stance of neutrality, and the therapeutic set-up of psychoanalytic practice, clearly excludes IP from consideration as a psychoanalytic system. However, it is a historical fact that for many years Adler was a colleague of Freud (not necessarily a student or disciple), and eventually became the first president of the Vienna Psychoanalytic Association. Evidence suggests that their collaboration began in 1899 (Handlbauer 1998) and Adler was a founding member of Freud's Wednesday discussion group (1902–11) which eventually transformed into the institution of psychoanalysis. But Adler always maintained his own unique views; views that often contrasted sharply with Freud's, particularly after their break, in the building of IP. It is unfortunate that Freud and Adler ended up locked in a rather bitter dispute, such that after their break they would never speak again. In the end, Adler's subscription to holism and teleology, his clear positioning of IP as a subjectively focused (rather than positivistic) psychology, and his emphasis on working with children through community-based *preventative* strategies further differentiates this system from most psychoanalytic approaches.

The word 'individual' has many meanings; some of which may be intertwined with 'individualism' and the political readings we may subsequently extract. Indeed, most Adlerians have no trouble accepting the individual as the applied site of focus, that it is right and proper to emphasize the individual within a Humanistic-liberal link. However, there are those of us who also recognize the need for simultaneous work within social institutions (especially schools) that go beyond this link. It is here that IP seems to have lost its original radical power as a method of psychology and community-based prevention that was heavily informed with both first-wave feminism and Marx's social theory. Today, most Adlerians work within established systems to instigate and encourage change. These programmes include teacher training and parent education, a lay counselling skill's movement, a philosophy of living and a method of counselling and psychotherapy. That these programmes are valuable and effective for individuals is not my criticism – that they have yet to contribute to any wide-ranging social change *is*, although this is my criticism of psychology in general, independent of the majority of schools in question.

That IP no longer promotes its radical heritage has inevitably disconnected it from a broadly based need to overhaul various social institutions (for example, schools). Moreover, through the example of the theory's traditional position on gender and homosexuality, I will argue that IP is in need of a radical injection, a return to its radical roots. Here, my perspective as an Adlerian is also profoundly shaped not only from the values I hold as an Adlerian, but also by my simultaneous subscription to aspects of critical psychology (Fox and Prilleltensky 1997), the pro-feminist men's movement and masculinity theory (Brod and Kaufman 1994; Horrocks 1994), gay and lesbian psychology (Kitzinger 1997; Kitzinger and Perkins 1993) and a limited use of deconstructionism within a postmodern analysis (Kulkarni 1997). By attempting to foreground my horizons, to use a term from philosophical hermeneutics[8] (Gadamer 1960), I shall attempt to make some of my prejudices known; such prejudices are what I bring to IP as a subject (among so many other things). Thus, as the label 'critical psychology' suggests, I take a critical view of psychology (including Individual Psychology) with a clearly stated view that psychology

- needs to adopt, according to Sloan, an 'ongoing willingness to call our own practices into question and to link our own local and global concerns as directly as possible to what we do professionally' (Sloan 1997, p. 103);

- should recognise that, as a discipline, it cannot divorce itself from the social and political circumstances through which it originated, maintains and continues to service;

- should emphasize the *individual* at the expense of oppressive social institutions rather than seeking ways of bridging the two so as to effect social change;

- is not objective or value-free; it is coloured by various assumptions, values and biases;

- ought to promote social justice rather than sustain and preserve the *status quo*.

I view IP as largely compatible with working towards solutions to the above points, but recognize the need to critique certain traditional Adlerian views, many of which continue to be upheld by contemporary Adlerians. In so doing, I seek genuinely to restore an appreciation of the concept of *oppression* back into the core of Adlerian theory, a concept that may be coherently linked with our central theoretical linchpin *Gemeinschaftsgefühl* (a feeling of community; social interest). Here, one concept directly fuels the other by arguing its solution. This repositing is not necessarily an infringement upon Adler's original thinking, as the following quote from his work *Social Interest* (1938) suggests,

> Suicide, crime, bad treatment of old people, cripples, or beggars; prejudices and unjust dealing with persons, employees, races, and religious communities; the maltreatment of the feeble and of children; marital quarrels, and any kind of attempt to give women an inferior position, and much else – ostentatious displays of wealth and birth, cliques and their effects on all the strata of society – all these along with pampering and the neglect of children, put an early end into the development [of community feeling] of a fellow being. (p. 281)

ADLER'S INFLUENCE AND VIEW OF HOMOSEXUALITY

Adler's original view of homosexuality was both harsh and judgemental. His passionate conclusions rang loudly in concert with the dominant pathology views of the day. That the concepts held simultaneously expose an active construction of an oppressive 'neurosis' is entirely consistent with feminist and social constructionist critiques of psychology and psychiatry (Foucault 1978). My critique will also expose an aspect of conservative conformism within IP, something which Adlerians have denied (Ansbacher 1985). In theorizing homosexuality, Adler made serious mistakes of judgement, as did almost all others who contributed to the topic during the earlier part of the twentieth century. Nevertheless, according to one account, Adler's view of homosexuality looked set to change a few years before his sudden death (while on a lecture tour in Britain in 1937). I am hoping that the reader will keep this point in mind. Adler obviously did not view homosexuality as always requiring treatment; he did make one exception, just a few years before his death. To illustrate, the following conversation was recalled by social worker Elizabeth McDowell. She had sought Adler's advice on her client 'John', a 21-year-old 'homosexual'. Upon her arrival at Adler's office, Adler reviewed the report of John and remarked,

> 'You say this – John – he is a homosexual?'
> 'Oh, yes,' Elizabeth replied.
> 'And is he happy, would you say?' asked Adler.
> 'Oh, yes,' Elizabeth replied.
> 'Well,' leaning back in his swivel chair and putting his thumbs in his vest, 'Why don't we leave him alone? Eh?'
> He did add a few words about how little was known about the sexual deviant, but the substance remained, 'leave him alone'. This was doubtless the most profound wisdom he could have shared with me. (Manaster et al. 1977, p. 82)

This is certainly a contradictory approach to dealing with 'homosexuality', especially when we compare Adler's guidance to Elizabeth with his writings and transcripts of his lectures, some of which argued compulsory treatment of individuals expressing homosexual behaviour (a view no longer shared by Adlerians, traditional or otherwise). Why did Adler decide to 'leave him alone?' Could it have been that his view of homosexuality was changing? This is possible, although his writings on the topic never reflected a change in attitude. Unfortunately, we simply do not know. It is, however, a very practical example of how we should critically heed the printed word and be wary of dogma. People can, and very often do, change their minds.[9]

Adler's written exposition attempted to portray 'the homosexual' as a 'failure', a 'coward' and one who 'lacks social interest'. These ideas were extensively argued in two of his papers: 'The Problem of Homosexuality' (1917) and 'Homosexuality' (1928) with excerpts of both papers appearing in Co-operation Between the Sexes (Adler 1978). These views of homosexuality mirrored the 'common-sense' views of the majority, views that continue to be rooted in heterosexist assumptions. That his analysis lacked a 'critical' component and focused instead on common-sense[10] assumptions draws attention to a

collusion between his theory and modernist notions of moral conformism. To remind us, Adler lived and worked in a period that,
within the Western world,[11] held a near universal condemnation of
homosexual acts and his theory reflects this.

Why should Adler's views matter at all, homosexuality notwith-
standing? My answer to this is to suggest that many mental health
practitioners use Adlerian-based principles and ideas within their own
disciplines, usually without any knowledge that these principles and
ideas had their therapeutic origins in IP. In his comprehensive
volume, *The Discovery of the Unconscious* (1970) Ellenberger cites
Hans Hoff's pronouncement that Adler

> inaugurated modern psychosomatic medicine, was the forerunner
> of social psychology and the social approach to mental hygiene, a
> founder of group psychotherapy, [and] that his conception of the
> creative self being in its goal-directedness, responsible for the
> life-style makes him the father of ego psychology. To this he [Hoff]
> could have added that Adler was the founder of the first unified
> system of concrete psychology on record. (p. 645)

Adler's influence on the formation of applied psychology has been
important but often overlooked by others in psychology. Ellenberger
also notes:

> It would not be easy to find another author from which so much
> has been borrowed from all sides without acknowledgement than
> Alfred Adler. His teaching has become, to use a French idiom, an
> 'open quarry' (*une carriére publique*), that is, a place where anyone
> and all may come and draw anything without compunction. (ibid.)

That Adler had a wide influence on the development of psychotherapy and counselling practice is important to recognize, specifically
because many Adlerian principles have been adopted wholesale by
other schools but without the central unifying construct of
Gemeinschaftsgefühl that underpinned and provided unity and coherence to all of Adler's theory. Here, Adler's influence has been noted
(Ellenberger 1970; Corsini and Wedding 1989; Ehrenwald 1991)
within Jung's analytical psychology, Humanistic models (for example,
Allport, Maslow), Existential approaches (Frankl, Rollo May), some
aspects of the cognitive schools (Beck), Transactional Analysis (Berne),
Rational Emotive Behaviour Therapy (Ellis), Reality Therapy (Glasser)
and various psychoanalytic ego-psychologies (Horney, Sullivan and
Fromm). Even Freud took up Adler's 'aggressive drive' (after an earlier

dismissal of the concept) long after Adler had abandoned drive psychology,[12] and Adler has been instrumental in forming an initial psychodynamic conception of narcissism (Ansbacher 1985). But the dissemination of Adlerian ideas is often a point of pride among many Adlerians, whereas I view it as a point of concern. Without Adler's central and unifying construct of community feeling, the principles digress further into an individualistic emphasis with all of the concerns that this individualism draws up (Fox and Prilleltensky 1997). More to the point, Adler's analysis was unable fully to capture the contradictions and oppression that gender conformities (and the sexual implications this conformity implies) have effected upon the discourse, despite the concept of community feeling.

The subjective focus on the individual in IP should allow us to begin to understand who the person is rather than what or why the person is. Unfortunately, it has been the pattern of many Adlerians to focus on the latter, a point of inconsistency within Adlerian theory. However, the Adlerian system has much to offer gay and lesbian people that is both encouraging and a means for facilitating the understanding and healing of mental distress. While various Adlerians proceed with an 'affirmative' or other non-pathology model, I wish to challenge those traditional Adlerians who are inclined to follow Adler's original ideas on homosexuality, to expose simultaneously these outdated conceptions.

Adler expressed the predominant views on 'homosexuality' of his day, thus he expressed the *Zeitgeist* on sexual morality that circulated prior to second-wave feminism and the gay and lesbian rights movement, both of which made their challenges and appearance approximately 30 years after Adler's death. Adler often expressed ideas that were, so to speak, ahead of his time. For example, we find his support and interest in feminism, his preventatively based community work, his desire to break down the power barriers in psychiatry and psychology, as motifs which did not receive wider attention until the 1960s and 1970s. However, Adler did not foresee the eventuality of a widespread movement to 'grant' gay and lesbian people equality based upon their sexual subjugation. Moreover, until recently there has been no Adlerian effort to extend the concept of community feeling, a concept which argues that social inequality (oppression) is at the root of the so-called 'neuroses', to lesbian and gay people. Have Adlerians simply become too conservative over the years?

The Australian sociologist Connell identifies Adler as one of the first theorists to argue a 'psychoanalytic' case for feminism, and such that was 'not found anywhere else until the 1970s' (Connell 1995, p. 16). Adler's insights into the dynamics (for example, inferiority, superiority and compensation) and oppressiveness of sexual inequality obviously predates the insights of second-wave feminism (Kurzweil 1995) and does not take into account the issues surrounding hetero-sexism. This is reflected in current Adlerian theorizing on homosexuality, where Adler's views have, until recently, remained unchallenged by most Adlerians. In addition, the emerging affirmative models developing within other approaches (such as Humanistic) have generally been ignored within IP. Indeed, it was not until June 1995 that the principal North American Adlerian Journal, *Individual Psychology*, devoted a volume of discussion surrounding the theory (with proposed revisions) and the special needs and issues that are relevant to the gay and lesbian populations. With the publication of this special issue, Adlerians have finally begun critically to examine their views and writings on homosexualities. Some offer well intentioned liberal solutions (Giovando and Schramski 1993) while others are explicitly conservative and offended by any attempts to legitimize 'perversion' as they have constructed it (Vervloet 1994).

NATURE, NURTURE OR NEITHER?

Whereas the discipline of psychiatry had initially established the medicalization of homosexuality, Adler (although a medical doctor himself) never viewed 'homosexuality' from a biological essentialist standpoint; rather, he viewed the 'problem' from an environmental position. This environmental position is seen as being under the service of a second variable, that of *self-stylized creativity*. The subjective uniqueness of how the individual makes creative use of her or his resources is the focus in our therapeutic work. Adler wrote:

Do not forget the most important fact that not heredity and not environment are determining factors – both are giving only the frame and the influences which are answered by the individual in regard to his stylized creative power. (Ansbacher and Ansbacher 1956, p. xxiv)

Adler subscribed to the dominant discourse and widely-held view of homosexuality as pathology. However, rather than view the phenomenon from the perspective of biological essentialism, he instead pathologized homosexual people via *neurosis*, which in IP is a social construct, a view also shared by the psychoanalyst Karen Horney (1937). Sometimes he would qualify this neurotic imposition in regard to homosexualities; Adler did admit: 'it would be a serious mistake to overlook that our state of knowledge is incomplete' (Adler 1978, p. 146). Subsequent Adlerian positions took little heed of Adler's warning and, with only recent exceptions, have clearly viewed homosexuality as a neurotic phenomenon, with the pathology justified through, among other things, an accusation of failure in community feeling. Many later Adlerians followed Adler's thinking on homosexuality by conceptualizing such behaviour as a social rather than constitutional 'problem'. Even more or less recent Adlerian positions (while not exclusive) have strongly affirmed this opinion: any arguments postulating a biological explanation are false (Rister 1981) or, according to Adler's son Kurt Adler, a deviation from Adlerian thinking (Adler 1994).

In terms of any so-called 'biological influence' that is only rarely stated but implicitly part of holistic thinking in IP (however minor), it must be viewed as subordinated to social and contextual realties in addition to self-stylized creativity. While I hesitate to frame sexual orientation using any reference to biological elements, it would, however, be remiss of me not to point out that a significant number of gay men frame their sexuality in non-choice and genetic terms (Marcus 1993). Can it be definitively stated that genes play *no* role in, for example, male homosexualities? Or, could it be that any role that genes may play is, in most cases, minor? Controversial evidence supporting a genetic basis to some homosexualities has surfaced in recent years (Hamer et al. 1995). The positivistic essentialism that underlies research of this kind has been sufficiently critiqued elsewhere. However, I am not about to dismiss *entirely* such 'evidence', nor the many subjectivities that make use of such 'evidence' when drawing meanings and attributions about their sexuality. We still do not know enough about the extent to which genes contribute to human behaviour. However, I am very cautious of this matter and suspect that many geneticists, biologists and sexologists largely overstate the 'interactional' role that biological variables may serve in human behaviour and that such overstatement can be quite dangerous. My own caution on this matter was deeply aroused through my readings of the Harvard biologist Ruth Hubbard (1990) and her critique of science and by other readings from the feminist critique of science (for example, Kitzinger 1987).

Sperry (1995) suggests that Adlerian theorizing of homosexuality is based upon the principles of *soft determinism* – that there are multiply determined variables contributing to sexual orientation which includes the idea of 'choice'. However, a pairing of choice with determinism may seem to be incoherent. What about those individuals who claim *no* choice in their sexual orientation, or those who claim *full* choice? Sperry's position also neglects to include an analysis of the role of gender in the maintenance of heterosexism and how heterosexism contributes to the mental health issues of gays and lesbians. Such arguments continue to locate determinants to sexual orientation within the individual (even the environmental determinants are explained only in individual terms), neglecting social and institutional bases. Sperry also neglects to differentiate lesbianism from male homosexualities within his brief analysis. While he does suggest that ideology plays a role in how we view sexual orientation, I feel that his representation of ideology is subsumed under the idea of determinism (however soft) and that his short comments leave a number of questions unanswered.

During the past 70 years, many Adlerians have written very strong statements that have sought to uphold the pathology status of homosexuality, thus contributing to an overall climate against the normalization of same-sex erotic acts. These views were not formally challenged until Kivel published her objections in *Individual Psychology* (1983).[13] That Adlerians appear to be divided on this issue is not surprising; most people in Western cultures are also divided on this matter.

SELF-STYLIZED CREATIVITY

The Adlerian emphasis on subjectivity and uniqueness of the individual within a social context contrasts sharply with the positivistic accounts offered by the discipline of sexology. Adler emphasized the subject (as opposed to the object) in a period when it was not at all popular to do so. Indeed, quantitative as opposed to qualitative (Adler's choice) methodologies were and continue to be overwhelmingly emphasized within psychology (O'Connell Davidson and Layder 1994).

Self-stylized creativity involves the synthesization of environmental influences, heredity and learning with the creative/purposeful aspects of our existence. Within this holistic mediation, the emphasis is placed on the subjective use of the 'givens' in life; here is where we place the greatest emphasis. The psychic creation of goals and the unique methods by which the individual strives towards these goals offers us a glimpse into the uniqueness of personality, and it reflects our own rhythm of movement in living. These two concepts, *personality* and *movement*, bring us closer to Adler's concept of *Style of Life*. We all have hands and palms and yet no two people have the same unique set of lines on their palms or finger tips. For 'the homosexual', the construction of a gay or lesbian identity is interwoven intrinsically with the same uniqueness of personality and movement that 'heterosexuals' display. In this context, the facet of Adlerian work which I find so rewarding is the humbleness of investigating the subjective life of the individual; a striving for understanding through the exploration of self-stylized creativity. That gays and lesbians can create personal and social identities and a sense of belonging in the face of such strong social, political, religious, and self-collaborating oppression (for example, low self-esteem and suicidal ideation) is truly remarkable. Indeed, I find that the only activity more rewarding than this individual work is group work, which I usually recommend for most clients simultaneous to individual sessions. My own experience in facilitating therapy groups for gay men has taught me more than all of my individual sessions with clients combined.

In addressing matters of self-stylized creativity, Adlerians employ techniques which explore the creative imagination. This includes the dialectical use of Adlerian-based dream interpretation, particularly the work of Leo Gold (1979); of client generated metaphors as outlined by Richard Kopp (1995); and the use of art in therapy such as the methods offered by Sadie 'Tee' Dreikurs (1986). In addition to creative work, individuals who sexually desire their same sex and appear for therapy usually need special encouragement from significant others in order to counteract the enormous social opposition against those who choose to live outside (as much as possible) a heterosexual paradigm. It involves a transformation of aspects of the self-concept (which is dialectical in the Adlerian model and not 'self-actualizing' within a predetermined framework) and the strengthening of self-esteem necessary to overcome a collaboratively imposed sense of inferiority. Adlerians focus on an appraisal of an individual's self-valuation. Sonstegard writes:

> Reorientation and redirection of mistaken goals requires restoration of the individual's faith in self so that he or she realises personal strength and ability and believes in his or her own dignity and worth. Without encouragement, counselling will not promote change. (Sonstegard 1996, p. 54)

Few 'homosexuals' have the necessary resources (from an early age) to counteract social and institutional messages which demand that 'being gay is not OK'. Thus, self-valuation and esteem is usually low in these individuals (especially prior to 'coming out'). Genuine encouragement is used to directively entice the client, to affirm their worth as human beings.

A reformulation of Adlerian theory in this context acknowledges a holistic frame of influences that contribute to the multidimensional antecedents in the individual's formation of sexual orientation (which implies direction *per se* rather than choice) but shifts the clinical emphasis to (ideally), among other things, an exploration of the creative imagination. We believe that this acknowledgement provides a better framework than the reductionism which is so much more pervasive within the institutions of psychiatry and psychology.

HOMOSEXUALITY AND 'NEUROSIS'

Richard Kopp notes that there were three phases in Adler's conceptualization of homosexuality:

1. 1900–1910: Organ Inferiority and homosexuality as a compensatory mechanism.

2. 1910–1920: Masculine protest and neurosis as exaggerated feelings of inferiority and consequent excessive compensatory striving.

3. 1928–1937: The theory was dominated by Adler's concept of social interest. (Kopp 1993)

Later Adlerians have generally located their theorizing of homosexualities within one of these three periods. For example, Krausz (1935) constructed homosexuality in terms of a 'compulsion neurosis' whereby the compulsion is expressed in same-sex acts or fantasies which serve the purpose of distracting the individual and protects him or her from feelings of inadequacy. These feelings of inadequacy are apparently related to the task of opposite-sex intimacy and marriage, with homosexuality acting as a defence against fulfilment of such a task.

Adler noted that the 'failure' of homosexuals to meet the task of heterosexual intimacy and marriage amounts to 'cowardice' and a 'faulty style of life'. Moreover, such a style of life is seen as grounded in the autoerotic and anti-social aspects of masturbation, 'so called homosexuality, which is only one of the many varieties of masturbation, often found among egocentric, vain adults who cling to the primary, autoerotic phase of the sexual function' (Adler 1978, p. 80). Adler also argued that the homosexual is characterized as one who fails to learn and behave within rigid sex-role stereotypes, thereby setting compulsory heterosexuality (conformity) as a mental health norm. For example, he ascertained that '[e]arly enlightenment regarding the unalterability of the sexual role and reconciliation to it' (ibid., p. 91) is a prerequisite to the development of a healthy sexual attitude in women. While Adler was a firm believer in the fundamental equality of the sexes, he never advocated androgynous, neuter or transgender forms of existence; instead, he discouraged children from a 'revolt' from traditional gender roles, a contradiction in the sense that he felt the rigidity and hierarchical construction of these roles were at the very root of neurosis. His view contrasts sharply with the post-Jungian position of Samuels who argues the opposite: that gender confusion is healthy and that monolithic and static expressions of gender are 'a most destructive con trick ... The problem is, in fact, gender certainty' (Samuels 1996, p. 86).

Family dynamics were often posited by Adlerians as sites to affect a child's acquisition of gender role stability (Powers et al. 1993). The interpersonal dynamics within the individual's family constellation have been argued by Adler (1978) and Pevin (1993) as a predisposing background factor in the development of homosexualities. In male homosexualities, a pampering mother was thought to provide the kind of warmth that the child feared never finding again; a domineering mother and a tyrannical father were thought to be most discouraging in terms of his approach to the opposite sex; a hostile and rejecting mother was thought to have permanently frightened boys from girls; and cross-gender behaviour was thought to result from striking uncertainty regarding sexual role (gender nonconformity).

Mosak (1983) disputed these claims arguing that, in his clinical experience, homosexuals come from a wide variety of backgrounds and that to resort to this kind of causal thinking is un-Adlerian. It is unlikely that family constellation and the resulting dynamics are causally linked to expressions of homosexualities. For example, family elements that may have been thought environmentally to 'cause' a homosexual orientation include children being raised by overtly homosexual parents. Such arguments have been used to prevent the legalized adoption of children by same-sex and homosexual parents for fear that these children may become homosexual themselves through modelling. In answer to such concerns, a study published in *Developmental Psychology* (Bailey et al. 1995) examined 55 gay or bisexual men and their 82 sons who were at least 17 years of age when interviewed. The researchers hypothesized two possible routes on environmental homosexual transmission: (1) a child may acquire sexual orientation by imitating (internalizing) his or her parent's sexual orientation; (2) through socialization the child may be reinforced in the probability of a homosexual status, especially if such a life course was not discouraged by the parents. The results of this research revealed that 90%[14] of the sons whose sexual orientation could be ascertained reported a heterosexual orientation. Thus, if an environmental influence from the gay parent was present, it is evidently weak and has no apparent bearing on the sexual orientation of the child in question. This theory, like earlier theories which suggest that a weak or missing father contributes to a homosexual orientation in gay men, remains empirically dubious.

FEELING OF COMMUNITY, SOCIAL INTEREST AND HOMOSEXUALITY

Adler viewed the individual as being embedded within a social fabric; how the individual finds his or her place and a feeling of belonging in society becomes the measure of mental health. Individuals who are raised to feel equal as members of their families develop healthy mechanisms of adjustment and are not preoccupied with hierarchical strivings to compensate for a felt lack of belonging.[15] They develop a *feeling of community*, the correct translation of the German *Gemeinschaftsgefühl*, rather than *social interest*, the concept which (until recently) replaced the former, particularly in America. Social interest was thought to be less 'spiritual' at a time when psychology was even more positivistic than it is today (Ansbacher 1985), and the term now refers to the line of action towards community feeling only.

Until recently, labelled and/or identified 'homosexuals' were thwarted from full participation within most communities unless they masked their sexuality under a heterosexual veneer. This thwarting of an individual's homosexual behaviour/identity expressions is representative of the lower and unequal status such identified persons are delegated to, a point that simultaneously demonstrates the inequality at the root of heterosexism. Nevertheless, the historical significance of the gay and lesbian rights movement is not limited only to the winning of legal and legislative battles towards equality, but also demonstrates the remarkable shedding of what was, and in some cases remains, a coercively imposed and constructed neurosis[16] towards an emancipated manifestation of sexuality and mental health. Thus, the contemporary gay and lesbian person is not suddenly 'healthy' due to changes and removals from systems of diagnostic nomenclature, but rather because gays and lesbians were able to organize a community and make use of this community to heal from an imposed and constructed neurosis. The result has been a shift from illness to affirmation. Social institutions (such as religion, law, medicine) with their pervasive heterosexist ideologies (and not necessarily the individual homosexual) attempted to block the expression of community feeling by reading 'homosexuality' as undermining such feeling. The blocking tactics (such as legal and religious sanctions) often reinforced an individual's inherent feeling of inferiority and resulting superiority compensations. Because we never lose our need to remain a part of a social group, previous attempts to ostracize 'homosexual' persons undoubtedly led to a certain measure of mental distress among those affected. The greatest damage human beings can do to other human beings is to marginalize and oppress; to prevent a feeling of belonging. On the other hand, it must be said that many creative compensations can be drawn from the margins, many of which point the way towards a transformative restoration of the original loss of community feeling. Nevertheless, oppressive movements are based on a lack of community feeling and endorse the neurotic compensation of superiority striving. In Adler's grand narrative, the result is mental distress and suffering. Does the mental health status of homosexual people then lie entirely within the individual or within social institutions?

Adler clearly believed that homosexualities and other 'perversions' violated the ideals inherent within the concept of community feeling. At one point he was so convinced of this premise that he wrote, 'surely no theory will ever influence society or social morals in favour of homosexuality' (cited in Mosak 1983). That history is beginning to prove Adler and others, such as various psychoanalytic thinkers (see the analysis in O'Connor and Ryan 1993) mistaken in regard to their heterosexist assumptions is not sufficient for celebration; rather, there remains a significant amount of theoretical revision and social change to be accomplished before we even begin to approximate an ideal community.

In a critique of the problem of homosexuality in IP, Carl Jylland (1990) found no evidence whatsoever of homosexuals demonstrating 'limited social interest'. In fact, Jylland found that many of the early recollections he examined and decoded contained significant variables pertaining to *mutuality*, actions that indicate community feeling, and the ability to interact co-operatively with others.

Social interest (community feeling) is not a concretized concept and is open to change in a time–space continuum as Kivel (1983) has pointed out. In the absence of any concrete evidence that would suggest an entire group of people lacks social interest, the only solution remaining for Adlerians is to look more closely at this concept with the aim of elucidating how it is possible that such an oppressive application could have taken place to begin with. It is something which Freudians, Jungians, Adlerians (and a host of others) must look at and learn from.

Community feeling is apparently an inherent potential in all people regardless of race, religion, colour or *sexual orientation*. However, as Adler pointed out, it must be taught and cultivated, particularly by teaching children the skill and value of co-operation rather than current Western cultural emphases on competition (for example, capitalism and resulting class struggles).

GENDERED ASSUMPTIONS

I am in agreement with Kulkarni who writes, 'it is gender which effectively "creates" sexual orientation. Without the concept of gender, the concept of sexual orientation is meaningless' (Kulkarni 1997, p. 16).

The concept of *gender* has evolved significantly into a powerful area of discourse within the social sciences, led largely by feminist analysis with support from the pro-feminist men's movement. However, this specific concept did not exist in Adler's day. Rather, it was the sexologist John Money (1985) who borrowed the term from linguistics back in the 1950s where it was used to refer to masculine and feminine speech particles. The term has since been widely disseminated throughout the academy, often deviating significantly from Money's original usage of *gender identity* and *gender role*.

Adlerians have assumed that a prerequisite for homosexuality is an impaired gender identity (King and Manaster 1973; Friedberg 1975; Adler 1978; Rister 1981). For example, Rister attempts to connect homosexuality to an impairment in gender identity, consistent with common myths and stereotypic language about homosexuals (that is, the 'sissy' myth – that 'sissiness' somehow causes homosexuality). She argues:

1. Male children with effeminate faces or body builds begin to develop doubts about their gender identity when they hear from others that they 'look like a girl'.

2. Inability to compete with other boys at traditionally male sports and games causes the boy to give up hope. As a result, the gulf between him and other boys widens and he takes up feminine activities instead.

3. If his genitals are small by comparison with the other boys, then he may be further reinforced in his inferiority. As a consequence, he may form the belief that he will never become a 'real man'. (Rister 1981)

In point 3, Rister makes two mistakes. First, she assumes that pre-adolescent comparison of penis size may lead to homosexuality, should the boy feel that he does not 'measure up'. This idea, in addition to being transparently laughable, is a regression of Adler's theory of homosexuality from his third phase (social interest/community feeling) back to his first phase (organ inferiority) and the positivism and essentialism he later abandoned. The second error is the assumption that the boy with the smaller penis may conclude that he is less of a man and that such a conclusion leads to a same-sex erotic orientation. This idea takes a 180-degree turn from the equally ridiculous theories of the past that suggested that homosexual males have bigger penises than heterosexual males (Tripp 1987). It is both silly and erroneous to relate penis size to sexual orientation. If Rister were correct in her thesis, then we would see a higher incidence of homosexualities among, for example, those with the birth defect of 'micro penis';[17] there remains no evidence that this is the case (Money 1988).

As various authors have argued (Bell et al. 1981; Bailey and Zucker 1995), cross-gender behaviour occurs with regularity in a significant number of homosexuals. Homosexualities and expressions of cross-gender behaviour constitutes a controversial discussion within literature on homosexualities. Bailey and Zucker (1995) note that if a child consistently engages in cross-sexual behaviour, he or she is more likely to grow up to regularly express homosexual behaviour than a child who maintains strict adherence to assigned sex role conformity. No doubt the regulatory nature of compulsory heterosexuality within the constructions of masculinity and femininity contributes to these observations, although the authors make no such reference to this point.

There are no solid conclusions as to why gender nonconformity is a variable in some children who grow up to principally desire their same sex. However, cross-sex behaviour cannot necessarily be ascribed as the cause of homosexualities (that is, boys who play with dolls do not grow up to be homosexual because they played with dolls). Here, the error made by some Adlerians is not necessarily in the observation, but in the interpretation of the observation; the assumption that gender nonconformity is devised as a safeguard against feelings of inferiority.

There are also a significant number of homosexuals who do not have a history of gender nonconformity. For example, in many cases, the discovery of exclusive or predominant homosexual feelings by those who do not have a childhood history of gender nonconformity may very well indicate needs which are different from those whose history is more clearly gender nonconformist. While an early sense of marginalization is certainly no 'picnic', such a sense may provide an impetus for developing life skills and coping strategies that would not necessarily be available to those who realize their homoerotic desires at a later age. Such individuals may, upon their discovery, be in a state of acute crisis. In particular, those who wish to conform to gender stereotypes within the boundaries of compulsory heterosexuality may be unable to reconcile their sexual desires with their gender identity (John Head 1997, personal communication).

Another Adlerian claim of aetiology attempts to correlate male homosexualities with women's political gains in the social/economic arena (Adler 1978; Rister 1981; Pevin 1993). This hypothesis assumes that during historical periods where women have gained socio-political power, so too has the incidence of male homosexualites increased. Apparently, male homosexuals have turned to homoeroticism in greater numbers during these periods in order to defend themselves from the resulting increase in male inferiority, an inferiority feeling which is intensified. This is apparently due to the power that women gain during these periods, which is perceived as threatening by the male in question. Thus, they 'retreat' into homosexuality in order to compensate for their lost power. I do not feel that there is really a way to prove or disprove such a broadly based construct as this. No doubt, when women increased their social power during specific historical periods, there probably was a rise in the overt numbers of male homosexuals too, as well as an increase in the acceptance of other civil/human rights. Another interpretation of this phenomenon may be that the rise in male homosexualities during these periods is due to the general loosening of sexual restraints during such periods that both women and homosexual men capitalize on simultaneously. This argument is more consistent with other arguments which purport that women have been controlled in part through institutionalized oppression that both regulates and stifles women's sexual expression; political and economic freedom for women entails, among other things, freedom from sexual constriction. To correlate women's upward mobility with increases in male homosexuality, as some Adlerians have suggested, and implying that this is a compensatory strategy for inferiority, is rather dubious. Moreover, such a theory generally ignores the social context of those periods.

A core tenet in Adlerian psychology is the promotion of a child's courage and movement towards healthy future goals; that is, the promotion of community feeling. However, the assumption that educating a fixed and unalterable sexual role will prevent homosexualities is not supported in the broader literature on gender. Indeed, such assumptions are viewed, by O'Connor and Ryan (1993) for example, as both causal and reductive. They have proposed that psychoanalysts adopt a critical attitude which is informed by postmodern thinking embedded in a 'post-phenomenological' approach, which eschews universal truths. I think that traditional Adlerians could benefit from such a position too. Furthermore, declaring that homosexuals 'lack courage' (as Adler often accused such individuals) must be challenged and disputed with force. Models of 'coming out'[18] did not exist in Adler's day and it was perhaps more common for homosexuals to *appear* 'cowardly', especially when so many spent a great deal of energy hiding their sexuality from others. However, today the act of 'coming out' requires tremendous courage, especially with the expressed hatred of homosexualities so apparent in many parts of the world. It is not uncommon for a person who 'comes out' to receive severe reactions from others, including family, friends and employers. 'Coming out' entails taking a great risk, especially that of rejection and condemnation from significant others. It is an act that usually requires tremendous courage and is far from being the product of a 'coward' – a statement which is a most offensive and duplicitous representation of lesbian and gay lives. To be fair, Adler was a very astute and gentle man, and it is with certainty that we can assume he would rapidly discard this notion if he were alive today. He was mistaken, but he also had, to use Dreikurs' phrase, the 'courage to be imperfect'.

The recent assertion of Gender Guiding Lines (GGL) theory (Powers et al. 1993) essentially confirms a contemporary and traditional assertion of Adler's assumptions of gender role conformity as essential to mental health. While there are many aspects of GGL theory which are unique, well structured and informative,[19] it is nevertheless unfortunately based upon an unexamined (and empirically barren) assertion of traditional binary notions of masculine/feminine and man/woman, as the following illustrates.

> Rejecting the same sex parent as a positive role model (like choosing the parent of the other sex as a positive role model), leaves the child feeling uneasy as to gender and what it means to be a man or woman ... Such a situation may lead to discouragement expressed through a reluctance to grow up and take a place as a man or a woman. (Powers et al. 1993, p. 363)

That GGL theory is imbued with heterosexism exposes an aspect of what Jacoby (1975) articulated as Individual Psychology's (and all so-called ego-psychologies') greatest weakness: that it upholds the *status quo* through its conformism. Exposing this conformism through an analysis of gender and heterosexism will, I assert, begin to break IP free from the dogma and oppressiveness of heterosexism.

HETEROSEXISM AND HEGEMONIC MASCULINITY

When I was a child, I recall being fascinated with my aunt's ability to knit. Without hesitation, she taught me how to hold the needles, start the yarn and do the various stitches. Later, she taught me to crochet. I also remember how my brothers teased me for this activity, how they policed my behaviour and tormented me for knitting. Eventually, I gave up. To pick up the needles brought instant shame. This was my first taste of *hegemonic masculinity*, the dominant form of prescribed behaviour for boys which is dogmatically imposed upon those assigned as males. At the core of hegemonic masculinity we also find *heterosexism* inasmuch as a 'real' man is determined to be avowedly heterosexual, as theorists such as Jung have argued (see Chapter 4, this volume).

Patterson defines heterosexism as

> an ideological system that denies, denigrates, and stigmatizes any non-heterosexual form of behavior, identity, relationship or community. Evidence of heterosexism can be found in religion, in law, in the media, and in the social sciences. (Patterson 1995, p. 4)

On the other side of the coin, less obvious is how heterosexism is used to control and restrict the behaviour of heterosexuals. In his research on male–male friendship, Miller wrote:

> the fear of being taken for a homosexual or, worse, becoming one is a main factor in the United States, in Germany, in Belgium, France, England and Switzerland, in Portugal, Spain and Italy, literally everyone I talked to mentioned it. The universality of this view was astonishing. (Miller 1992, p. 129)

Most people, including many lesbians, gays and bisexuals, are socialized into holding heterosexist assumptions, although this arguably falls within a degree continuum, with gays and lesbians probably expressing the least amount of heterosexism. We generally accept heterosexism because, only with rare exceptions, we learn from early childhood about heterosexuality, and to *be* heterosexual in our behaviour. We incorporate heterosexual imagery from a multitude of sources: television, cinema, fairytales, cartoons, books, advertising, the Internet, heterosexual role models, and so on. In most cases, the non-heterosexual image remains invisible, rebuked, laughable or unexplained. This is the process of learning to be heterosexual that is both culturally embedded and actively promoted in our society. However, learning to be heterosexual also means learning not to be homosexual. The widespread condemnation of homosexual behaviour is known to children who will 'name call' with words like sissy, poof, bender, shirt-lifter, fairy, queer, faggot, etc. This is not intended to imply that children necessarily understand what a 'homosexual' is, but they do understand that to refer to someone *as if* they were 'homosexual', is insulting and derogatory. Learning this is what Herek (1995) refers to as *psychological heterosexism*, which is the individual incorporation of cultural heterosexism. As an alternative to internalized homophobia, psychological heterosexism is exemplified in the common experiences of feelings of disgust, embarrassment, shame, hostility and moral condemnation in regard to homosexual acts. The principal means by which a young person is identified as a potential target of heterosexist discrimination is through, for example, the stereotype of the 'effeminate male homosexual'. Thus, anyone who does not conform to expected gender role behaviour is subject to heterosexist discrimination, regardless of whether they are 'homosexual' or not.

Heterosexism is my own preferred term in describing all manners in which expression of heterosexual status is elevated over homosexual. In this sense, heterosexuality occupies a hegemonic position, as viewed in a hierarchical sense and it conceptually demonstrates the social inequality that homosexuals are faced with.

A report in *The Times* of London illustrates the blatant institutional heterosexism which exists within, for example, the British Military. An individual representation of this homophobia was quoted in the report. According to one Royal Marine:

> If a known homosexual was in the Marines and had started to suffer from hypothermia I would not share my body heat with him. I'd rather he died. (Evans 1996, p. 6)

MASCULINE PROTEST

As one of the forerunners to a modern study of gender in psychology, Adler pursued his concept of the *masculine protest* at the expense of his relationship with Freud. Adler introduced this concept in his 1910 paper 'Psychological hermaphroditism'. Here, he was not referring to any biological notion of hermaphroditism but to the apparent presence of ascribed character traits of both sexes that are present in the psyche.

When one psychological attribute of either so-called male or female traits predominates to the extreme, mental distress (neurosis) ensues. The striving to overcome the weaker 'feminine' attributes and to aspire towards 'masculine' attributes was argued to be the psychic material in which a person models a striving for power that could lead to neurotic experiences and he insisted that the masculine protest is at the core of neurosis. It is also the fundamental psychic material by which psychological inequality is reproduced. He argued that through our biased apperception, we create our *fictions* of what is weak and what is strong. These fictions are largely gendered (ascribed and pervaded with 'masculine' or 'feminine' status). Adler also argued that a hierarchical striving towards masculine fictions does not acknowledge aspects of masculinity as desirable. For example, Adler wrote, 'To this is added the arch evil of our culture, the excessive pre-eminence of manliness' (cited in Connell 1995, p. 16).

We might consider that Adler was initially on the right track with his analysis of masculine protest but ended up sacrificing this concept to the dominant discourse of the day; retreating into the sexual stereotyping and staticness of the binary masculine/feminine polarity prevalent for his time. In the end, Adler replaced his *masculine protest* with a series of other concepts. As Ansbacher (1985) has noted, these concepts included will to power, superiority striving, conquest, security, perfection, an exaggerated personality ideal, success as subjectively defined, overcoming, movement from a felt minus to a felt plus and the safeguarding of self-esteem. The final culmination was reached when all of these previous concepts were collectively subsumed under the concept of community feeling. However, by abandoning the masculine protest, Adler also gave up an analysis of the power dynamics in gender. Yet Adler's original insight, that many pathological problems in psychiatry/psychology are rooted in masculine protest (akin to being 'gendered'), remains quite sharp. A more contemporary and non-Adlerian treatment is offered by Busfield (1996) in her analysis of gender issues and psychopathology which echoes some of Adler's original observations. My own interest and research goals (Shelley 1997) seek to return to Adler's original concept of the masculine protest; to address the problems within this concept so that an Adlerian critique of, for example, *masculinities* may again take a place within various gender debates.

Aspects of the traditional Adlerian position on lesbianism appear to be consistent with some of the subjective experiences lesbians have reported (Kitzinger 1987). These aspects assume that the root of lesbianism is to be found in the masculine protest, where the dislike of the feminine role is so 'extreme' that the woman in

question 'retreats' into homosexuality as a protest against patriarchal power structures (Ansbacher and Ansbacher 1956). Although
this theory may prove consistent with the subjective experiences of
some lesbians, perhaps it also echoes certain popular notions of
lesbians as 'man-haters', a notion that is far too general and
sweeping. A dislike of patriarchy does not necessarily translate into
a hatred of men (although it certainly may in some cases).
Moreover, Adler's use of the word 'retreat' is objectionable for its
allusion to cowardice or withdrawal. Excepting these criticisms, the
masculine protest does appear to be significant for some lesbians.
For example, some lesbian women identify as lesbian for political
reasons and they construct their sexuality in direct reaction to the
oppressiveness of patriarchy. It needs to be emphasized and
acknowledged that there are many attributions lesbians make about
their sexuality which most theorists in psychology have failed to
grasp. Obviously, where traditional Adlerians part company with, for
example, postmodern accounts of lesbianism, is in the construction
of this 'retreat' as neurosis.

In general, traditional Adlerians have focused their criticism on
male homosexualities. Scant attention has been paid to lesbian
issues: not because some Adlerians do not or have not disapproved
or pathologized the lesbian subject; more likely it is due to other
factors. In particular, if we keep in mind the effeminate stereotype
of the male homosexual, society would probably have more difficulty
with the male subject adopting what is perceived to be a
'cross-sexual position', especially when this implies taking a lower
status. Masculinity is an achievement based upon a strict
construction of hierarchical and competitive structures. The 'privi-
lege' of masculinity is easily exposed in the example of 'sissy' boys.
'Sissies' receive a heavier penalization for their cross-sex behaviour
(downward movement) than do 'tomboys'[20] (upward movement)
who are less likely to be penalized for their behaviour, provided they
move towards more feminine behaviour after puberty, as Greenglass
(1982) has reported. Indeed, tomboy behaviour appears to be
tolerated provided it is not associated with lesbianism. Largely,
lesbians have remained exempt[21] from both the legal and psychological persecution campaigns which have been directed overwhelmingly against gay men. This exemption has not been a totally saving
grace – it has meant that lesbians have had a history of invisibility,
which is currently being addressed by many lesbian groups who are
seeking greater visibility in both the gay and straight communities.
This invisibility is, however, also subjected to the wider oppression
lesbians experience as women.

THE EDUCATION OF CHILDREN

Adler emphasized the role that institutional education (schooling) plays in the moulding of an individual. Consequently, he spent a great deal of his time training teachers in the principles of Individual Psychology, principles which emphasize community, co-operation, sharing, mutual respect, equality, encouragement, individual responsibility (where appropriate) and democratic values. Adler believed that solid training for children in these principles would provide a powerful 'inoculation' against future mental disturbance so that individuals would be equipped to meet the demands of life. His efforts were rewarded by a revolutionary educational project in post-First World War Vienna where the entire Viennese school system implemented Adler's ideas. Maddox writes:

> After the collapse of the Hapsburg empire, the Social Democrats of Austria were determined to create a new culture which would free man from the oppressive forces of feudalism and the inequalities of capitalism. They realised that education played an important part in this transformation and decided to implement Adler's ideas which laid great emphasis upon the development of the communal spirit and reflected the ideals of the enlightenment as well as socialism. (Maddox 1997, p. 45)

Unfortunately the scheme was dismantled, along with Adler's Viennese child guidance clinics, after the fascist uprising in Austria during 1934. Nevertheless, Adlerian optimism in educational reform has continued through to this day and teachers from around the world continue to be trained in Adlerian approaches to education, an approach which emphasizes co-operative rather than punitive discipline, equality, assisting children to overcome feelings of inferiority, and so on (Adler 1970; Albert 1989).

There is great potential for schools to be implemented as sites to train youth in community-building values. A mandate for training students in social living is possible. So is the potential for training youth in the values of tolerance and equality with sensitivity to such matters as racism, sexual equality, heterosexism and other important issues. Researchers at Canterbury Christ Church College in the UK are currently examining the need for resources and discussion of homosexuality in secondary schools. The project aims to implement the following resources:

1. For staff and students to gain greater understanding about homosexual relationships within the context of all kinds of relationships.

2. For young people to gain an insight into the feelings of young homosexuals and 'difficult' adolescent feelings.

3. For schools to begin to see the need to address homosexualities within the wider context of equal opportunities, bullying and prejudicial attitudes.

4. For the school community to go some way towards overcoming misconceptions and myths about homosexual relationships and feelings.

Learning to be tolerant of difference is just as possible as learning to be non-violent. Myriam Miedzin (1991) reports that the Hutterite community in the US is unanimous in training their children (particularly boys) to value community, charity, love and non-violence. This is a co-operative effort by both families and teachers; violence is now practically unknown in this community. Is it possible for other communities to learn from the example set by the Hutterites?

The idea of extending the role of the school to train the young in social living is consistent with the pastoral care model in place within British schools (for example, PSE: Personal and Social Education). This model embraces the idea of care for the general welfare of the students rather than an exclusive focus on academic achievement. Nevertheless, the basic practice of the school in England has generally not been one of an institution tolerant of sexual difference. As Mac an Ghaill (1994) has convincingly argued, schools may be viewed as complex arenas of gendered and heterosexual behaviours and ideologies which significantly impact the development of the student's emerging identities. In Mac an Ghaill's research on masculinity and schooling, he found few teachers who would be willing to discuss their views on masculinity without feeling that the enquiry constituted a critique or a divergence into 'homosexuality'. Moreover, none of the teachers he had interviewed were prepared to counsel gay or lesbian youth or to provide a positive view of homosexualities within the curriculum, due to the perception that Clause 28 of the 1986 Education Act (which prohibits the 'promotion' of homosexuality) prevented them from doing so. The absence of any formal reference to homosexualities, particularly in a positive sense, allowed the dominant heterosexual ideology to prevail. The result for the lesbian and gay students was summed up by Mac an Ghaill:

> heterosexuality was presented as natural, normal and universal, simply because there are no alternative ways of being. The students emphasised the personal isolation, confusion, marginalisation and alienation that this engendered. (1994, p. 161)

Alternative schools have been created for gay, lesbian, bisexual and transgendered students in the US and Canada as a short-term solution to the problems Mac an Ghaill has identified in his research. Such alternatives may help in the short term, but is segregation the solution we require?

THERAPY

Adlerian psychotherapy tends towards a *brief* as opposed to a long-term psychotherapy model which is directive when necessary (Life Style assessment, Socratic questioning, the use of interpretation, confrontation, paradoxical intention, art, and so on) but is also non-directive if the moment requires it. Adlerians are trained to practise therapy as a creative art form. Like playing the violin, there are many levels of competence for the use of Adlerian principles and techniques and it generally takes years of study, training and experience before one becomes a therapist (as in most other schools). We do not necessarily practise from a stance of neutrality in our work but allow ourselves to enter into the subjective world of our clients, to attempt to see with their eyes, hear with their ears and feel with their hearts. Our work is subjectively focused, empathically based and dialectically engaging. We do not encourage clients to depend on therapy; rather, we encourage community feeling – as quickly, deeply and transformatively as possible.

Most children internalize the message that 'homosexuality is wrong': it is a message that is often bombarded at us on all levels, conscious and unconscious; it takes root in our beliefs and becomes represented individually through the creation of guiding fictions. In most of us, homosexuals included, the inner dimension of our attitudes resonates with the social induction of collective beliefs about gender and homosexuality (men are ... , women are ...). Maylon writes:

> Since homophobic beliefs are a ubiquitous aspect of contemporary social mores and cultural attitudes, the socialisation of the incipi-

ent homosexual individual nearly always involves an internalisa-
tion of the mythology and opprobrium which characterise current
social attitudes toward homosexuality. (Maylon 1985, p. 60)

I am not of the opinion that homosexual clients should *only* receive
service from self-identified homosexual therapists. Certainly, a gay or
lesbian therapist can model positive aspects to their clients; however,
an attitude of affirmation or a willingness to explore the oppressive
dimensions to gender and sexuality takes precedence over the sexual
orientation of the therapist. Moreover, additional training, when
absent from the standard training curriculum, can be installed as a
mandatory component for therapists in training who intend to include
'homosexuals' in their practice caseload. Hopefully, additional training
will allow practitioners to be aware of and more sensitive to the special
needs of this population. Clark states, 'Certainly no non-gay [or
lesbian] therapist should assume competence in serving gay clients
without retraining and gay oriented supervision to unlearn the
prejudices and misinformation acquired in life and in professional
training programs' (cited in Rochlin 1985, p. 27). Is it possible for a
therapist who has not confronted his or her own homophobic/
heterosexist attitudes to facilitate the often complicated process of
facilitating a client to challenge and give up his or her heterosexist
material?

By using a framework which does not ignore issues of oppression
and emphasizes the elements of encouragement, choice, compassion
and community feeling, the Adlerian practitioner will have much to
offer those clients who seek help in sorting through gender and
sexuality issues. With these tools, and by non-judgementally accepting
people as they are, Adlerians may assist troubled individuals with their
forward movement towards a stable lesbian, gay, bisexual, transgender
or heterosexual identity. The alternative is to oppress, to fail to listen
to him or her and to practise discrimination – one of the major barriers
to the full realization of community feeling and social equality. To
re-focus on questions of equality is paramount as equality and its
social expression are a central tenet of Individual Psychology (Dreikurs
1971). Many Adlerian counsellors and psychotherapists have come to
understand this and are putting into practice these positive tools in
their work with clients who bring sex and gender issues into the
therapy room.

If a therapist is not sure of his or her heterosexism, he or she
may find it useful to engage in some self-questioning and
examination: 'Am I comfortable talking about lesbian/gay sex? Do I
even know what kinds of sexual acts lesbians and gays practice? Do

I feel I am condoning sinful/immoral behaviour? Do I respect my client's homosexuality?' These are only a few of the many issues I believe all therapists must resolve before they engage in any work with clients, especially those who identify as non-heterosexual.

THE BRIEF CASE OF 'MR J'[22]

Mr J, a 35-year-old white male, was referred for therapy by his family physician. He presented with depressed mood, low self-esteem and sexual identity issues. Initially, Mr J was reluctant to reveal his feelings about his sexual orientation and was insistent that I 'make him straight'. Up to this point in his life, he had had some limited homosexual experiences and his only long-term relationship, which he described as very unsatisfying, had been with a slightly older woman (three years' duration).

Mr J was initially uneasy in answering questions about his sexual issues, so, rather than press sexual identity issues, we spent the first five sessions preparing the Life Style assessment. Through this process, I was able to establish excellent rapport with Mr J and collect valuable information on his social and individual history.

After a rapport was established, we spent several sessions discussing sexuality. Here, Mr J revealed that he was able to perform sexually with women but found such experiences ungratifying. His exclusive fantasy repertoire consisted of male erotic material. At this point in the therapy, Mr J became more comfortable in revealing his feelings.

In attempting to understand an individual's sexual orientation, I find it crucial to find out which sex (or both sexes in the case of bisexualism) the individual romanticizes, or is capable of falling in love with. Mr J revealed an exclusive romanticization of males, even though his history up until that point had been principally heterosexual (at least behaviourally). I was careful not to 'steer' him in any direction, but rather to allow him to reveal what was there in as unbiased a manner as possible. Even when his sexual orientation seemed clearer to me, my role was to listen non-judgementally and not to act directively or to impose my feelings about his situation on to him.

Intervention with Mr J took place only to confront his cognitive distortions and biased apperceptions regarding gay men. This was done in the manner of *Socratic questioning* (Stein 1991). Here, in a dialectical spirit, we would explore and discuss his beliefs and ideas regarding gay men, which subsequently challenged the very basis of his psychological heterosexism.

In session twelve, Mr J meekly announced: 'Maybe I might be able to learn to accept being gay?' He then revealed the following dream to me:

> I was in Vietnam, I was in an aeroplane with a co-pilot and we were shot down. I was surprisingly calm under the circumstances; my co-pilot lay dead beside me. Later, I was captured and tortured by the Viet Cong. When I went back to Canada, I told his daughter about her father's death.

Under facilitation, Mr J examined this dream and concluded that the dead co-pilot was actually his former heterosexual self (self-ideal): his fiction of what he 'ought' to be. The dream is a dream of change. Mr J felt that the torture element in his dream represented the attitudes of society at large and his fear of being ridiculed for being 'queer'. A core fiction and basic mistake that Mr J had held was, 'I'm less than others, I'm not equal.' Up until this point, he had used his sexual impulses as self-justification of his felt unworthiness.

The next few sessions were spent examining Mr J's general basic mistakes, which were extracted from his early recollections. We agreed that the negative self statements he used to maintain his depression were probably related to his unfortunate early life, a consequence and resultant strategy of being raised in a highly dysfunctional family. He had blamed himself for the poor state of his family life: 'Maybe if I'd been a good boy, or what they wanted me to be ... .' I pointed out to him the social and economic circumstances his family had had to endure (unemployment, heavy debts, isolation) and attempted to point out the socio-political dimensions which supported his family's dysfunction. However, these beliefs proved to be a 'hook to hang more evidence of my essential worthlessness on', and Mr J was reluctant to give up these mistakes. They became convenient excuses which Mr J used creatively to avoid making those structural changes that were in his, rather than 'society's' domain.

Further manifestation of Mr J's inferiority feelings were made clear in his abhorence of being delegated to a 'minority status', as revealed in the following dream:

> There was an Indian Chief called McDermot and he assisted in the Manitoba Rebellion. He had a beard and a Mountie hat. He sat on his horse. He was pointing west and I was looking east and we were on the prairies. We rebelled and he ended up dead and I was alive. I was a minority.

Mr J's enmity at being a minority (gay) became something of a stumbling block at this point in the therapy. He did not want to give up the attractiveness of the heterosexual male ideal, the Mountie figure, the tall man on the horse – slick and shiny, with his broad hat of authority. To kill him is to rebel, to take another direction of movement that leads to being a 'minority', to despair. The direction is either conformity or nonconformity. This dream seemed to reaffirm his inferiority feelings and temporarily slowed down the movement of the therapy. 'I don't want to be one of THEM!', he once cried out in anger. Soon after, he revealed the following early recollection to me which uncovered his feelings of shame and embarrassment for being sexually 'different'.

Age: 7. There were three boys, I was one of the three. The rest were girls and we were signed up for figure skating. We had to wear leotards. This was at a winter carnival with lots of people. I felt really embarrassed [he slipped here and said 'bare-assed'] and feminine. People made jokes. I didn't want to do it but I had to. What was worse was the girls were better figure skaters.

Most vivid part of memory: Doing the bunny hop and falling on my arse.

Feelings in this memory: embarrassment, humiliation.

This memory relates to the deeper gender fictions Mr J held. These fictions were held in place by the emotional chains of his feelings of shame. Shame and guilt are expressions of the more common feelings presented, especially apparent when many clients begin to challenge the basis of their psychological heterosexism. Indeed, we can feel guilty for challenging the historical weight of this institution. Subsequent sessions were spent desensitizing Mr J to his guilt and shame for becoming gay. This is where encouragement and understanding become among our most valuable tools as Adlerian therapists.

Mr J's greatest forward movement occurred after revealing the following dream:

I was out in the wilderness. I was on a crew that changes the train tracks. In the dream there is a blur between the real and model train tracks. We were a crew of about 25 guys. It was around 1900 and today simultaneously. We replaced a rail that was smaller than the actual rail needed but it would still allow the train to pass if it went slowly. To hold the rail on to the tie were clips. The clips were bright pink where I was working, while the others were multi-coloured. The foreman said: 'That won't work', and I replied: 'Yes it would, provided the train went slowly.' The tracks were in a mountain area leading into a tunnel. The group of guys were near the tunnel, about 5 kilometres from where we had worked. An old steam engine came by speeding and to my amazement the train didn't derail in the area where we did the work. The train went through the tunnel and some time passed and we became old men. We heard a rumour that the train had eventually derailed, but this was only a rumour, it didn't derail. When we heard the rumour the tunnel closed and became solid rock and we were trapped in the mountains. There were other dead-end lines and when we realized this we all declared our territory by shouting: 'This is my line!' When we were old men, I was looking down on the scene as it had all become a model railway.

Mr J created this dream as a prelude of what was to come. We mutually agreed that the train represented Mr J moving forward as a result of his work on creating a new sexual identity (symbolized by the pink tie clips). The passing of the speeding train over the clips indicated the intention of durability in terms of our therapeutic work. However, the rumour of the future derailment indicated that Mr J expected problems as a result of accepting his homosexuality. Here I reminded him that it was only a rumour and that the train did not actually derail. Thus, his ultimate goal was to 'stay on track'. The dream reflected his intentions.

The consequences of not accepting his sexuality were clearly represented in the dream too. Here, the tunnel became solid rock and he remained trapped in the mountains. In the end, life did not seem real (indicated by the model railway) and he became old in a world not real to him (the world of pseudo-heterosexuality).

Shortly after this dream, Mr J began dating men and announced his sexuality to some significant others. And through this process he is learning how to respect himself, to share love, and to give up his depression. He is happier being 'out' and living life on-track as a gay man. He now makes use of his time by working as a volunteer in a local gay youth group and has become more political in working for change within our heterosexist system. In increasing his community feeling, he has learned to channel his anger constructively into working for social change.

CONCLUSION

Adlerian approaches to counselling and psychotherapy (both individual and group) have much to offer the gay and lesbian client. I chose to practise the Adlerian approach for a number of personal reasons, which are summed up in the idea of community feeling combined with Adler's general optimism in human beings. I also strongly support the Adlerian commitment to bring the skills necessary for some semblance of community feeling to the masses rather than to support an elitist psychological approach of expert–client. Unfortunately, Adler's early attempts to break down psychoanalytic jargon in order that lay people may share (even in a limited way) in this understanding was seriously criticized by Freud and others (Jacoby 1975). Within this critique, Adler has been accused of having attempted to 'water down' psychoanalytic ideas, of attempting to undo the subversive potential of these concepts. Nothing could be further from our truth. There is nothing more subversive than a widespread movement to develop community feeling. Those of us who practise IP know the challenge of our concepts; that they might be read on many levels – from common sense through to deeper and more complex understandings of what these concepts may be. Indeed, Adler sought to subvert the bourgeois elitism and overt conservatism at the heart of Freud's psychoanalytic circle. He did not succeed, and instead, broke away from this group to develop his own school and to further develop his concepts. But Adler's original message, that therapy is best practised as a collaborative activity between, as much as possible, two people striving towards an equal relationship, is a message that has fallen on deaf ears within the overall discipline of psychology. For this reason, Adlerians have continued to argue their version of psychology and psychotherapy.

This chapter has attempted to demonstrate that traditional Adlerians have failed 'homosexuals' in the very way that we, as Adlerians, have tried so hard to overcome the tyranny of a lack of community feeling in Western society. The only way forward is to separate traditional Adlerian assumptions about gender and sexuality from our core concepts; to cast these oppressive ideas into the abyss of history so that we may emerge with the dialectical possibility of creating a truly better world where we all feel that we belong; where we can be a community.

NOTES

1 Adlerians have not differentiated the pluralism within homosexualities and, like so many others, view same-sex love within the monolithic representation of *homosexuality*. My occasional use of 'homosexuality' rather than homosexualities is to refer to historical representations only or to avoid confusion.

2 Ansbacher (1985) writes: 'It must be stressed that good adjustment in the sense of social interest does not mean conformity. Rather, it often means nonconformity as progress and improvement of a situation require. It may mean disobedience and rebellion, where conformity would mean self-centred shirking of responsibility' (p. 205). Unfortunately, this argument has not been accepted by traditional Adlerians in terms of sex and gender.

3 I am in agreement with most postmodern sentiments, even with the stated difficulties in defining the term. However, I do not necessarily accept the idea that there is 'no objective truth' (although I remain suspicious of claims of objectivity). Rather, I think that there is a middle ground to be found between the rationalist project of the Enlightenment and postmodern accounts.

4 My lack of German and Italian prevents me from citing the innovations brought forward by theorists at the Adler Institutes in Torino, Zurich, Vienna and Berlin. Moreover, the preference of many Adlerians to carry forward their innovations through an oral-performance tradition (rather than writing) should not allow me to ignore the outstanding work of figures such as Manford Sonstegard, Oscar Christensen, Leo Gold, Jim Bitter and Sophia De Vries (among many others!).

5 I prefer the label 'Indivisible Psychology' and would propose this to Adlerians if I felt that they would adopt it as an alternative to 'Individual Psychology'. I continue to find the 'individual' problematic. However, many Adlerians refer to their school as 'Adlerian psychology' which is also preferable to 'Individual'.

6 Adler sometimes preferred 'unaware' or 'non-conscious' rather than 'unconscious'.

7 I prefer Keith Silvester's (1977) unpublished ideas on co-transference rather than transference/countertransference as conceptually more consistent with the Adlerian model, even though Silvester is not an Adlerian.

8 I am indebted to Claudette Kulkarni (1997) for introducing me to Gadamerian hermeneutics.

9 A good example of this would be the Adlerian Manaster, who co-wrote an overtly heterosexist article on male homosexuality (King and Manaster 1973) but has recently expressed a contrary opinion which does not appear to support a pathology viewpoint any longer (Manaster 1996).

10 Adler implied that 'common sense' is really a striving for reason. In this sense, I support Adlerian emphases on 'common sense'. I do not necessarily support the unexamined moral conformism that is often bound to notions of 'common sense', as this can lead to dangerous problems; homosexualities are a case in point.

11 An obvious liberal exception would be France, a country that decriminalized homosexual relations in 1789.

12 Upon hearing that Freud had taken up the aggressive *drive*, Adler replied: 'I

enriched psychoanalysis by the aggressive drive. I gladly make them a present of it' (Ansbacher and Ansbacher 1956, p. 38). Adler did not negate the importance of aggression in neurosis. He did, however, eventually dispute the legitimacy and utility of drive psychology.

13 Prior to Kivel's 1983 article, there were Adlerians who did not accept these negative ideas about homosexuality. However, their silence is reflected in the absence of a written objection prior to Kivel's article.

14 The rate of homosexuality in the sons was 9%, which can be argued to be higher than other population-based surveys (as in Kinsey's conclusion of 4%). However, the higher rate in this study can be explained by *concordance-dependency ascertainment bias*, as the study authors have argued.

15 What individuals also need, I argue, is a social and political awareness of what it is they are adjusting to! In this regard, the concept of adjustment ought not to be divorced from the historical, institutional and contextual elements that provide an all-important means to address clinical issues of adjustment.

16 Foucault's (1978) poststructuralist analysis has helped to shed greater light on this matter. In many cases, the clients themselves colluded with this view, insisting that they were/are 'perverted' or otherwise 'sick'.

17 'Micro penis' is a relatively rare 'defect' where the penis size is 2.5 standard deviation units below the mean for the age. In some cases, the penis is slightly larger than an average clitoris with hypospadias features, requiring urination in a sitting position.

18 'Coming out' is the term used when homosexuals begin to synthesize their same-sex feelings into a gay, lesbian, bisexual or transgender identity. It is expressed when the individual feels comfortable enough to announce his or her sexuality to significant others.

19 Gender Guiding Lines theory is an extension of Powers and Griffith's (1987) method of establishing a client's *gender guiding lines*, an aspect of Life Style assessment. I have found their work on gender guiding lines to be both exceptional and enormously useful. Here I differentiate between the utility of gender guiding lines' assessment from my differences with the underlying theory.

20 A 'tomboy' refers (in a rather sexist way) to a girl who is perceived to be more masculine in behaviour than other girls.

21 An exception to the legal debates would be the attempt by the British Parliament to criminalize lesbian sex in 1921, an attempt that was rejected by the House of Lords. Moreover, there are some examples of horrific psychiatric 'torture' of lesbian women by the psychiatric and medical professions that, Falco and Garrison (1995) point out, have included lobotomy, clitordectomy, hormone treatments and electroshock therapy. Moreover, there are some examples of a lesbian 'illness' model in the psychological literature, an example of which Falco and Garrison have cited is the 1954 text by Caprio, *Female Homosexuality: A modern study of lesbianism*. I do not underestimate the sad toll that these approaches have taken on lesbians, I just wish to make the point that most anti-homosexual campaigns have been (historically) directed against gay men.

22 I have taken care to conceal the identity of this individual.

REFERENCES

Adler, A. (1938) *Social Interest: A challenge to mankind*, London: Faber & Faber.

Adler, A. (1970) *The Education of Children*, Chicago, IL: Henry Regnery Co.

Adler, A. (1978) *Co-operation Between the Sexes: Writings on Women and Men, Love and Marriage, and Sexuality*, (eds) H. Ansbacher and R. Ansbacher, New York: Anchor Books. (Note: This is a collection of previously published and unpublished papers by Adler with editorial comments by Ansbacher and Ansbacher. All of Adler's papers were written prior to 1937.)

Adler, K. (1994) 'Responses', *Individual Psychology*, 50 (3): 316.

Albert, L. (1989) *Cooperative Discipline*, Circle Pines, MN: American Guidance Service.

Ansbacher, H. L. (1985) 'The Significance of Alfred Adler for the Concept of Narcissism', *American Journal of Psychiatry*, 142 (2): 203–6. (Note: For details on social interest/community feeling, see reprint of this article in *Adlerian Yearbook*, London: ASIIP, 1997).

Ansbacher, H. L. and Ansbacher, R. (eds) (1956) *The Individual Psychology of Alfred Adler*, New York: Harper Torchbooks.

Bailey, J. M., Bobrow, D., Mikach, S. and Wolfe, M. (1995), 'Sexual orientation of adult sons of gay fathers', *Developmental Psychology*, 31 (1): 124–9.

Bailey, J. M. and Zucker, K. (1995) 'Childhood sex-typed behavior and sexual orientation: A conceptual analysis and quantitative review', *Developmental Psychology*, 31 (1): 43–55.

Bell, A., Hammersmith, S. and Weinberg, M. (1981) *Sexual Preference*, Bloomington: Indiana University Press.

Brod, H. and Kaufman, M. (eds) (1994) *Theorizing Masculinities*, London: Sage.

Busfield, J. (1996) *Men, Women and Madness: Understanding Gender and Mental Disorder*, London: Macmillan.

Connell, R. W. (1995) *Masculinities*, Cambridge: Polity Press.

Corsini, R. and Wedding, D. (eds) (1989) *Current Psychotherapies*, fourth edition, Itasca, IL: F. E. Peacock.

Dreikurs, R. (1967) *Psychodynamics, Psychotherapy and Counseling*, Chicago, IL: Alfred Adler Institute.

Dreikurs, R. (1971) *Social Equality: The Challenge of Today*, Chicago, IL: Alfred Adler Institute.

Dreikurs, S. T. (1986) *Cows Can be Purple: My Life and Art Therapy*, Chicago, IL: Alfred Adler Institute.

Ehrenwald, J. (ed.) (1991) *The History of Psychotherapy*, London: Jason Aronson Inc.

Ellenberger, H. F. (1970) *The Discovery Of The Unconscious: The History And Evolution Of Dynamic Psychiatry*, London: Penguin Press.

Evans, M. (1996) 'Three Quarters of Service Personnel Support Ban on Homosexuals', *The Times*, 5 March 1996, p. 6.

Falco, K. and Garrison, M. (1995) 'Steps Toward a Lesbian Friendly Life Style Interview', *Individual Psychology*, 51 (2): 129–43.

Foucault, M. (1978) *The History Of Sexuality: An Introduction*, vol. 1, New York: Vintage.

Fox, D. and Prilleltensky, I. (eds) (1997) *Critical Psychology: An Introduction.* London: Sage.

Friedberg, R. L. (1975) 'Early Recollections of Homosexuals as Indicators of their Life Style', *Individual Psychology*, 31 (2): 196–204.

Gadamer, H. (1960) *Truth and Method*, trans. J. Weinsheimer and D. Marshall, New York: Continuum.

Giovando, K. and Schramski, T. (1993) 'Sexual Orientation, Social Interest, and Exemplary Practice', *Individual Psychology*, 49 (2): 199–204.

Gold, L. (1979) 'Adler's Theory Of Dreams: An Holistic Approach To Interpretation', in Wolman, B. (ed.) *Handbook Of Dreams: Research, Theories And Applications*, New York: Van Nostrand and Reinhold Co.

Greenglass, E. (1982) *A World of Difference: Gender roles in perspective*, Toronto: John Wiley & Sons.

Hamer, D., Hu, S., Pattatucci, A. M., Patterson, C., Li, L., Fulker, D., Cherny, S. S. and Kruglyak, L. (1995) 'Linkage between sexual orientation and chromosome Xq28 in males but not in females', *Nature Genetics*, 11.

Handlbauer, B. (1998) *The Freud–Adler Controversy*, Oxford: Oneworld Publications.

Herek, G. M. (1995) 'Psychological Heterosexism in the United States', in D'Augelli, A. R. and Patterson, C. J. (eds) *Lesbian, Gay and Bisexual Identities Over the Lifespan: Psychological Perspectives*, Oxford: Oxford University Press.

Horney, K. (1937) *The Neurotic Personality of Our Time*, New York: W. W. Norton & Co. Inc.

Horrocks, R. (1994) *Masculinity in Crisis*, London: Macmillan.

Hubbard, R. (1990) *The Politics of Women's Biology*, London: Rutgers University Press.

Jacoby, R. (1975) *Social Amnesia: A Critique of Conformist Psychology from Adler to Laing*, Boston, MA: Beacon Press.

Jylland, C. (1990) 'Early Recollections of Homosexual and Heterosexual Males, unpublished Doctoral dissertation, Chicago: Adler School of Professional Psychology.

King, M. and Manaster, G. J. (1973) 'Early Recollections of Male Homosexuals', *Journal of Individual Psychology*, 29: 26–33.

Kitzinger, C. (1987) *The Social Construction of Lesbianism*, London: Sage.

Kitzinger, C. (1997) 'Lesbian and Gay Psychology: A Critical Analysis', in Fox, D. and Prilleltensky, I. (eds) *Critical Psychology: An Introduction*, London: Sage.

Kitzinger, C., and Perkins, R. (1993) *Changing Our Minds: Lesbian Feminism and Psychology*, New York: New York University Press.

Kivel, C. I. (1983) 'Male homosexuals in a changing society', *Individual Psychology*, 39 (3): 218–21.

Kopp, R. (1993) 'Responses', *Individual Psychology*, 49 (2): 216–21.

Kopp, R. (1995) *Metaphor Therapy: Using client generated metaphors in psychotherapy*, New York: Brunner Mazel.

Krausz, E. O. (1935) 'Homosexuality as Neurosis', *International Journal of Individual Psychology*, 1: 30–9.

Kulkarni, C. (1997) *Lesbians and Lesbianisms: A Post-Jungian Perspective*, London: Routledge.

Kurzweil, E. (1995) *Freudians and Feminists*, Oxford: Westview Press.

Mac an Ghaill, M. (1994) *The Making of Masculinities, Sexualities and Schooling*, Buckingham: Open University Press.

Maddox, C. (1997) 'Alfred Adler's Philosophy of Education', *New Analysis: Journal of Psychoanalytic Social Studies*, Summer 1997 (2): 45–7.

Manaster, G. (1996) 'The Structure of Neurosis: A Contemporary Critique', *Individual Psychology*, 52 (4): 363–71.

Manaster, G., Deutsch, D., Overholt, B. and Painter, G. (1977) *Alfred Adler: As we Remember Him*, Chicago, IL: North American Society of Adlerian Psychology.

Marcus, E. (1993) *Is it a Choice?* San Francisco, CA: Harper Books.

Maylon, A. K. (1985) 'Psychotherapeutic Implications of Internalised Homophobia in Gay Men', in Gonsiorek, J. C. (ed.), *A Guide to Psychotherapy with Gay Men and Lesbian Clients*, New York: Harrington Park Press.

Miedzin, M. (1991) *Boys Will be Boys*, London: Virago.

Miller, S. (1992) *Men and Friendship*, Los Angeles, CA: J. P. Tarcher Inc.

Money, J. (1985) 'Gender: History, Theory and Usage of the term in Sexology and its Relationship to Nature/Nurture', *Journal of Sex and Marital Therapy*, 11.

Money, J. (1988) *Gay, Straight and Inbetween: The sexology of erotic orientation*, New York: Oxford University Press.

Mosak, H. (1977) *On Purpose*, Chicago: Alfred Adler Institute.

Mosak, H. (1983) 'A Range of Comments on Homosexuality and Kivel's Article', *Individual Psychology*, 39 (3): 222–36.

O'Connell Davidson, J. and Layder, D. (1994) *Methods: Sex and Madness*. London: Routledge.

O'Connor, N. and Ryan, J. (1993) *Wild Desires and Mistaken Identities: Lesbianism and Psychoanalysis*, New York: Columbia University Press.

Patterson, C. J. (1995) 'Sexual Orientation and Human Development: An Overview', *Developmental Psychology*, 31 (1): 3–10.

Pevin, D. (1993) 'The Individual Psychological Viewpoint of the Psychosexual Disorders', in Sperry, L. and Carlson, J. (eds), *Psychopathology and Psychotherapy: From Diagnosis to Treatment*, Muncie, IN: Accelerated Development.

Powers, R. L. and Griffith, J. (1987) *Understanding Life-style: The Psychoclarity Process*, Chicago, IL: Americas Institute of Adlerian Studies.

Powers, R. L., Griffith, J. and Maybell, S. A. (1993) 'Gender Guiding Lines Theory and Couples Therapy', *Individual Psychology*, 49 (3 & 4): 361–71.

Rister, E. S. (1981) 'The Male Homosexual Style of Life: A Contemporary Adlerian Interpretation', *Individual Psychology*, 37: 86–93.

Rochlin, M. (1985) 'Sexual Orientation of the Therapist and Therapeutic Effectiveness with Gay Clients', in Gonsiorek, J. C. (ed.) *A Guide to Psychotherapy with Gay Men and Lesbian Clients*, New York: Harrington Park Press.

Samuels, A. (1996) 'In Praise of Gender Confusion', *Soundings*, (2): 85–90.

Shelley, C. (1997) 'The Psychology of Men's Power', *Achilles Heel*, Summer/Autumn, 22: 19–22.

Shulman, B. (1973) *Contributions to Individual Psychology*, Chicago, IL: Alfred Adler Institute.

Slavik, S. and Croake, J. (1998) 'What is Psychological Tolerance?', *Adlerian Yearbook*, London: ASIIP, pp. 92–103.

Sloan, T. (1996) *Damaged Goods: The Crisis of the Modern Psyche*, London: Routledge.

Sloan, T. (1997) 'Theories of Personality: Ideology and beyond', in Fox, D. and Prilleltensky, I. (eds) *Critical Psychology: An Introduction*, London: Sage.

Smuts, J. C. (1926) *Holism and Evolution*, London: Macmillan.

Sonstegard, M. (1996) 'The Phases of Counselling', in Hooper, A. (ed.) *Adlerian Yearbook*, London: ASIIP.

Sperry, L. (1995) 'Sexual Orientation and Psychotherapy: Science, Ideology, or Compassion?', *Individual Psychology*, 51 (2): 160–5.

Stein, H. (1991) 'Adler and Socrates: Similarities and Differences', *Individual Psychology*, 47: 241–6.

Tripp, C. A. (1987) *The Homosexual Matrix*, New York: New American Library.

Vaihinger, H. (1911) *The Philosophy of 'As If'*, London: Routledge and Kegan Paul, 1965.

Vervloet, S. (1994) 'Random thoughts on the homosexual life-style', *Individual Psychology*, 50 (3): 318.

6 Cognitive Analytic Therapy and Homosexual Orientation

Chess Denman and Petrus de Vries

Cognitive Analytic Therapy (CAT) is a brief focal structured therapy (devised by Anthony Ryle and outlined in Ryle 1990, 1995 and 1997) which draws on elements derived from the cognitive therapies and elements derived from psychoanalytic psychotherapy, particularly object-relations theory and attachment theory. It is not, however, a hybrid therapy because it fuses these borrowings into its own well developed theoretical conception of human functioning. Our aim in this chapter is, first, to outline the theoretical foundations of CAT, and then to describe and account for the theoretical position CAT and cognitive therapy take in relation to sexual orientation. We then move on to develop CAT theory in the area of sexual orientation, illustrating this theoretical perspective with a case example.

THE THEORY AND PRACTICE OF COGNITIVE ANALYTIC THERAPY

CAT theory begins with the concept of a procedural sequence. Procedures are sequences of thinking, feeling and acting which humans use to achieve their aims. A procedural sequence involves defining an aim, evaluating the environment, planning an action, acting, evaluating the results of the action and discontinuing, repeating or revising the procedure. Aims may be simple, such as eating; or complex, such as passing an exam. They may be intrapersonal – controlling one's temper; giving up smoking; having a bath, or interpersonal – challenging one's boss; making love; playing with one's children. The cognitive processes which enact and evaluate them may be highly conscious (for example, our plan for writing this chapter) or largely automatic (for example, a baby rooting for the breast). Procedures allow for an analysis of experience and behaviour which welds thinking, feeling and acting together into a single unit centred around motivation and specifically on an aim.

Procedures have a circular interaction with the environment (inner or outer) in which they are deployed. This involves learning and change through checking and revision. The circular interaction encourages good (aim-achieving) procedures and weeds out ineffective ones. Normally, therefore, procedures should be subject to revision if they do not succeed in achieving their aims or if the side-effects of achieving the aim are unacceptable. Some procedures, however, fail to be revised appropriately and these maladaptive procedures produce difficulties in achieving aims and ultimately may result in psychopathology. So, from a CAT perspective all psychopathology involves either malfunctioning procedures which have for some reason not been revised or abandoned, or a restricted range of procedures which cannot deal with the task in hand. Procedures are being devised, learned, modified and abandoned all the time, although as development proceeds we tend to lay down a large repertoire of procedures to deal with most situations.

Sometimes procedures are not revised because they were devised and used in haste or desperation and the individual has had no leisure to revise them. For example, following a bereavement a widow might stuff all financial papers (normally dealt with by her partner) into a drawer and not look at them. Sooner or later the effects of this faulty procedure will come home to roost, perhaps in the form of angry letters from the bank. Even when they do, she cannot bear to look – her husband dealt with all that. 'Adjustment reaction' is the term we use to describe the kinds of psychopathology encountered in these occurrences.

The key therapeutic strategy in such situations is to liberate the potential for new procedural sequence development (in this case by working on the mourning) and then to help the individual through the inevitable pains of the trial and error learning which will be involved in developing new procedural sequences. Much new procedural learning is generally automatic and in consequence not very conscious. However, it is possible to take a hand in new procedural learning in a more conscious way. CAT draws heavily on the specifically human capacity to use higher functions to remedy defects in lower order functioning. Self-conscious self-reflection is a tool we all use to plan new action and CAT conceives of self-conscious self-reflection as being capable of devising new procedures to try out, and of assisting in evaluating and altering existing procedures. These capacities are prominently drawn on in CAT's therapeutic methods for dealing with adjustment reactions.

More often problems are long-standing and reflect the operation of maladaptive procedures which fail to be revised because they are in some way insulated from revision. For example, a man may become depressed because he feels that others hate and avoid him. On the rare occasions when he does venture out into the social world he interacts hesitantly and in a preoccupied way expecting rejection. Being with him is not very rewarding. After a while people leave and he gathers evidence for his view that people hate and avoid him. This man's procedures for dealing with others take the form of a self-fulfilling prophesy and form a vicious self-reinforcing circle (called a 'trap' in CAT). Their morphology does not include a valid checking and revising element and so they are never challenged and revised. As a result, the depression fuels itself.

CAT's theory of psychopathology gives considerable weight and time to exact descriptions of the way in which procedures have become faulty, either because of environmental circumstances or because they are insulated from revision for a range of reasons. This description may then be used by the patient in a conscious way to recognize the operation of maladaptive procedures and to begin to revise them.

A second key area of CAT theory is a fusion of a Vygotskian view of the social nature of thought and development (Vygotsky 1986) with aspects of object-relations theory (see, for example, Leiman 1995). For CAT one of the most important structuring features of a human infant's life is the social world into which it is born. Immediately, all around the developing child are other humans who are involved in mediating the affective and cognitive life of the child using sign systems – principally language. It is because of this mediation that thought (conceived of in CAT as an inner conversation) develops. Thought, self-reflection, language/communication and human relationships form for CAT the largest part of the human condition and all are dialogical processes. Self-reflection, self-management and human relationships also involve aims and therefore are structured as procedural sequences. Their special dialogic form is encapsulated in their particular name – reciprocal role procedures (RRPs). A highly simplified example is that of a three- to four-year-old girl enacting with her mother several sequences in which she is clearly testing out the consequences of disobedience. Each time as she disobeys the injunction she watches mother to see what the reaction will be. It could be a number of different things: a scolding; mother laughing as she becomes aware of the element of game-playing; eventually being ignored. Some time later, the child can be seen playing with a toy elephant. Repeatedly the elephant is naughty in some way. The child, as 'mother', scolds and admonishes, inventing new transgressions, new punishments, and new scenes of forgiveness too.

From a CAT perspective this vignette describes a process in which a child is learning and then practising a range of RRPs centring around scolding and being scolded. It is important to notice that the child learns both the scolding and scolded roles. In future interpersonal interactions she might take up either position depending on the situation. The enactment of these RRPs by her in relation to herself (caring for, punishing or forgiving herself) will contribute to the way that she deals with herself. It is also important to notice that the child makes something of her interaction with her mother. Her behaviour towards the toy is not just a copy of mother's behaviour toward her, but an interpretation of that behaviour in the context of the child's appreciation of its social meaning. The range of a child's social experiences as it develops conditions the development of its growing repertoire of RRPs. But it is not just the blunt fact of these social experiences which is important. Rather the internalized repertoire of RRPs represents the child's active construction of its social experiences. When parenting is inconstant or confusing, children may misconstrue what is occurring around them and internalize RRPs which are founded on that misconstruction.

A crucial feature of RRPs in interpersonal relationships is the way in which they elicit reciprocation from the environment. In relationships, if one individual operates a particular RRP in relation to another, then there will be strong pressure for the other to relate back using a similar RRP. This is a universal feature of human interaction so that, for example, adopting a dependent role tends to elicit control and support; adopting a domineering role might elicit either conformist or rebellious (but rarely neutral) reciprocal roles in others. If an individual suffers from faulty or maladaptive interpersonal procedures in a particular area which are for some reason not revised, then the elicitation of congruent reciprocations from others often ensures that again and again he or she will re-enact the same bad relationship story.

RRPs function vitally in the intrapersonal world to help us manage and reflect on experience. From the very moment a child is born it is subjected to long stretches of running commentary from its caregivers which describe and interpret its presumed experience ('Oh, look, you've been a bit sick. Never mind, mummy wipe it up then, yes, there we go. Look over there it's sunny today ...', and so on). This running commentary which later develops into a dialogue ('What did you do at school today? Did you enjoy it?', and so on) is part of an RRP which we might call 'concerned interpreter parent'–'observed and cared-for child'. In CAT theory this RRP and others like it are internalized and form part of an internal self-reflective and self-monitoring function capable of interpreting experience, interrogating it and ultimately capable of planning future self-management.

Difficulties during childhood may restrict the range of reciprocal role procedures which are learned in a number of ways. In serious psychopathology the procedures themselves may be harsh and unhelpful if crucial aspects of childhood experience were harsh and unhelpful, forming, for example, the reciprocal roles 'bullying–bullied' or 'abused–abusive'. The range and flexibility of the roles and the procedures which enact them may also be restricted, leading to stereotyped responses in certain or many situations. The procedures may be malformed and lack appropriate checking and correcting mechanisms in the manner described above. Finally, the self-management procedures derived from these reciprocal role procedures may be rudimentary or positively unhelpful.

In considering psychopathology CAT does not set a developmental timetable for the acquisition or damage of procedures and in consequence there is no presupposition that early damage is pre-eminently responsible for later psychopathology. Vulnerabilities to different kinds of difficulty will open up and close down depending on what the child makes of experiences at a particular time, and may be quite idiosyncratic. Additionally, children are not passive recipients of relationship experiences; rather, they are active participants in relationships and may, building on what they already have, either contribute to or ameliorate the psychopathological situation in which they find themselves. However, in general, it is repeated exposure to inconstant, abusive or in other ways procedurally damaging experience which lays down faulty procedures and it is the continued experience of emotional and social deprivation which restricts the range of RRPs.

CAT's distinctive claim is that faulty or restricted RRPs account for most of the psychopathology dealt with routinely by psychotherapists. Comparison of RRPs with other theoretical entities invoked by different schools of psychotherapy can be used to chart the similarities and differences between CAT and the ways other therapies describe psychic functioning and psychopathology. Clearly, RRPs describe the self's transactions with itself and others in ways which are similar to descriptions given in object-relations theory. Simple extensions of the theoretical perspective already described allow for descriptions of the phenomena of transference, countertransference and projective identification as special cases of the general tendency to deploy RRPs in particular situations and to elicit reciprocal responses from the therapist. CAT differs from object-relations theory in many ways, but, most importantly in its consistently Vygotskian focus on social learning, in having no use for the concept of a part-object and in its failure to invoke the notion of unconscious phantasy to describe and explain the phenomena under discussion.

CAT's theory of RRPs is also similar to the theory of schemata which underpins Cognitive Behaviour Therapy's (CBT) developing approach to character pathology (Young 1990). In CBT, schemata are learned patterns of thought which underpin emotion and action. RRPs, although in some respects embodying similar ideas, are unlike schemata in that they are not conceived of as enduring templates which structure higher level interactions. Rather, they are actively formed and reformed structures which involve thinking, feeling and acting, and are repeatedly enacted in the world and subjected when healthy to revision and modification. So CAT and CBT differ over the extent to which the structures which underpin action, emotion and belief are thought to be permanently encoded in memory. CAT also adopts a consistently more interpersonal focus than CBT in its description of mental processes, in the practice of therapy and in its concept of psychopathology.

CAT's theory is put into clinical practice in a therapy which seeks to elicit the patient's co-operation in jointly delineating and then revising the faulty procedures or areas of procedural restriction which are currently causing interpersonal difficulty. The therapy is therefore co-operative, and self-consciously educative. In CAT the therapist and patient work jointly and CAT therapists argue strongly that, in the simple act of coming to therapy, the patients, however damaged or ambivalent, thereby announce that they are at least partly concerned for themselves. It is this self-concerned part which the therapist will try to work with. CAT therapists also share their understandings very openly with their patients. They do not make interpretations or keep things back for fear of being wrong or imposing their view on the patient. Instead they stress equality, joint working and co-operation and achieve this by sharing the contents of their reflections with the patient while being very evidently influenced in their conceptions by the patient's response to what they say.

CAT is a technically difficult therapy. It consists of a wide range of different techniques bound together by a complex theory and what follows necessarily compresses a complex and subtle process into a flat, brief description.

The therapy starts with the patient's story. The therapist listens but also asks questions and spends the first two sessions trying to gather a history, make a list of the main problems the patient complains of (called 'target problems') and, crucially, tries to make a relationship with the patient. In two further sessions the therapist and patient try to discover the maladaptive procedural sequences which result in the target problems – the CAT term for these particular procedures is 'target problem procedures' (TPPs). In doing so therapist and patient may use various active information gathering techniques such as keeping a diary, or filling in questionnaires, as well as examination and discussion of elements of the transference and, crucially, of the therapist's countertransference.

In the fourth session the understanding which the therapist and patient have come to (called a 'reformulation') is shared with the patient in written format. This is a retelling of the patient's story and a recasting of their difficulties into a new understanding based on the RRPs involved. The reformulation is worked on by patient and therapist over the next few sessions. It is revised and negotiated and, if necessary, struggled over. In further sessions the patient and therapist try to identify the operation of the problematic RRPs in the session (transference and countertransference) and in the patient's life. Again there may be psychoanalytic-like interpretations involved and also cognitive-like monitoring procedures, but the key CAT techniques used will be accurate description and joint reflection. The aim is always to aid and strengthen self-reflection generally and to develop specific capacity to identify problematic procedures.

Once recognition is reliably established the patient is in a position to alter these procedures. Here the therapist may nudge a little, brainstorm different ways of behaving with the patient, or make specific suggestions. However, this is usually not necessary because, often, once the patient can see a maladaptive procedure operating he or she will begin spontaneously to revise it by trying out all kinds of new ways of behaving. Some of these will be wise, in the therapist's view; others not, but all will be different from the pattern that went before. The last sessions (therapy generally lasts 16 sessions) centre on saying goodbye, a process which often involves examining old losses and the RRPs for dealing with them.

ATTITUDES TO HOMOSEXUALITY IN
COGNITIVE ANALYTIC THERAPY, BEHAVIOUR THERAPY
AND COGNITIVE BEHAVIOUR THERAPY

Reviewing publications about CAT with an eye to inspecting its attitude to sexuality and sexual orientation is a remarkably brief task. Ryle's work contains only a single reference to sexual orientation. In his first book on CAT, Ryle (1990) reprints Malan's list of exclusion criteria for brief therapy, among which homosexuality appears, and opines that none of Malan's criteria apply to CAT.

CAT's silence on sexual orientation and sexuality generally stems from its view of human motivations as derived from needs for attachment, security and mastery, and its concentration on interpersonally learned procedures for meeting these needs. Thus, for CAT, sexuality is not at the centre of human psychology nor is it the mainspring of psychic development. This is not to say that CAT is incapable of developing its theoretical tools to encompass and describe difficulties and pathologies of sexuality, just that this task has not been the first on the theoretical agenda.

Drawing on the theoretical base outlined above let us sketch out how homosexual orientation might be viewed within CAT. However, before this development can be done it seems important to say something about theoretical and clinical views of sexual orientation in the cognitive and behavioural therapies from which CAT draws, largely because they have had a reputation for aggressive attempts at altering homosexual orientation.

In the early days of behaviour therapy there were clearly a number of practitioners who used classical and operant conditioning methods in an attempt to alter sexual orientation with varying evidence of success. As the 1960s and 1970s progressed, however, there is evidence of increasing disquiet in the literature on two counts. First, it began to become clear that behavioural therapy was not an effective means of altering sexual orientation (McConaghy 1976). More importantly, ethical questions were raised about attempts to alter patients' sexuality. The retreat of the behaviour therapists on ethical grounds was conducted in waves. First coercion/persuasion of unwilling patients to submit to therapy was discouraged (Phillips et al. 1976), then the therapy of patients who requested treatment of so-called 'ego-dystonic' homosexuality was questioned on the grounds that internalized homophobia and social repression might be the driving force behind the request (Davidson 1977). Finally, completing the volte-face, behavioural and cognitive therapists turned their attention to ways of altering the ego-dystonic nature of homosexual orientation or treating associated difficulties rather than altering the orientation itself (see, as an example in relation to couples, Kaufman et al. 1984). The cognitive therapies were begun rather later in the history of this debate and, broadly speaking, inherited a more liberal view of homosexual orientation. Beck's Cognitive Therapy does not pathologize or even theorize homosexual orientation and, most probably, a modern cognitive therapist would tend to view sexual orientation as in large part a biological trait.

The modern practice of Ellis's Rational Emotive Behaviour Therapy also does not involve a pathologizing view of sexual orientation, but Ellis himself is a different matter. He began life as a sex therapist and was actively involved with the Mattachine society (an early American homosexual grouping). Ellis seems to have been vociferously of the view that homosexuality was a neurotic condition involving a phobia of women which would respond to treatment (see Bayer 1981). However, in his later writings, as he develops Rational Emotive Therapy into a formal system, there is no hint of his pathologizing stance towards sexual orientation; indeed, in this case the silence on the subject of sexuality could almost seem to represent an embarrassed awareness of a previous gaffe.

Broadly therefore, in relation to the current practice of cognitive and behavioural therapies, it seems fair to say that homosexuality is not viewed as a pathology. While there may be individual practitioners with idiosyncratic views, awareness of the history of behaviour modification in the field and the ethical turnaround which followed, it has generally meant that cognitive behaviour therapists will not accede to a patient's request for therapy designed to make him or her heterosexual, but would, with the consent of the patient, try to focus on the reasons for making the request.

COGNITIVE ANALYTIC THERAPY FOR PATIENTS WHO ARE GAY OR LESBIAN

The focus in this section will be on problems which are specific to gay men and lesbians. Space considerations mean that not all such problems can be discussed. In consequence we have chosen those problems which particularly illustrate aspects of CAT practice in this area.

Just as a gay man or a lesbian may grow up without evidence of psychopathology so also they may show pathologies which are quite un-related to their sexual orientation. In such a case CAT would treat the patient in the same way as it would treat any other patient. There may also be cases where a patient's sexual orientation intersects with his or her psychopathology in ways which may either increase or diminish that pathology. Here the issues which arise concerning sexual orientation would be dealt with by CAT insofar as they were relevant to treating the main problem. This is in line with CAT's focal approach to patients' problems. Notwithstanding this, some commonalities can be identified between the psychologies of many gay men and lesbians who have prob-lems associated with their sexuality. These commonalities include issues related to identity formation, 'coming out', coping with homo-phobia and unfairness, issues concerning HIV, particular relationship issues, and alcohol and drug abuse. In all of these areas we will see that the commonalities are due to the interaction between social experience of the individual and his or her sexual orientation.

Identity Formation

Most gay men and a significant proportion of lesbians report knowing that they were 'different' in some way from a very young age. In gay men this knowledge seems either to coalesce around a greater than usual number of feminine qualities or to manifest as a clear-cut sexual interest in boys and men. Either way, many children who grow up to be gay or lesbian experience significant social and parental disapproval on account of their early difference. Children respond to parental disapproval in a number of ways which may be more or less adaptive, but parental disapproval is hard to ignore and many gay men and lesbians have in consequence an internal RRP of the form 'critical disapproving authority/parent' in relation to 'criticized subordinate/ child'. The criticized and subordinate part may also be either self-concealing, defiant, crushed or self-accusing, depending on temperament and the balance of other developmental forces in childhood. Such an RRP is likely to be activated when the patient experiences him- or herself in a position of authority or in the subordinate role, and can create difficulties in either situation. Clearly it can make for considerable difficulty in claiming a secure place in the world – a task which is in any case tougher for gay men and lesbians than for many others.

Parental anxiety is also a response of parents to their perception of the 'difference' of their child and consequently a feature of the childhood of some gay men and lesbians. Here the RRP which is built up will have in part the form 'anxious and possibly intrusive parent'–'aware-of-being-observed child'. Again the child may respond in an additional range of ways which can include either secrecy or acting up.

The common feature of all of these RRPs is the way in which they jeopardize an untroubled and authentic sense of self when they are enacted in adult life. For this reason many gay men and lesbians come to the task of articulating their identity as adolescents, already burdened with RRPs which jeopardize their chances of achieving this aim. The girl who responds with secretiveness and self-accusation may become a lesbian who conceals her sexual nature apart from furtive lapses which provoke bursts of self-recrimination. The boy who responds with defiance and acting-up may become an 'in your face' screaming 'queen' – 'We're here, we're queer, get used to it' becoming the child's cry to the parental world.

But are either of these responses necessarily pathological? How can the pathological nature of an identity be judged? Not easily. Consider a gay man who escapes from the difficulties of establishing a sexual sense of self by the complete submergence of all sexuality – leading a celibate life. Judging this choice to be pathological might involve ruling that members of religious orders who vow celibacy are pathological. Indeed, behind many gay and straight identity choices will often lie quite subtle balances of malignant and benign RRPs. CAT's theory of pathology deals with this moral and therapeutic difficulty by acknowledging that each and every RRP was formed in an environment in which it was in some sense adaptive. It is the persistence of the RRP into other environments in ways which cause grief to the individual which focuses the eye of therapist and patient upon them and marks them out as pathological because of their role in causing current difficulty. The secretive lesbian might be jeopardizing her chances of close friendships with other women; the 'in your face' 'queen' might have difficulties expressing fears and doubts about his role, and the celibate gay man might wish to explore sexual expression.

Another common reason for difficulty in establishing a gay or lesbian identity are faulty assumptions about the nature of the identity which one is proposing to adopt. Such faulty assumptions may take various forms, but one common form is called, in CAT, a 'dilemma'. Dilemmas are false choices or narrowed options. For some gay men who have had no experience of the gay scene their sexuality may appear to them to offer a stark choice between a life of celibate repression or furtive promiscuous couplings in public toilets. The effect of a dilemma is to block behaviours which might lead to experiences which could challenge it. A gay man locked into this dilemma might never explore his sexuality, choosing the repressed celibate role and, consequently, would never have experiences which would challenge the accuracy of this way of thinking. Equally, he might plunge into a promiscuous gay life thinking it his only option. Such a plunge would be more likely to result in new experiences but he might, because of his assumptions, choose venues and structure his meetings so as to make any experience other than a brief sexual encounter unlikely. Again the effect of the dilemma is to set up a situation in which experiences that challenge it are unlikely.

For CAT what marks this hypothetical patient's world-view as psychopathological is the narrowing of the range of options which appear viable to him and the insulation of this narrowed view from experience-driven revision. An important consideration in working with a gay man stuck in this particular dilemma would be for the therapist to hold clearly in mind the distinction between the patient's negative evaluation of promiscuous and anonymous sex and the therapist's own views about the morality or otherwise of such sexual encounters. Some gay men who have anonymous sexual encounters do so because they like and enjoy it and say that it suits them. From a CAT perspective such a gay man is not presumed, as a result of his preference, to have pathology in this area.

Our hypothetical patient with the 'either celibate or promiscuous' dilemma who took the plunge and began to investigate the gay scene might develop in a range of ways. First, he might have a bad experience which confirms his horror and return terrified to a life of celibacy and isolation, possibly interspersed with further forays now seen by him as 'lapses'. Second, he might discover that not all gay men have primarily anonymous sex and so change his dilemma-driven thinking for the better. As a result he might embark on differently structured relationships with more commitment or he might continue to have anonymous brief sexual encounters, but now because he prefers them rather than because he is forced into them. Third, he might discover a taste for sexual promiscuity and non-commitment and thoroughly enjoy and value his new-found sexual freedom, assuming that all gay men are like this. Interestingly, in this last case his dilemma would actually stay intact although his distress would evaporate. He would become in this respect like everyone else: all of us have illogical or undeveloped areas of belief or prejudice (which may be more or less revisable given experience) but which, because they do not currently happen to cause distress, do not present as difficulties to a psychotherapist.

Any discussion of identity remains incomplete without a large 'health warning'. Social and cognitive convenience force us to speak of identity and particularly homosexual identity as a fixed or stable entity. Indeed in this discussion we have focused chiefly on individuals who are in one crucial respect already sure of one aspect of their current identity, that is on gay men and lesbians who are sure that they are homosexual. Their attitude to this identity may be to refuse it, to seek to change it, to ruefully accept it or to joyfully embrace it, but in all cases they (and we) assume that there is some solid thing to take up an attitude to. However, identity is much more slippery than that. Arguably while homosexual acts and possibly homosexual inclinations seem fairly universal, an identity as a homosexual is both a culturally and historically specific phenomenon. Many commentators argued that homosexual identity is socially constructed (notably Weeks 1985) while others are associated with the view that it is innate (for example, LeVay 1993).

Most CAT therapists would, I think, be inclined to a middle position acknowledging, first, that homosexual and heterosexual inclination almost certainly have to a greater or lesser extent a biological basis and, second, that there are brute facts of biology which are culturally and historically invariant. However, what a culture makes of these 'facts' may be hugely variable. Only a culture can 'make something' of the facts, and only by making something of the facts can cultures contemplate them. This making something of our natures is the work of social construction.

However, even if identities were entirely socially constructed this would not necessarily devolve much choice in matters of identity and identification on to the individual. We are irremediably born into and conditioned by – even constructed by – a culture which we may ultimately come to influence but do not initially choose. Therefore it is the experience of all members of our culture, gay or 'straight', that identity formation does involve measuring (more or less consciously) the self against a range of more or less stereotyped identities which are, as it were, on offer.

Such an analysis sits rather oddly in the space between debates among those we might call biological or psychological positivists (a group which would include some behaviour therapists and some Kleinian analysts) and postmodern social theorists (including analysts in the Lacanian tradition, some feminist therapists and many psycho-analytically inspired literary theorists) about the role of nature and nurture and the plasticity or otherwise of the psyche. This is because CAT's theory of society and culture (which is central to CAT's theory of development and learning) is based on the work of Vygotsky carried into the West by Brunner (see, for example, Brunner 1986) and continued in Russia by Bakhtin (Clark and Holquist 1984). This intellectual tradition has been neglected until recently by psychoanalysts, behaviourists, Lacanians, feminists and literary theorists alike but CAT theorists consider that it offers a subtle and sensible way to analyse the interactions between nature and nurture and between the individual and the social origins of attitudes and behaviour.

'Coming Out'

'Coming out' is a possibility for gay men and lesbians which does not confront most members of the straight community. As an act and experience it has a specific form. From the perspective of the straight world it represents repeated announcement of a new and rather intimate fact about an individual. From the perspective of the gay world it represents the breaking of secrecy and the repeated challenge of assumptions of heterosexuality. As an act it partly announces, partly claims, and partly forms an aspect of the person's identity. Consequently (and unsurprisingly), difficulties in identity formation may well hinder or threaten a successful coming-out process.

However, despite the simplifications involved, we want to consider coming out as a repeated act (it is actually best thought of as a continuous activity) of self-revelation and identity definition. This continuing act of coming out has problems of its own as well as being linked with related difficulties involved in establishing a stable identity. Considered as such, coming out is also a task with special difficulties. However well or badly it is done, coming out in a conversation immediately increases the level of intimacy and self-revelation on the part of the gay person. Generally, the conventions of conversation allow for gradual increases in intimacy reciprocally on both parts. In a carefully engineered conversation to a specific individual, part of coming out to that person involves managing the intimacy of the conversation to fit the level of intimacy of the self-revelation. But in a conversation about other matters where the sexuality of the gay person must be revealed to avoid deception (for example, a conversation about bringing partners to the staff party) there is a sudden intimacy bump. This is especially marked when the coming out is embedded in a conversation about a different topic in which the inter-locutor has made a heterosexual assumption. Gay men and lesbians have to learn special methods for managing such conversations.

For these reasons as well as many others, coming out is not an activity for which a gay person is likely to have built up, as a result of childhood learning, a secure and flexible procedural sequence. Conse-quently the psychopathological difficulties which centre on coming out often have the same form as adjustment reactions. The difficulties do not arise from repetitively enacted faulty procedures but from an absence of suitable procedural repertoire. Early comings out use sketchy, poorly nuanced procedures. They may be too loud, too subtle, or inappropriately timed – the most common problem here is remaining silent when one should speak, or speaking up when silence would have been wiser.

CAT deals with difficulties around these areas by pointing out to the patient the way in which he or she is faced with the task of developing new procedures. The therapist can reframe some of the difficulties in the coming out process as the inevitable trial and error learning involved in developing, testing and establishing a new set of procedural sequences. CAT places considerable weight on the value of higher functions in altering and guiding other procedural sequences. Consequently, a more self-conscious and self-reflective consideration of the task of learning a good way of coming out which works for the patient would be regarded as highly beneficial.

Coming out in small ways can be contrasted with coming out in big ways. Indeed for many the term 'coming out' generally implies the once-and-for-all task of telling significant others (often parents) about oneself. Struggling with, thinking about, and resolving the emotions around telling or deciding not to tell significant other individuals about one's sexual orientation are frequent tasks in therapy. Here there may be maladaptive procedural sequences in play which manifest themselves as 'snags' – subtle negative aspects of goals. Snags are very similar to the faulty basic assumptions of cognitive therapy. Common coming-out snags include 'If I tell my mother it will kill her'; 'If I tell my father he will never forgive me.' In procedural sequence terms, snags represent negative anticipatory evaluations of the likely outcome of achieving an aim which act to halt the enactment of the procedural sequence designed to achieve that aim. Since the evaluation of the outcome involves making assumptions about how things will go in the future, and since the negative evaluation prevents the enactment of the procedure, the assumptions are not revised and snags halt the procedure.

CAT reserves the term 'snags' for evaluations which are clearly unlikely to be realistic. For example, a mother is unlikely literally to die if told about her child's sexual orientation. Added to these are snags which are self-evidently self-defeating: for example, 'If I tell my parents I am gay they won't ever have discovered this fact for themselves and I want them to have known I was gay without being told because this would prove to me that they were genuinely interested in me.' But some negative evaluations of the environment are realistic. Some parents never do forgive their gay sons and lesbian daughters. Part of overcoming snags involves taking the plunge. What if the therapist cannot judge if the plunge may truly prove disastrous? In such a situation a CAT therapist would probably rely heavily on the joint nature of the work with the patient. The therapist would explain what a snag was to the patient and point out that some of the patient's worries and problems about coming out might be snags, but would also explore the possibility that the worries and problems were realistic. There are, after all, some situations in which coming out to someone is either inadvisable or unkind to an individual who is him- or herself too damaged to cope.

Coping with Homophobia, Unfairness and HIV

Discussion of coming out and particularly of situations in which coming out might not be advisable leads on to a third important domain for gay and lesbian patients. Homosexuals get a poor deal in society and the advent of HIV has piled further tragedy and difficulty on to that rotten deal. This deal is not a piece of gay or lesbian psychopathology. It should be challenged and altered in all possible circumstances. An effect of the bad deal is to force psychological development in certain areas on gay men and lesbians – development which straight people do not have to undertake. It challenges gay men and lesbians to develop procedures which are strong and flexible in the area of coping with unfairness and disadvantage. In this area gay men and lesbians need to be more healthy than straights just in order to survive. Furthermore, persistent disadvantage and unfairness is a poor environment in which to develop strong and flexible procedures.

For a start, in a sufficiently damaged world no procedure may be successful in, say, helping a gay man get a job as a primary school teacher or preventing a lesbian from being thrown out of the army. If procedural learning is driven by evaluation of outcome it will take a particularly steady period of thought for an individual to realise that a failed procedure is perfectly adequate and that in this case the world is at fault. CAT theory makes it easy to see how a persistent experience of disadvantage – for example, in getting a certain kind of job – can lead to a sense that all one's efforts fail. This then becomes internalized as the thought that one is no good at the job along with more generalized thoughts that perhaps homosexuals should not want or get such jobs any way. These thoughts can seem quite reasonable given the feedback, but they are unwarranted because the feedback is not real feedback but prejudice driven by bigotry. Once an individual notices that he or she is not getting valid feedback from the world because of prejudice he or she can begin to throw out the internalized self-evaluation based on that feedback. However, the individual is then faced with a second problem (also not faced to such an extent by individuals who do not experience prejudice) of evaluating the feedback he or she does get. Some gay men and lesbians may swing for a while too far in the other direction and interpret any criticism as driven by prejudice.

Locating difficulty in the world runs against the thrust of therapy. As therapists our natural tendency is to want to identify problems where the locus of control lies within the patient's orbit. For as long as a person says, 'It is all the problem of my husband/wife/mother/ child/boss', therapy has little in the way of change to recommend. As soon as the patient asks what he or she can do or wonders why he or she continues to put up with the situation, then therapy can intervene. In Western culture we are conditioned to believe in responsibility, self-reliance and, broadly speaking, the fair reward of merit. Thus, helping gay men and lesbians come to terms with what might be termed a reasoned paranoia will often involve the construction of new procedures and the development of new sensitivities which run counter to the cultural current. An important element will be the therapist's capacity to spot where the patient may be blind to the effect of homophobia – either internalized or on the part of others – on his or her life. Therapist and patient will have to be quick to spot where therapy must end and political action begin.

Work with individuals who are HIV+ represents another, and in many ways, very similar area. From a CAT perspective infection with HIV is not a psychopathology (as some have implied – see Burgner 1994) but a circumstance which may require special adaptive effort on the part of the individual. CAT may be helpful to people who are making this adaptive effort, particularly when they suffer, like many physically ill patients, from pre-existing maladaptive assumptions about their causal role in bad things which happen to them, or have problematic procedures in the area of receiving care.

However, the main point about HIV is the way in which it has been responded to adaptively. HIV does represent something special to gay men. For both gay men and lesbians a vital part of adaptation in Western culture involves developing ways to respond to unfairness. HIV seems the ultimate unfairness and additionally one with no abusive perpetrator involved – although the response of some to people with HIV has been bluntly abusive. From a childhood perspective HIV is an unfairness which offers no offending other against whom one could bear witness to the 'parents' and gain redress. The response of the gay community to this unfairness in its positive aspects (from the 'quilt' through to the establishment of hospices) and its negative ones (including the anger, blaming and false starts on causation) is a model for others on how a community can respond to unfairness adaptively.

Relationship Issues

The concept of RRPs allows CAT to analyse the interplay of relationships in a complex and subtle way, but also in a way which can easily be explained to those patients for whom interpersonal relationship issues form a very considerable part of their difficulties and struggles. CAT does not theorize lesbian or gay relationships as pathological in any way by virtue of their being homosexual ones. However, there are differences in relating between gay men and lesbians and straight people; clearly, part of the structure of all interpersonal relationships is affected by the effects of the sexual possibilities which may be expressed in them. This means that for gay men and lesbians the structure of all their relationships will be somewhat different than that of straight people. For example, the female friendships of lesbians carry an undertow of sexual possibility in the same way that male–female friendships do for heterosexuals. Yet in Western culture non-sexual intimacy between women is far more possible than similar intimacies between men and women. Lesbian friends may have to negotiate a far greater area of bodily intimacies, sexual possibilities and sexual risks than a straight man and a straight woman in a friendship. By the same token the men who lesbians are friendly with are not (generally) sexual objects and may know this, either liking it or resenting it or having no settled view. So, for a lesbian, negotiating friendship relationships will not be the same as for a straight woman. She may do it well or badly, bringing to it pre-existing adaptive or maladaptive patterns, but the struggles will be somewhat different from those faced by a straight woman in this area. Consequently, it is possible to argue that in everyday life the psychology of gay men and lesbians will be different from that of straight people and for much the same complex tangle of social and personal reasons that the psychologies of men and women differ.

One area of putative relationship psychopathology which has commanded considerable interest in the lesbian community centres on the concept that some lesbian relationships are subject to periods of intense fusion followed by rows which may be violent to regain distance and reunion. Such relationships, it is often added, tend to be sexless, and this is explained as a consequence of the fusion involved. CAT can be used in a couples context. The focus is on delineating the reciprocal role procedures that each member of the couple tends to use and showing how they interact either positively or negatively. A CAT therapist would tend to see the pattern of closeness followed by rows followed by closeness not in terms of distance regulation within the relationship but in terms of the procedural sequences which founded it.

In practice, the procedural sequences which may be operated by both parties in a 'fused' lesbian relationship often vary. However, one quite common pattern is for both partners to have difficulties with aggression and assertion founded on the basis of the dilemma, 'Either I bottle things up and stay frustrated or I let them out and make a terrible mess.' Such a dilemma all to frequently forms an almost routine part of female children's socialization, with its general concentration on order and control and its lower tolerance of bad (aggressive) behaviour and encouragement of good (mild-mannered) behaviour. The presence of such a dilemma in both parties, generally accompanied by the snag, 'If I shout at her she will leave me', clearly militates in favour of the pattern of periods of profound calm followed by massive rows. Once both parties have been given the formulation (and supposing that it fits), then therapy can centre on stimulating them to revise their procedures. Revision might encourage a capacity for more open expression of dissent in everyday life and the capacity to 'stage manage' rows.

Alcohol and Drug Abuse

Another area in which there is evidence of difficulty in the gay and lesbian community is substance misuse – primarily alcohol. The reason for this is probably fairly mundane. There is considerable evidence that alcoholism rates are related to occupational exposure. The gay and lesbian club scene does depend fairly heavily on drinking and, in some settings, on drug abuse. Consequently, it is probable that a greater proportion of the gay and lesbian population are at risk than their equivalent straight counterparts. Some succumb.

Substantial alcohol abuse makes psychotherapy of any sort difficult but is particularly problematic for therapies where a large cognitive element is involved and where 'homework' needs to be done. While it may be possible to show how (as is often the case) drinking excessively is the outcome of one or several maladaptive procedures, it can be difficult to get the person to focus on this fact in a constructive way because the alcohol use results in a reduction of the availability to memory as affectively 'real' of the experiences which provoked it. Broadly speaking therefore, CAT therapists look first to alcohol and drug dependency services in treating patients who present with substance misuse. However, it is notable that no empirical research has been carried out to investigate this clinical lore.

A CASE EXAMPLE

Let us now look at a case example which involves many of the theoretical issues discussed in relation to sexual orientation. We are grateful to the patient we describe for giving us permission to use his therapy as an example. All identifying biographical details have been disguised to protect the identity of the patient.

Jonathan, aged 28, was referred to the Psychotherapy Department with a history of depression, anxiety and social isolation. He was certain of his homosexual orientation but had never had any sexual experience or intimate relationships. He identified his 'lack of self-confidence' as primary focus and expressed the hope that he could change this through therapy. He was offered 16 sessions of CAT with a trainee (Petrus de Vries), supervised by Chess Denman.

In the first few sessions Jonathan's life-story was explored. He was the third of four children and worked as a low-level clerk in an office in spite of graduating from university with a degree in history. His parents were separated and his father, who became a Baptist minister later in life, reportedly always had very high expectations of his children and often put down their achievements.

He was educated at grammar school where he had few friends and was regarded by staff as timid, not confident and academically 'not up to standard'. At his single-sex 'old-fashioned' boarding school, he was teased, ostracized, sometimes bullied and humiliated. He recalled that he first became consciously aware of his homosexuality at the age of 15, but never expressed this to anyone.

In his pre-assessment questionnaire he wrote:

> I am homosexual. As yet I have not had any sort of relationship. I would very much like to form a relationship and have met a few people whom I developed very strong feelings for. They were, however, not gay themselves. At present I feel lonely, isolated, uncertain of which direction to take. I am also developing a sort of hopelessness over the situation. I do not feel confident generally, and am unsure of whether this matter should be a priority.

Very early on, therefore Jonathan identified a link between his sexuality and confidence, but expressed a sense of confusion about ways out of his predicament.

At college he performed better academically but remained 'reclusive' with only a small group of student friends (all of them older than him). Since entering full-time employment, he had usually found jobs to be dreary and demoralizing and had felt victimized on more than one occasion.

During the course of telling his story, Jonathan realized that, in addition to having poor self-confidence in all domains of life, he also put himself down a lot. The confidence factor affected him in social situations, where he would 'clam up', as well as in his sexual life, where, in spite of a lot of thinking, he never acted on his desires. He described writing lots of notes asking himself questions about his isolation. He had a persistent 'sinking' feeling, felt uninteresting while interacting with others and was aware of an ambivalence between wanting to get more involved and wanting to pull away in social contexts.

All four of the introductory sessions led to emotionally invested discussions about his father. Jonathan's father wanted the children to be musical and play the instruments he chose. In all aspects of their lives he wanted the best for his children and, having decided what was best, forced it on them – 'If he thought it was best, he'd get us to do it.' Jonathan remembered his father's tales of a brilliant academic career at Oxford, with an overwhelming sense of inability to reach such an equivalent level. He also realized that the image of his father was interwoven with thoughts about religion and the 'rights and wrongs' of homosexuality.

However, all through his adult life Jonathan had tried hard not to think about his sexual orientation too much. Homosexuality, in his mind, was linked with the promiscuous gay scene, the spreading of disease, and getting emotionally attached to people. These internal images were blocked out by pretending that his sexuality was not there, ignoring it as unimportant, and hoping (as his mother had once told him) that he would 'grow out of it'. Together, in the initial sessions, we explored his long-term relationship goals. He wished for a lasting monogamous relationship. His ideal relationship was one of 'fulfilment, richness and an inner sense of happiness and self-assurance', ideals which were in strong contrast with his perception of general gay promiscuity.

He remembered his first attempts at coming out to his family with discomfort. While at university he talked first to his elder brother:

'I think I'm gay.'
'You can't be', his brother responded. 'How do you know you're gay?'

Jonathan had no answer, as he had never had any relationships and for him sexual orientation was defined and confirmed by sexual activity. Jonathan's brother told his mother, who 'had to tell' his father. Father was very upset and confronted Jonathan with the issue. Out of fear of condemnation, Jonathan retracted his initial tentative coming out. He told his father that he probably was not homosexual and everyone buried the issue with great relief.

As the shared understanding of his life-story increased, the therapist and patient identified target problems and set off to explore the maladaptive procedural sequences responsible for them. Asked to think about possible processes which lead to his difficulty in having a stable sense of identity, Jonathan returned to the third session with an elaborate diagram of downward-spiralling arrows, able to recognize the self-perpetuating nature of his poor self-confidence, yet unable to imagine a solution.

At the start of the fourth session Jonathan described a 'slipping sensation' with a fear that he was moving away from 'the issue'. He expressed the need to be reassured that he was doing the right thing, that he was focusing on the right area. At this point, the therapist read out his reformulation letter to Jonathan:

Dear Jonathan,

You have come for Cognitive Analytic Therapy, looking for help with your self-confidence which you have been struggling with for some time.

We are now at the fourth session and are getting to the stage of reformulation, trying to see what we've done so far. This is my letter to you, to try and express how I understand your problems and to think with you, how we should proceed from here.

Here is your story:

You are the second child and the eldest son of parents who have had hopes and wishes for you and your life. Very early on, however, you realised that yours were different desires. Your father wanted you to play the violin but you liked the piano. He wanted you to enjoy sports, but you didn't. He wanted you to like girls, but you didn't ...

You thought that you were wrong and feared that you would be despised at home and at school. Yet more and more you became convinced of your 'differentness'. The fear of your father's anger and rejection by others made you turn inward, keeping to yourself your wishes, your dreams and ideals. This stopped you from ACTING, responding to your wishes and desires.

Throughout your school years, being teased and called names and later on at university, you became more and more withdrawn into a fantasy world of hope and desire, free of conflict (like with your father). Sometimes the anger inside escaped with 'tantrums' towards friends (even those you most liked or desired).

Even the most difficult step of telling your family that you are gay, was met by shock, surprise, your mother's hope that by the end of therapy you would have changed and your statement to your father 'perhaps I'm not'. The increasingly painful fear that perhaps nobody will ever understand or know how you feel, reconfirmed all the existing thoughts. This increased your awareness of your differentness, and also increased your uncertainty about your identity.

In your daily life, even now, this has prevented you from achieving in the work sphere, it has prevented you from finding intimacy in relationship and has prevented you from feeling a sense of self.

Discussion about your family has always led to your father, and even though you are always quick to state your respect and love for him, an enormous sense of anger is always present when we talk about him ...

... We have identified a number of target problems for therapy:

· assertiveness

· intimate relationships, and what we shall call

· 'unfinished business with your father'.

You also described very vividly the process or procedure which you felt is affecting your life:

· Sense of individuality (your nature, strengths, weaknesses and being able to like that) leading to:

· putting yourself down (feeling 'different', not as good/don't fit in)

· turning in on yourself (brooding, sitting alone, isolating self)

which affects the way you see yourself, and affects the way you see others (as normal, perfectly friendly with each other).

One's personality or identity to a large extent is made up of 3 key elements: memories, desires and social interaction. We could represent it like this:

memories

[temperament]

desires   social interaction

Looking at your negative process, which spirals your thoughts down, as you put it, there is a great arrow at the bottom, feeding back to the top.

Your negative process or procedure continually gives negative feedback to your 'sense of identity'. By doing that you deprive yourself of the very components of your identity – memories, desires and social interaction.

In the 12 sessions that lie ahead we will look at these more closely, firstly to understand them, secondly to recognize them, then to ACT! We may find ourselves re-enacting through the process of transference some of the anger, differentness and other emotions. It would be very important for us to talk about these and use them.

I hope that gradually over the course of our therapy, you will learn more about yourself to help you find your individuality, sense of self and confidence to lead a more fulfilling life.

Jonathan felt enormously reassured by the confirmation of his thoughts (and repetition of his own target problems) and followed the statement about acting by saying, 'What if I did something drastic?'

Sessions 5–11 provided (with hindsight) an interesting period of transference and countertransference. Jonathan was very keen to please and diligently completed homework assignments for the (father-figure?) therapist, while the therapist became deeply proud of his patient's (son's?) progress and this dynamic was also re-created in the supervisory sessions between therapist and supervisor. In the context of this positively toned relationship Jonathan increasingly recognized the internal operation of a prohibitive 'NO'-voice and a mental image of his father in a forbidding and prohibiting role at the thought of a supposedly illicit sexual desire.

The reciprocal role pattern of Jonathan's relationship with his internal father can be characterized as 'prohibiting and forbidding'–'prohibited and forbidden' because of desiring the wrong things. The relationship with the therapist represents another reciprocal role pattern – that of encouraging and supporting, to supported and eager to please. These two patterns probably both represent aspects of Jonathan's relationship with his father but they are unduly dichotomized, probably because of Jonathan's father's incapacity to speak directly about his loving and admiring but also hopeful and fearful feelings towards his son. It might have helped therapy at this point to have added this understanding more explicitly to the reformulation letter.

The therapist suggested more specific mental exploration tasks in therapy and set 'homework' tasks for the periods between sessions. All were related to Jonathan's stated aim of overcoming his fears and anxieties in relation to the gay scene and to forming a gay relationship. Jonathan agreed to 'try something and see what happens'. The therapist's aim with Jonathan was to see how 'trying something' would affect his target problem procedures. However, Jonathan found it extremely difficult to mobilize himself to act, although he did manage to confront some socially difficult situations. For example, he confronted a flatmate about non-payment of rent: an 'experiment' which resulted in payment of the rent and a better atmosphere in the flat and which also served to disconfirm Jonathan's prior fear of catastrophic consequences.

Jonathan did, however, get information leaflets about gay groups and clubs and brought them to his therapy session, but he continued to feel that something was holding him back. As the sessions progressed, the therapist started to recognize his own restlessness for his patient to 'perform', and acknowledged his anxieties about the enormous power invested in the therapy by his patient. Jonathan started to describe a growing sense of 'fighting inside', but also a growing sensation of 'what I might be about'. Jonathan's sense of emptiness and lack of identity had been conceptualized as a result of his fear about what exploration of his desires might result in. This led to using a range of avoidant procedures to restrict feeling and limit action and relationship. These avoidant procedures had the effect of depriving Jonathan of those experiences which comprise a sense of identity and which 'fill' the self with memories and desires. His relationship with his therapist was growing in complexity and, in consequence, was beginning to generate exactly the kind of experiences which form and stabilize a sense of identity.

Jonathan's parting statement at the end of one session that he 'might have some news next week' seemed teasing and alerted therapist and supervisor to the possibility of erotic elements at play in the relationship. Jonathan's weeks started to get better with a 'growing sense of self' in social situations, yet persistent uncertainty regarding how to mobilise his long-dormant desires: 'How do I bring them to life?'

Jonathan met a gay man at work and decided that he was going to approach him for advice on how to meet people. In the following session he carefully described a growing anxiety prior to the planned meeting, avoiding the person all day at work, and a sense of withdrawal just prior to the act of talking to the man. Jonathan recognized this as a pattern, not only in his sexual life, which was characterized by florid fantasy but non-activity but also in social interaction where, at the point of possible intimacy, he would 'withdraw', fearing that something would 'go wrong'. He realized that his fantasy world of desire was probably a comfortable place to withdraw into, and he acknowledged the possibility that therapy was also a place in which to withdraw into a fantasy world.

By failing to recognize and point out the somewhat idealized reciprocal role relationship between therapist and patient, the therapist and supervisor had run the risk of creating in therapy an idealized but unreal location where problems of anxiety and social failure (things 'going wrong') were not present. Fortunately both Jonathan and his therapist were then able to recognize the possibility of retreating into therapy being a similar kind of danger to retreating into sexual fantasy.

Jonathan returned to session 13 thinking about making an effort to act, being acutely aware of his own snag of withdrawal ('I desire relationships and fantasise about them but never initiate them for fear of what may go wrong') and saying, 'I have to be honest, I do fantasize a lot but then fear failure in real relationships.'

As CAT therapy approaches the final sessions, the therapist may well count down the sessions explicitly with the patient so that the ending is always on the table. In addition the therapist and patient spend time together reviewing what has been achieved and what remains to be done.

In session 14 (with the patient aware that only two sessions remained) regret and risk were evident and Jonathan expressed with sadness how he felt that his sexual desires and the lack of sexual contact were the 'pinnacle' of all his mental work: 'I didn't realise how much I thought about it.' He stated emphatically that he needed to do something. Therapy was drawing to a close with a lot of thinking and talking about acting, but little or no acting having taken place. Therapist and supervisor speculated about possibilities of outcome, and planned a 'goodbye' letter for session 15 to allow a response by the patient at session 16.

Jonathan came into session 15, head down after not such a good week. He described a sense of failure and fear, hopelessness and worry. The therapist used this as an opportunity to read the goodbye letter:

Dear Jonathan,

This is your goodbye letter.

Almost 16 sessions ago you came to the department for CAT with the specific aim of working on your self-confidence. During the first 4 sessions we tried to put together some basic pieces to identify a few TARGET PROBLEMS

1. *Assertiveness*

2. *Intimate relationships*

3. *'Unfinished business with your father'*

and a basic TARGET PROBLEM PROCEDURE, which you described as a 'downward' spiral. At the time we planned to look at these in order to understand why this has evolved, how to recognize when it happens in your life, and then to ACT.

Thinking back on the subsequent sessions, you have brought interesting and very valuable ideas to therapy. 'What if I do something drastic?', you asked, wondering if it will 'jolt me out of it'. We had discussions about the 'triangle' of memories, desires and social interaction and the whirlpool of negative thinking. You started to identify things in your daily life and realized that you could affect them both positively and negatively.

Gradually you developed a growing sense of self. You felt more comfortable with your family, talked to your housemate about rent, got more involved in your hobby. You started to think and talk about your father in a more neutral, less threatened way. Later on you spoke to a girl at work and approached John [the gay colleague] to talk to him. They may feel like small things looking back, but at the time each one was a great achievement.

As you started to feel 'more solid', you also, however, recognized a fear of success. 'What is holding me back?', you asked many times. That was the point when you made the realization about the WORLD OF FANTASY, that place, easy to be in, perfect, harmonious. You realized how much you have learnt to live in it over the years. Then, as you felt momentum, and the possibility of success, the WITHDRAWAL PHENOMENON would prevent you from leaving the security (or insecurity?) of fantasy.

This you felt vividly in many of your interactions. Even when we started to talk about your deep sexual wants, the sensation of withdrawal was there. Perhaps the withdrawing can come in different guises: putting off things, thinking things over and over and over, talking about it too much, writing lots of notes ...

You know your ideals. You strongly feel that you haven't reached them. Importantly, you also told yourself how much of a 'pinnacle' your sexual desires are. And for how long you haven't thought of it (another withdrawal).

'Perhaps I should close my eyes and do it.'

I think, Jonathan, you have worked very hard in therapy. At times you felt positive and optimistic. During other sessions there was a lot of anger and frustration. My feeling is that you have invested a lot in the therapy. Perhaps even that 'this could be the making of me' (as you thought when you went to university). Remember that the investment was in yourself. And that you did the brave work and ran your own errands.

What now? What happens after therapy?

I wonder. Will you continue to work on the ideas developed in therapy? The fantasy world which you want to leave, the withdrawing back into it at the point of possible success, remembering to close your eyes and just do what you want to do. Or perhaps continue for a short while until the momentum disappears, until reality becomes too uncomfortable?

I hope that this improved vision of yourself, being less intimidated by others (including your father), knowing that you can get what you want, will help you to go out into the world and fulfil your plans and desires step by step.

A key feature of the goodbye letter in CAT is the way in which it reviews therapy honestly, in both its positive and negative aspects. This letter aimed to hold positive hopes for Jonathan while not minimizing and ignoring difficulties and continuing threats to well-being, and in the session Jonathan and the therapist were able to look at sadness and worries as well as achievements.

Jonathan came to the final session with his goodbye letter.

Dear Dr de Vries,

There is nothing in your letter which I would disagree with. Indeed, the contents describe very vividly much of the feelings and thoughts that I have had in connection to my therapy. I think that my 'goodbye' to you should include a statement of how I feel at the moment – a 'snapshot' of me right now, if you like.

To begin with I can safely say that the 'investment I made in myself' (as you put it) has proved rewarding in some ways which I will describe ... I knew about a third of the way through the sessions that I had been on the right lines all along ... You, as a 'mentor' have helped me to very positively develop themes which I am now going to do my best to build upon.

... I still lack assertiveness; I am still unsure of the direction in which to turn re sexuality ... Yet, in spite of this, I am increasingly more aware of the fantasy world in which I live; the world which I have previously taken for granted as 'normal' and as real as everyone else's ...

I am feeling a little frightened. Is this it? Am I 'cured'? What will I do without Dr de Vries? How will I know if I am doing the right thing? What on earth will I do if I feel I cannot cope? These are just some of the questions I am asking myself as I sit here and write to you. I feel a constant need for reassurance, but there are elements within me which help me to reassure myself.

... It is a pity I have not been able to report a sexual act to you in the last part of my therapy. But on the other hand, this may be down to the pace which I move at ... I hope that, when I see you for the final time in three months' time, something of a change will have occurred.

From a prognostic point of view Jonathan's goodbye letter was very encouraging. Although his practical life-changes in therapy had been limited, the letter reveals and charts the development of a very much increased self-understanding.

At his three-month follow-up, Jonathan revealed that he had been to a local gay pub on a number of occasions. He picked up someone after the fourth visit and had oral sex, his first sexual encounter ever. 'I've never been more sure that I was gay.' The following morning, having felt great the night before, he awoke with anxiety and panic about AIDS and phoned his mother and an AIDS advice line. He got some leaflets about safe sex and was reassured.

Jonathan experienced a slow process of increase in his self-confidence, but reported that he was now able to speak his mind and not fear others. Even in talking to his mother about his sexual activities (a further act of coming out) he felt less threatened and more sure of himself. He said that he had found the therapy 'enormously helpful', and was able to say, with some embarrassment, that he may have had a slight 'admiration' for the therapist. He added that the ongoing therapeutic relationship prevented him from withdrawing in the manner of many previous similar (non-therapeutic) situations.

The therapist agreed to see the patient for one further follow-up three months later.

By the six-month follow-up, Jonathan appeared a changed man. Relaxed, and with a different haircut, he had moved house and was the main tenant in a house shared with two other men and a woman. His housemates viewed him as the 'most stable' of them all and regularly asked him for advice on their own lives and relationship issues. One housemate (who described himself as 'as close to gay as a heterosexual man can be') in particular expressed the wish to be 'as sorted out' as Jonathan.

By now, Jonathan had had further sexual interactions, frequented the gay pub and felt very comfortable about it. At feedback he reflected that he could now see that all people have their own problems. He mentioned that he saw his father and that they had an 'intimate discussion' about his anger and his sexuality. His father said that he would always love him. Jonathan felt moved at the thought that his father (once strong and scholarly) ended up having a rather sad life, separated from his wife and children, and lonely.

After initial ambivalence about a further follow-up, Jonathan agreed that he did not need to see the therapist for review. He was invited to write to the therapist at the department with a nine- to twelve-month report.

Supervisor's Commentary

This was the therapist's first effort at Cognitive Analytic Therapy and, with hindsight (always a valuable instrument), the therapy had two major problems. First, the whole therapy has a distinctly directive cast and, second, there were a number of areas in which the technique of CAT could have been better implemented. Both therapist and supervisor colluded together with the, at times, openly stated and consciously pursued aim of helping Jonathan to have sex. This did happen for Jonathan but there were risks and disadvantages in this way of proceeding. First of all, it may have failed to occur and this might have left Jonathan re-experiencing the same coming out and then going back in that he had suffered in relation to his first attempt to talk to his family. Second, as a strategy it failed to challenge his equation of secure homosexual identity with sexual activity.

All CAT therapies are to some extent directive in nature. Objections to this directive stance include worries that it may impose the therapist's solution on the patient (an experience which many gay men and lesbians have had in relation to attempts to alter their sexuality in both behavioural and analytic treatments) and suggestions that while the patient may comply with the directives, doing so blindly may limit insight. CAT therapists combat these objections as follows. First, they emphasize that the directive elements of CAT are collaboratively agreed within a joint structure. Second, they point out the value of experience in developing new capacities for self-reflection. The structure of directed activity in Jonathan's therapy was enclosed within a joint and collaborative effort by patient and therapist. Additionally, the new experiences which Jonathan had, evidently stimulated his self-reflective capacities and were also discussed and reflected on in therapy.

In relation to various technical aspects of CAT it is possible to criticize some elements of the reformulation letter as not reflecting and charting an accurate understanding of the nature and operation of maladaptive procedural sequences. While it is important to point this out in the context of a chapter which may be presenting CAT to some who are unfamiliar with it, there is a much more important feature of the letter which offsets by far any technical worries. This is the way in which it was a joint production by therapist and patient. Much of the understanding about identity (and the diagram related to it – which is not part of CAT theory) was produced by the patient and therapist together in their discussions in sessions 2 and 3. CAT, drawing on the ideas of Vygotsky and Winnicott emphasizes that the reformulation should be a joint production and should represent a joint tool for self-reflection. In the case of Jonathan this feature of the reformulation letter was very strong, and for this reason the letter needed no revision.

Ultimately, however, the therapy was highly successful. Brief treatment works especially well in cases where restricting procedures can be removed to allow new experiences which, in turn, stimulate further self-reflection and new emotional and cognitive learning.

CONCLUSION

A CAT perspective on therapy with gay men and lesbians has been outlined and illustrated with a case example. In some ways what CAT has to say specifically about homosexual orientation may seem limited. CAT is silent on the putative origins of sexual object choice and it does not have a track record of homophobia to contend with or a series of pronouncements on the subject by prior masters to contend with, interpret or reject. However, we trust that the discussion and case example have shown that as a therapeutic modality CAT is able to make a valuable offer to gay men and lesbians who are in some kind of psychological trouble. That offer comprises active listening and joint reflection which culminates in an accurate description and reformulation of the problems and experiences of the patient. This is followed by a phase of therapy which emphasizes the recognition of the problematic procedures operating in life and then turns from simple (or not so simple) recognition to active revision of those procedures.

CAT stresses joint working and collaboration but it also makes a virtue of its brevity. For CAT, life is always a better thing to be doing than therapy, and the aim is for the patient to return as fast as possible to a life unencumbered by this strange and artificial relationship called 'therapy'. These features of CAT make it able to respond to the cogent criticisms of *all* therapy offered by some lesbian critics. Kitzinger and Perkins (1993) argue that therapy medicalizes the problems of everyday life, offering cures to normal states of mind; that it personalizes the experience of oppression and thus makes political action to defeat oppression less likely; that it takes over and professionalizes the human relation of friendship, and that it claims a fraudulent expertise. All this, they add, is done in the context of a relationship characterized by a major inequality of power. CAT therapists would find themselves in tune with very many of these criticisms, especially those regarding long-term therapies. CAT aims to overcome them by explicit and open sharing of the therapist's understandings with the patient, by emphasizing joint working and by getting out as fast as possible in favour of life. Specifically in relation to oppression, CAT would be on the side of the resistors of oppression and would see a failure to fight oppression as a psychopathological response to victim status. CAT would be very sensitive to the charge that therapy was replacing friendship. Normally, if someone's life lacked close confiding relationships which were experienced as being at a level of intimacy at least as deep as that achieved in therapy, CAT would take this as evidence of psychopathology. A CAT therapist would seek to make such a lack in someone's life a direct focus of treatment.

In two areas CAT would take exception to Kitzinger and Perkins' analysis. CAT therapists do not accept that all the psychological suffering which they see in their patients falls within the orbit described as 'Ordinary feelings, painful reactions to the normal vicissitudes of life ...' (Kitzinger and Perkins 1993, p. 76). More commonly (and particularly because CAT is a therapy practised predominantly within the National Health Service), the patients seen in CAT have severe and disabling neurotic and personality problems which means that they lead lives characterized by severe distress in which they cannot work or relate to others or enjoy themselves.

Another area of disagreement is the area of fraudulent expertise. Kitzinger and Perkins cite JoAnn Loulan who compares the work of the therapist to that of the car mechanic but adds that therapy is 'unlike car repair which can be learned, one cannot learn to be objective about oneself' (Loulan 1990, p. 95). Kitzinger and Perkins disagree with Loulan about the existence of the type of expertise (that is, psychological expertise) she claims for therapists. CAT therapists do claim an expertise in a particular model of understanding some kinds of human difficulty; however, unlike Loulan, they aim to pass this expertise on to the patient. The experience of CAT therapists and their patients is that it is not a difficult skill to teach and that once patients acquire it they are able to use it as a tool to improve their lives.

REFERENCES

Bayer, R. V. (1981) *Homosexuality and American Psychiatry: The Politics of Diagnosis*, New York: Basic Books.

Brunner, J. (1986) *Actual Minds, Possible Worlds*, Cambridge, MA: Harvard University Press.

Burgner, M. (1994) 'Working with the HIV Patient: A Psychoanalytic Approach', *Psychoanalytic Psychotherapy* 8 (3): 201–13.

Clark, K. and Holquist, M. (1984) *Mikhail Bakhtin*, Cambridge, MA: Harvard University Press.

Davidson, G. C. (1977) 'Homosexuality and the Ethics of Behavioural Intervention: Homosexuality, the Ethical Challenge', *Journal of Homosexuality* 2 (3): 195–204.

Kaufman P. A., Harrison E. and Hyde M. L. (1984) 'Distancing for intimacy in lesbian relationships', *American Journal of Psychiatry* 141 (4): 530–3.

Kitzinger, C. and Perkins, R. (1993) *Changing our Minds: Lesbian Feminism and Psychology*, London: Only Women Press.

Leiman, M. (1995) 'Early development', in Ryle, A. (ed.) *Cognitive Analytic Therapy: Developments in Theory and Practice*, Chichester: John Wiley.

LeVay, S. (1993) *The Sexual Brain*, Cambridge, MA: MIT Press.

Loulan, J. (1990) *The Lesbian Erotic Dance*, San Francisco, CA: Spinsters Book Company.

McConaghy, N. (1976) 'Is a homosexual orientation irreversible?', *British Journal of Psychiatry* 129: 556–63.

Phillips, D., Fischer, S. C., Groves, G. A. and Singh, R. (1976) 'Alternative behavioural approaches to the treatment of homosexuality', *Archives of Sexual Behaviour* 5 (3): 223–8.

Ryle, A. (1990) *Cognitive Analytic Therapy: Active Participation in Change*, Chichester: John Wiley.

Ryle, A. (1995) *Cognitive Analytic Therapy: Developments in Theory and Practice*, Chichester: John Wiley.

Ryle, A. (1997) *Cognitive Analytic Therapy for Borderline Personality Disorder: The Model and the Method*, Chichester: John Wiley.

Vygotsky, L. (1986) *Thought and Language*, Cambridge, MA: MIT Press.

Weeks, J. (1985) *Sexuality and Its Discontents*, London: Routledge and Kegan Paul.

Young, J. E. (1990) *Cognitive Therapy for Personality Disorders: A Schema-Focused Approach*, Sarasota, FL: Professional Resource Exchange Inc.

7 Acceptance and Construction: Rational Emotive Behaviour Therapy and Homosexuality

Emmett Velten

This chapter, written in late 1997 and early 1998, will show the development and historical contexts of Albert Ellis's viewpoints about personality theory, sexuality and homosexuality. He continues to develop and modify his ideas. At 84, Ellis still sees more than 100 clients a week, trains therapists, and travels widely throughout the world to give talks and workshops. He has been enormously productive, with almost 70 books and 800 articles published.[1] A survey in the early 1980s of the clinical and counselling members of the American Psychological Association found Ellis the second most influential theorist and practitioner (Smith 1982) – most influential was Carl Rogers; Sigmund Freud was third. A similar survey of Canadian psychologists ranked Ellis first, Rogers second and Aaron Beck third (Warner 1991). A survey of the membership of the American Association for Marriage and Family Therapy (AAMFT) ranked Ellis fourth most influential among family therapists, following Virginia Satir, Freud and Rogers (Sprenkle et al. 1982).

SEXOLOGY AND SELF-HELP

From early childhood, Ellis inclined to efficiency and rationality. When he was a toddler, his mother referred to him as 'my little scientist'. At about the time of his bar mitzvah, Ellis began his lifelong reading and application of both classical and modern philosophy. By the age of 16, he was reading Epictetus, Spinoza, Bentham, Kant, Dewey and Bertrand Russell. (Some 20 years later, Russell endorsed Ellis's viewpoints on sexual freedom and mores, calling them 'wise and enlightened' in comments on *The Folklore of Sex* (Ellis 1951a).) This philosophical bent is very apparent in the humanistic orientation of Rational Emotive Behaviour Therapy (REBT). REBT concerns itself with how people can create an effective, happiness-enhancing philosophy of life and with how they create, maintain and can mitigate psychological disorders. In his twenties, Ellis wrote his first self-help book, never published, 'The Art of Never Being Unhappy'.

Besides his natural bent toward efficiency and rationality and his interest in philosophy, another personal factor influenced Ellis's development of an active-directive therapy style, with its strong emphasis on real-life work and practice. As a youth and well before he had any notion of studying psychology, Ellis overcame his own severe social phobias related to meeting and dating women and to public speaking. He did so by applying methods he derived partly from philosophy and from the writings in the late 1910s and early 1920s of the Behaviourists John B. Watson and Mary Cover Jones.

Using some of Watson's findings and the practices of the Greek orator, Demosthenes, as chronicled by Plutarch, Ellis worked on his own social phobias. He resolved to force himself to sit next to every woman alone on a park bench at the Bronx Botanical Gardens – in those long-ago days, a beautiful and completely safe environment – and within one minute start a conversation if it killed him. So he did. In one month he sat on the same bench with 130 women, about 30 of whom promptly got up and left. This left a sample of 100, which, Ellis says, was very good for research purposes. He had pleasant conversations with them about their reading, their knitting, current events, the weather, and so on. He made only one date, and she did not show up. Ellis is fond of pointing out that B. F. Skinner might say that his sitting and conversing behaviour should have extinguished, due to lack of reinforcement, but such was not the case. For Ellis saw that nothing horrible happened, that he could do it, that he could stand the anxiety, that the anxiety would fade, and that he got plenty of conversational practice. His efforts with the second 100 women, Ellis comments, turned out much better.

Ellis also directly tackled his public speaking phobia through his work after college as a paid revolutionary for a collectivist organization. The latter sought a classless society and opposed the brownshirt movement – then fairly strong in the US – that favoured Hitler and Mussolini. After a couple of years he broke with them because of their dogmatism and the purges and show trials in Stalin's Soviet Union in the 1930s. Ellis became the leader of the youth group in the organization. Week after week, by uncomfortably speaking before groups, he forced himself to overcome his public speaking phobia. Again, he found that repeated, *in vivo* exposure to the feared stimuli, without running away, led to a rapid reduction in the phobia. He is fond of commenting that it was not long before they could not keep him away from the public speaking platform, he enjoyed it so much.

In the mid-1930s when he was in his early twenties, Albert Ellis began his career as a sexologist. This was years before he entered graduate school at 28 at Columbia University in 1942, and almost a quarter of a century before he first named in January 1955 the new system of therapy he had been developing since 1951. After he entered the City College of New York at 16, Ellis read voraciously on the subjects of sex, romance, love and marital relations (Bernard 1986; Wiener 1988). He gradually found he could give useful advice on those topics to friends and acquaintances, who began to consult him. After a passionate, unhappy first love affair and marriage in his twenties, Ellis continued to read everything he could find on sex, love and relationship problems and customs, and to counsel friends and acquaintances. He decided he would seek a professional degree to back up what he was already doing. Ellis often remarks that he might not have later developed an active-directive form of psychotherapy were it not for his earlier work as a relationship and sex counsellor. Those problems require an active-directive style.

Ellis wanted to study marriage therapy and sex counselling, which were not available as subject areas in those days, so he chose the next closest thing, clinical psychology. He entered Columbia University in 1942, obtained his Master's degree in 1943, and began a part-time practice as a psychologist, while continuing his graduate studies. His first doctoral dissertation, supported by his faculty advisers, pertained to the love emotions of college women (Ellis 1949). After he completed the research and the writing of the dissertation, two key faculty members in the psychology department completely opposed his project or any other thesis on love. They were afraid there would be controversy surrounding Columbia if it became known that a dissertation about sex and love research had been approved. Ellis then completed a second dissertation, this one on the decidedly non-controversial topic of the psychometric properties of psychological tests.

ELLIS TACKLES CENSORSHIP AND PSYCHOANALYSIS

Having earned his doctorate in 1947, Ellis immediately returned to his main interests – sex and marital issues and therapy, romance and love, and sexual mores and customs – and he began to write prolifically on those topics. Those days, half a century ago, were very different from present-day America. Sex was not just taboo, but writings about sex were censored or banned, and writers and publishers could be – and were – censored and jailed. A few mainstream books that dared to allude to or depict homosexuality, such as Edward Sagarin's *The Homosexual in*

America in 1951 and Gore Vidal's *The City and the Pillar* in 1948, created public sensations. Court cases raged, or had raged in the previous decades, involving *Ulysses*, *Lady Chatterley's Lover*, writings of Henry Miller, *Fanny Hill*, and nudist magazines. Could such books and magazines be brought into the country? Could people read them freely? Sell them? Send them through the mail? Ellis testified in court for the nudist magazines, against sex censorship, against the prosecution of homosexuals, and against rigid laws governing sexual practices. Ellis and the famous civil liberties lawyer, O. John Rogge, persuaded the US Supreme Court to allow news-stands to sell nudist magazines. One of the most famous court cases was the obscenity trial in 1956 involving Allen Ginsberg's book of poetry, *Howl*, for its explicit homosexual references. The trial, which Ginsberg won, helped make *Howl* an American all-time best-selling book of poetry.

In the late 1940s and the 1950s, publishers rejected or heavily bowdlerized many of Ellis's manuscripts pertaining to sex (Ellis 1957a; 1965a). Newspapers, such as the *New York Times*, refused all advertisements for sexually oriented books, even if they were clinical and scientific. Ellis's writings were exceptionally explicit. He discussed sex techniques and problems in great detail and strongly championed people's rights – including women and homosexuals – to sexual enjoyment, expression and freedom. Ellis attacked and satirized the rampant sexual mythology, the censorship and prudishness and the old-fashioned ideas that he thought needlessly hampered people in their pursuit of happiness. In 1956, Ellis founded and served as the first president of the Society for the Scientific Study of Sex.

Ellis wrote numerous books and articles pertaining to sex therapy, sexual practices and customs, dating and mating, marriage and marriage therapy. A reading of these tomes, some of them now almost half a century old, reveals Ellis's use of numerous modern sex therapy techniques and methods. Further, Ellis debunked the idea that sex equals intercourse. He described methods for communicating with one's partner, asserting one's sexual desires, taking interpersonal risks in dating, and combating prudishness and guilt over sex. In *Sex Without Guilt* (1958), for instance, Ellis applied his REBT approach to specific sexual problems and issues such as masturbation, petting, premarital relations, adultery, censorship, female frigidity, and male inadequacy. He ended the book with a chapter titled 'The Right to Sex Enjoyment'. Some of the more famous titles include

1951: *The Folklore of Sex*
1953: *Sex, Society and the Individual*
   (which includes an article on the myth of the vaginal orgasm)

1954: *The American Sexual Tragedy*
1954: *Sex life of the American Woman and the Kinsey Report*
1958: *Sex Without Guilt*
1960: *The Art and Science of Love*
1963: *If This be Sexual Heresy ...*
1963: *Sex and the Single Man*
1963: *The Intelligent Woman's Guide to Man-hunting*
1976: *Sex and the Liberated Man*
1979: *The Intelligent Woman's Guide to Dating and Mating*

Although Ellis wrote prolifically on sexual, marriage and relation-ship issues, his private practice dealt with a full range of people's problems. His Master's-level training was in Carl Rogers' client-centred therapy, which he used for clients without sex problems. It was probably a poor fit for someone as active and directive as he. In the mid-1940s, Ellis developed an interest in psychoanalysis. When Hitler assumed power in Germany in 1933, what had been a sizeable immigration to the US of psychoanalysts, virtually all Jewish, became a flood. Like everyone who was anyone in intellectual, literary or liberal circles in New York, Ellis was in psychoanalysis. His analyst, a psychiatrist from Karen Horney's Institute, later arranged a formal training in psychoanalysis for Ellis, who then practised psychoanalysis and psychoanalytically oriented therapy for about six years.

Frustrated by what he saw as the inefficiency of psychoanalysis and analytically oriented therapy, Ellis began to develop his therapy by turning to the same sources he had used in developing himself. Parallel to, but following by a few years his radical stances on sexual issues, Ellis also began to develop original ideas as a psychotherapist. He combined ideas from philosophy and early Behaviourism with his action-oriented, problem-solving style, to formulate a briefer therapy. New York City was then, and remains, the world capital of psycho-analysis, and at first Ellis's efforts were to reform psychoanalysis from inside. He recommended that psychoanalysis – whether classical, or neo-Freudian like Horney's and Adler's approaches – adopt the scientific method, change according to empirical studies, be more active and directive with patients, and become much briefer (Ellis 1950; 1956a).

Before 1953 was over, Ellis gave up his efforts to reform psycho-analysis and he told his clients to stop referring to him as a 'psychoanalyst'. When he received telephone calls from prospective clients who thought he still practised analysis, he would try to talk them out of wanting psychoanalysis and he urged them instead to consider the brand of brief, solution-focused therapy he was developing. In January 1955 he named it 'Rational Therapy'. His first cognitive-behavioural self-help book on non-sexual issues, *How To Live With A Neurotic*, was published in 1957. In 1961, Ellis changed the name of his psychotherapy to 'Rational Emotive Therapy' (RET) to reflect the connection between meanings, purposes and emotion. In early 1993, he again modified the name of the therapy he created to its present-day name, 'Rational Emotive Behaviour Therapy' (REBT). Ellis inserted the word 'Behaviour' to emphasize that change of overt behaviour, along with changes in cognitions and emotions, is (and always has been) a goal and method of this therapy.

Having first tackled the forces of censorship and prudery about sex that dominated American life despite some legal victories for freedom of expression, in 1953 Ellis also challenged psychoanalysis. The latter was the prevailing belief system in educated circles in New York City and throughout the US, and comprised the core psychiatric viewpoint about homosexuality as a sickness. What were Ellis's beliefs about homosexuality? How did they fit in with and differ from American culture's viewpoints about homosexuality as a sickness, a sin, and a crime?

In elucidating these points, it will be useful to sketch some of the historical and cultural forces that characterized and affected American society from the mid-1940s to the mid-1970s. These forces also characterized and affected the homophile movement, which became known as Gay Liberation. I will show which of Ellis's viewpoints regarding homosexuality changed appreciably over the years, and which changed little. Some of his viewpoints first made him a hero to the homophiles and then a villain to segments of the gay rights movement.

IN THE MATTACHINE SOCIETY

Ellis was an early champion of homosexual rights, a fact consistent with his philosophy of Humanism and utilitarianism, including his advocacy of people's rights to sexual freedom. He gave a number of talks to meetings of the Mattachine Society, the first of the homophile organizations in America, officially formed by Harry Hay in 1951. Hay named the Mattachine Society after the secret society of medieval court jesters who voiced unpopular truths from behind a mask. In the 1948 US presidential campaign, Hay had formed a 'Bachelors for Wallace' group, supporting a strongly left-wing independent candidate, Henry Wallace. After that, Hay began to look for people to help him create a homophile organization. Ellis published several papers in the *Mattachine Review* as well as in *ONE*, the publication of One, Inc., another homophile group (Ellis 1955; 1956b; 1957c; 1959; 1964; see also Ellis 1951b). The Mattachine Society made Ellis an honorary member in approximately 1953, at about the time he was formally breaking with psychoanalysis. Not only did Ellis champion the right to diverse, consensual sexual expression, but he taught methods of unconditional self- and other-acceptance as a therapeutic strategy and as a philosophy promoting happiness and mental hygiene. He strongly advocated an end to persecution of homosexuals, including their entrapment by the police on 'morals' charges, and he recommended decriminalization of homosexual practices. In *ONE* in 1957, Ellis published his paper, 'How Homosexuals Can Combat Anti-homosexualism.'

The modern, especially younger, reader might be quite surprised to learn that Ellis's talks at homophile meetings and his publications in their journals clearly stated his belief that homosexuality was an emotional disturbance whose cure he outlined. As an illustrative quote, consider the following from Ellis's 1963 book, *If This Be Sexual Heresy*:

> Very rarely, in my many psychotherapeutic relationships with homosexuals, as well as in my non-therapeutic friendship with many of them, have I found one who is not *generally* disturbed and whose homosexuality is not a direct function of his or her general disturbance. For many reasons such as these, confirmed lesbians and their 'gay' male counterparts are emotionally sick and aberrated. True, our repressive and punitive society unfairly tends to make them even sicker by its anti-homosexual attitudes and persecutions. But they were disturbed long before they became homosexual, and only very rarely as a direct consequence of their becoming so. (Ellis 1963a, p. 212)

I will now discuss the conclusion Ellis had at that time that homosexuality was an emotional disturbance, a viewpoint he no longer holds. In doing so, I will show (1) what Ellis's theories were, though they have changed somewhat, about inborn sexual preferences; (2) what his theories were, and remain, about the development of sexual identities; and (3) how his ideas fitted in with, or clashed with, American cultural norms of those times.

SEXUAL PREFERENCES AND SEXUAL IDENTITIES

Ellis has consistently voiced his belief that there is no monolithic route followed in reaching one's sexual practices and identities. He believes few people are born exclusively homosexual or heterosexual, but are born 'ambisexual' (bisexual) or 'plurisexual', with usually rather slight biologically based leanings in various directions. By 'plurisexual', Ellis means prone to become sexually aroused and to achieve orgasm in a number of different ways. These include (a) masturbation, (b) heterosexual contacts, (c) homosexual contacts, (d) sex with animals, (e) sex with inanimate objects, and (f) thoughts, fantasies and dreams. For various biological, social, personal and unknown reasons, people learn to prefer and train themselves in one mode of sexual expression over another. For example, in his 1965 book, *Homosexuality: Its Causes and Cure*, Ellis said that most homosexuals could become heterosexually or ambisexually oriented if they worked at it long and hard enough (Ellis 1965b, p. 269). In a 1986 interview, he added:

> My contention is that *any* person, with enough effort, can change his or her heterosexuality, homosexuality, or bisexuality – even though they may still be born with some strong *tendencies* to be the way they now are. (Wiener 1988, p. 102)

Again, in an interview with Michael Bernard in 1986, Ellis remarked:

> If they were more flexible I think that just about all homosexuals could enjoy heterosexuality and just about all heterosexuals could enjoy homosexuality. But they both tend to be rigid and they both tend to from early age onwards. (Bernard 1986, p. 264)

Regarding the biological basis of sexual preference, Ellis (1976) reviews the opinions of a variety of sexologists, and states:

> My guess? That *some* confirmed homosexuals may well have a *slight* physiological predisposition to avoid heterosexual, and de-vote themselves to homosexual, relations – just as, I believe, most heterosexuals have a *slight* physiological predisposition favoring heterosexuality. But largely, I feel, humans tend to feel innately bisexual or plurisexual and can fairly easily train themselves – usually for psychological reasons – to avoid one major mode of sexuality (such as homosexuality *or* heterosexuality) and to exclu-

sively or mainly enjoy another mode. As a result of their self-training they *feel* much more comfortable with the mode they choose, *view* it as their 'natural' bent, and falsely conclude that they *had* to choose it. (Ellis 1976, p. 298)

Campbell summarized Ellis's position by saying:

The fact that both homosexuals and heterosexuals tend to deny that they have bisexual capacities and the fact that heterosexuals often become homophobic and that homosexuals become hetero-phobic is largely because they are turning rational preferences for one form of sex into irrational fixations and compulsions. *Preferential* homosexuality and heterosexuality are healthy; *rigid, obsessive-compulsive* sexuality in both gay and straight individuals is neurotic. (Campbell 1985, pp. 177–8)

Regarding 'compulsive heterosexuality', Ellis has the following to say in *Sex and the Liberated Man* (1963):

Can you, in such circumstances, actually change your neurotic ways and begin to enjoy sex-love relationships on a noncompulsive basis? Yes, you can – just as compulsive homosexuals can, if they really want to, work at their problem and make themselves into enjoying bisexuals. For although sex disturbances easily arise, usually 'unconsciously,' in the sense that you do not will to bring them on, they stem largely from self-conditioning procedures; consequently, you almost invariably have the power to recondition yourself, if you want to take the time and trouble to do so.

Don't forget, in this connection, that so-called normal sex pleasures also originate in self-conditioning. As a human, you almost always have innate plurisexual tendencies – you can get aroused and come to orgasm in a fairly large variety of ways. You also may have innate tendencies to prefer one or a few of these ways to others. (Ellis 1976, p. 302)

Ellis remarks that:

My philosophy almost exactly follows, as it has for many years, that of Identity House, a counselling centre in New York specifically designed to serve the gay and bisexual community. Its philosophy bases itself on 'the ideal that one's sexual identity should be a freely chosen expression of that which is most natural to and rewarding for each individual.' (ibid., p. 299)

Ellis's ideas about humans' innate plurisexual leanings have not changed much, though he now agrees that many people have definite inborn leanings toward one form of sexual expression over another. Given those ideas, as well as his strong advocacy of civil rights for homosexuals, why did Ellis at one time nevertheless see homosexuality as an emotional disturbance? Let us now take a look at American society of the 1940s and 1950s, its treatment of homosexuals, and its viewpoints about homosexuality.

McCARTHY AND THE BOYS OF BOISE

The late 1940s and the 1950s were a time of intense conservatism in the US and of immense fear of the 'Red menace'. Beginning in the late 1940s, US Senator Joseph McCarthy spearheaded active witch-hunting of communists and other 'subversives', especially homosexuals (Rovere 1959). Homosexuals were generally despised and considered mentally ill and unstable as well as criminals and sinners. McCarthy and most government officials contended that homosexuals who worked for the government could easily be blackmailed into turning government secrets over to the communists. McCarthy's name is immortalized in American dictionaries in the term 'McCarthyism' – the practice of alleging disloyalty with little or no evidence, or using unfair investigative techniques to restrict dissent or political criticism. As well as McCarthy's committee in the Senate, the House of Representatives had the House Un-American Activities Committee (HUAC), which also investigated subversive activities. HUAC hauled numerous writers, professors, activists, intellectuals and movie stars before Congress and the cameras to testify against each other or to defend themselves against real or manufactured connections, usually as youth, to communism. Many careers and lives were destroyed.

McCarthy often alluded to his list of hundreds of 'known' communists working for the State Department. Investigators unearthed almost no communists, but many hundreds of homosexuals worked for the State Department and other branches of the federal government. The McCarthy hearings were broadcast nation-wide on television, and thus the entire nation learned of the 'subversive menace' of 'homosexuals', 'pixies', 'fairies', 'perverts' and 'deviates' – all terms used repeatedly during the hearings. This fanned the fears of the populace. Often subjected to gruelling interrogations with promises of leniency if they named other homosexuals, hundreds of homosexuals with government jobs were identified and fired. In time, McCarthy's tactics became so obnoxious and bizarre that he became unpopular and his fellow senators censured him, which ended his committee and his career.

In 1955, another unsavoury and sensational story about the homosexual menace in the US hit the media. This story and investigation lasted a year, with one shocking development or rumour after another; hundreds of lives were ruined, and there were arrests, trials and prison sentences ranging from six years to life imprisonment. Frank Gerassi's 1966 book, *The Boys of Boise*, chronicled this saga – set in Boise, Idaho – in a richly detailed and documented picture of political skulduggery and police-state tactics. The scandal began because several members of the ruling clique in Boise wanted to 'get' a politician whose son was homosexual. By the time the story broke, the boy was a US Army cadet at the elite West Point Academy, which dismissed him immediately, devastating both his family and his career. By the time the scandal died down, the police had interrogated approximately 3 per cent of Boise's 50,000 residents and had arrested and jailed dozens of men.

The story about the 'homosexual underground' in Boise appeared and reappeared in newspapers throughout the US. Editorials in newspapers and magazines such as *Time* either viewed with alarm or earnestly discussed the homosexual menace to the youth of America, and reported the salacious details and rumours. These included the rumour that the 'homosexual underground' chartered airliners for homosexuals from around the world to visit Boise, to sodomize teenage boys. The investigating authorities held mass meetings in Boise high school gyms, brought in a special prosecutor, and flew psychiatrists in from out of state (Boise had only two psychiatrists) to counsel victims. Both senators from Idaho returned home from Washington, DC, to the scene of the disaster to do what they could to 'help' their constituents. In one astonishing incident, a jailed homosexual was photographed (by a camera belonging to the prosecuting attorney), having sex with another prisoner. His sentence, which had been mere months, was then extended to seven years in prison.

The unparalleled furore about the boys of Boise powerfully reinforced anti-homosexual prejudice. Boise was exceptional only in the intensity of its witch-hunting folly. More quietly, with less hysteria and media coverage, the same stories, the same tactics, the same ruined lives were commonplace in America of the 1950s. Typically, small reports would appear in local newspapers, complete with names and addresses, of people arrested on, or fired for, 'morals' charges.

HOOVER, THE FBI AND ELLIS

A prominent spokesperson of the homophile movement, Donald Webster Cory (the pseudonym of Edward Sagarin) of the Mattachine Society, endorsed Ellis's views publicly and in writing, a fact used against Sagarin politically in 1964 when activists were voted into leadership of the Mattachine Society. Ellis and Sagarin co-authored a book on nymphomania and Sagarin wrote the introduction to Ellis's 1965 book, *Homosexuality: Its Causes and Cure*. The Federal Bureau of Investigation (FBI) did not endorse Ellis's views; instead, it investigated him. According to Wiener (1988), Ellis's FBI file said he took 'an extreme position in condoning homosexualism and premarital intercourse'. The file linked him to the Mattachine Society and stated that he had published a paper in 1952, entitled 'On the Cure of Homosexuality'.

The FBI, formed in the early 1900s to fight crime, eventually compiled massive files on people and causes that seemed, however remotely, to be anti-*status quo* or un-American, including those with liberal political viewpoints or those that challenged racial, artistic, literary or sexual norms. The FBI compiled voluminous files on newspeople, politicians, artists, movie and television stars, writers, professors, protesters, left-wingers and revolutionaries, as well as homosexuals, their supporters and their organizations. For example, the FBI bugged the home, telephones and hotel rooms of Dr Martin Luther King, Jr, the civil rights hero and Nobel Prize winner, looking for connections to communism or any juicy titbits that might be useful in dealing with him politically.

J. Edgar Hoover, chief of the FBI from 1924 until his death in 1972, was virulently anti-homosexual, very prejudiced against blacks, Jews and Latinos, refused to hire women as agents, and was extremely conservative politically. He had many quirks, ranging from not allowing bald men to serve as FBI agents to refusing to admit there was any such thing as the Mafia. Ironically, Hoover was well-known as a homosexual, and his long-term companion, Clyde Tolson, was associate director of the FBI. A biographer reported that US presidents sometimes – very much in private – referred to Hoover as 'a queer' (Summers 1993). However, he had at his command potentially incriminating or embarrassing information about so many well connected people, or could easily obtain such information, that he was very dangerous, valuable and untouchable.

HOMOPHILES, CIVIL RIGHTS AND GAY LIBERATION

Ellis's position against persecution of homosexuals might seem rather tame to the younger, modern reader. In the context of that historical period, however, Ellis's views were outspoken and radical – more so, in some ways, than those of the homophile organizations themselves. Early homophile organizations, according to sociologist and historian of the gay and lesbian movement, Barry D. Adam (1987), changed and developed as American culture changed and developed, and they had activist and accommodationist/assimilationist phases. The aim of the accommodationists/assimilationists was to obtain rights through education and through looking and acting as normal as possible, not offending anyone, and appealing to people's compassion. In 1951 when the Mattachine Society was founded, Senator McCarthy's power was at its zenith. In the same year, the Black Cat, a bar in San Francisco, won the legal right in the California Supreme Court to serve alcohol to homosexuals. (In 1955, however, California's legislature made it illegal to serve alcohol in 'resorts for sexual perverts'.)

Initially, the Mattachine Society was activist and left-wing. Its founder, Harry Hay, had been a card-carrying communist for many years. When he established the Mattachine Society, he recommended that the American Communist Party, which did not support homosexual rights, expel him. Open-mindedly, however, the party allowed him instead to resign as a 'security risk'. Hay established a system of secret 'cells' of Mattachine members, to attempt to protect them from police surveillance, arrest and public exposure. Central to his system, as the Mattachine Society grew, were groups of no more than ten members. Each group had a leader who *memorized* names, addresses and telephone numbers of his group members; they wrote down nothing. The other early organizers of the Mattachine Society had also been communists or fellow travellers.

At the Mattachine Society's convention in 1953, the assimilationists – referred to by Hay as 'middle class' – took over. When the HUAC forced Hay before it to testify, it knew of his communist past but not of his organizing of homophiles. In 1954, the same year the Supreme Court declared racial segregation in American public schools unconstitutional, the US Post Office banned *ONE* from being mailed. The Supreme Court overturned this ruling in 1958. By 1959, the Mattachine Society presented itself only as a group interested in the problems of homosexuality, rather than as a 'rights' organization (Martin and Lyon 1972; Adam 1987). The pioneering lesbian organization, Daughters of Bilitis, founded in 1955, was also accommodationist. Its formal objectives included education of the 'variant', development of a library on the 'sex deviant' theme, and promoting a mode of behaviour and dress 'acceptable to society'. It later added the aims of participation in research projects, investigation of the penal code as it pertained to homosexuals, and promotion of change through due process in the state legislatures. Several years after its founding, activists briefly took over the Daughters of Bilitis, which soon resumed a more accommodationist stance (Martin and Lyon 1972).

Historians of gay liberation such as Altman (1971), Katz (1976), Bayer (1981), Adam (1987), Bérubé (1990) and Shilts (1993) indicate that the rise of the civil rights movement of American Negroes – with mass marches, political pressure, protests, sit-ins, and legal action beginning in the late 1950s – spurred renewed militancy among the homophile organizations. In 1964, the Mattachine Society's activist slate of candidates won election over the accommodationists. Especially in New York, San Francisco and Los Angeles, activists began to push for reform. In 1964, the Society for Individual Rights was founded in San Francisco. It held forums for political candidates and sponsored social events and fund-raisers for its members. One watershed occurred when police photographed and harassed hundreds of politically active, influential 'straight' people, including many clergy and attorneys, as they crossed police lines at a fund-raiser in San Francisco in 1965 – the same year Ellis's book *Homosexuality: Its Causes and Cure* was published.

HOMOSEXUALITY AND MENTAL ILLNESS

In the documentary, *Before Stonewall* (1986), activist Frank Kameny states that younger gay people in 1986 could scarcely believe that only 20 years earlier a roomful of 100 gay people would earnestly discuss whether they should take the position that they were *not* mentally ill. Earlier in the homophile movement, it appears, many considered it a good idea to say that homosexuality was a disease because it could win sympathy and compassion. It could also enlist the support of medical and other educated authorities. This was similar to the use of the 'disease' concept by Alcoholics Anonymous (AA): if it's a disease, then the people 'with it' cannot be blamed. Harry Hay's preliminary concept paper for the Mattachine Society directly compared it to AA as a 'service organization'. In the earlier days of the homophile movement, Ellis's combination of 'it's a sickness' and his demand that all discrimination against and persecution of homosexuals be ended, easily made him a hero. The 'disease' idea not only had political advantages, but homophiles also widely believed it. Later, as lesbians and gays became more militant after successes of Negroes in obtaining civil rights, 'it's a disease' became decidedly unpopular. (Though never an official diagnosis in the *Diagnostic and Statistical Manual of Mental Disorders* (DSM), as late as 1964 an entire issue of *The Journal of Social Issues* was devoted to 'Negro American Personality'.)

Nevertheless, why did Ellis, hardly one to agree with mainstream ideas, originally consider homosexuality a sickness? In brief, because of its self-defeating aspects, which he particularly saw in a clinical population. The cultural context was the McCarthy witch-hunts, the rampant entrapment of homosexuals on 'morals' charges by police vice squads, the publication in newspapers of names and addresses of arrested and fired deviates, the threat of blackmail of gays in government, and the boys of Boise. These hysterias showed American society's powerful prejudice against homosexuality. Ellis's theory that people are naturally plurisexual and train themselves into various orientations and practices based on small leanings, may have increased his perception that homosexuals defeated themselves needlessly. Ellis defined – and defines – neurosis as self-defeating behaviour. Also, many homosexuals said they had no choice and that their sexual orientation was predetermined, whereas Ellis thought that people unconsciously trained themselves into their choices based on small initial leanings. Therefore, he disagreed with them and saw their insistence about their 'natural' bent as rigid irrationality.

Times changed, and so did Ellis. In 1968, the first organized disruption by gays at a convention of the American Medical Association took place in San Francisco. Gay students picketed a psychiatric seminar on homosexuality at Columbia University in New York. The Stonewall Inn bar riot took place in Greenwich Village in June 1969. Within a year, gays protesting the diseasing of homosexuality had disrupted a number of psychiatric and psychological conventions and conferences.

In 1973, the Council of the American Psychiatric Association (APA) voted unanimously to remove homosexuality from the DSM. Arguments from traditionalists in the APA, however, resulted in a referendum on the issue by the full membership. Adam amusingly points out:

> The result of this curious spectacle of defining pathology by plebiscite was a vote of 58 percent for deletion and 37 percent for retention in 1974. In the end, the new diagnostic manual included a compromise category that continued to allow psychiatrists to 'treat' people unhappy with their sexual orientation. (Adam 1987, p. 82)

However, as Adam may not have realized, the APA had by 1968 distinguished between ego-dystonic and ego-syntonic homosexuality and had explicitly stated that homosexuality *per se* was not a psychiatric disorder (APA 1968). In 1987, the APA removed the *term*, 'ego-dystonic homosexuality', from the revision of their third DSM, but retained the concept, as was true of the fourth (and, at the time of writing, current) manual.

In August 1997, the other APA, the American Psychological Association, took a formal position on conversion or reparative therapy for homosexuals (American Psychological Association 1997; Haldeman 1997; HRC 1997). It did not condemn the therapy, indicating that it did not want to get into the business of siding for or against specific types of therapy. Its resolution, entitled 'Appropriate Therapeutic Responses to Sexual Orientation', addressed misconceptions about sexual orientation. The resolution rejected the 'illness' model of same-sex sexual orientation and disavowed portrayals of lesbians, gay men and bisexuals as mentally ill due to their sexual orientation. The resolution also required psychologists who provide services to lesbian, gay, bisexual, and questioning individuals to disseminate accurate information about sexual orientation. It required them to provide informed consent as to the treatment offered, to offer information about alternative treatments and to practice in a non-discriminatory manner that lets the individual safely explore issues of sexual orientation.

HOW DID ELLIS'S POSITION CHANGE?

Ellis's position on the biological determination of homosexuality has changed toward the idea that a rather larger number of people than he originally thought are born with definite leanings one way or the other. From his citations of LeVay's work and others, he is ready to accept research conclusions. He still holds to his plurisexuality theory and to his belief that sexual identities and, to a large extent, sexual preferences, are constructions. The views he did change considerably are those to do with homosexuals being emotionally disturbed.

In 1976, eleven years after his book on homosexuality, Ellis stated in *Sex and the Liberated Man*:

as we – meaning heterosexual society – take more liberal attitudes toward fixed homosexuals and allow them to do what they want with their sex lives, with a minimum of interference and persecution, the happier and less disturbed they seem to feel and behave. (Ellis 1976, p. 296)

In Bernard's *Staying Rational in an Irrational World* (1986), Ellis indicates that he no longer thinks that childhood experiences affect whether someone becomes homosexual. Rather, he thinks homosexuals very early choose their orientation and train themselves into it, refusing to try anything else. Then he remarks:

> But the same thing goes for most heterosexuals. They tend to train themselves to be attracted to members of the other sex and then rigidly refuse to consider anything else. So I think it's the profound absolutistic thinking, the obsession, the compulsion, which we bring to our childhood and which we prejudicedly maintain later, which makes so many of us compulsively straight or gay. (Bernard 1986, pp. 263–4)

In a 1992 article in *The Humanist*, entitled 'Are Gays and Lesbians Emotionally Disturbed?', Ellis says:

> Sexual sanity, then, like nonsexual sanity, largely consists of noncompulsiveness, personal experimentation, and open-mindedness. It involves sticking to pathways that do not entail too many practical disadvantages and, perhaps, above all, accepting yourself and utterly refusing to put yourself down even if you do the wrong thing and indubitably behave self-defeatingly. (Ellis 1992, p. 35)

He then adds that, 'Sexual pathology is independent of the issue of sexual preferences', and, 'In terms of sexuality, the person's particular preference isn't the basis for determining the question of psychological normality' (ibid.).

RATIONAL EMOTIVE BEHAVIOUR THEORY AND THERAPY

Rational Emotive Behaviour Therapy (REBT) is a comprehensive and complicated form of therapy, and it is far beyond the scope of this chapter to do more than allude to a few aspects of its practice. To learn about that, the reader is referred to such sources as Dryden and DiGiuseppe (1990), Walen et al. (1992), Dryden (1994, 1995a, 1995b), Ellis (1995) and Ellis and Dryden (1997).

The practice of REBT has with it a personality theory; some ideas of which pertain to sexual preferences and identities. A principal idea in the theory is REBT's view that people largely construct, deconstruct and reconstruct their personalities and identities. The tendency to construct, assumes REBT, is innate. It includes leanings and talents, the ability to think, and the tendency to think about one's thinking. It includes one's rational and irrational beliefs, as well as one's infer- ences, intentions, decisions and will.

As we build ourselves, we select raw materials. Those available include various teachings and standards of the general culture and sub-cultures, the family, the world of work, the peer group, and so on. We can also create new ideas and actions and experiment to see how they work. At any age, our personalities can be 'works in progress' rather than 'finished products'. We, the builders – with work and practice – can redesign ourselves within limits, according to conditions and according to our intentions.

People can do this construction work throughout life, and it has little intrinsic connection to age. By providing restrictive blueprints, cultural standards can, however, limit people's expression of their tendencies toward self-construction. In the developed nations until quite recent times, opportunities for females to develop themselves were relatively limited. The same has been true of people who prefer to behave homosexually. In most Western cultures, older people remain rather limited in the roles they are 'allowed' to play: for example, they are expected to change themselves less as they age, rather than continue to experiment and develop. However, an elder movement toward more flexible options and greater opportunity for self-construc- tion is gaining steam (Ellis and Velten 1998).

According to the REBT viewpoint, 'gay', 'lesbian' and 'bisexual' are personal and social constructions. In their efforts to gain rights to express themselves and live how they desire, people in recent years have built sounder frameworks for these constructions. People's individual and collective efforts are transforming the meanings of 'gay', 'lesbian' and 'bisexual': once they were synonyms for mental illness, crime and sin, but now they are coming to mean an acceptable, healthy lifestyle, which is available for people to consider. Through the media, as well as word of mouth and visible personal examples, healthful constructions of 'gay', 'lesbian' and 'bisexual' have become much more available in today's world. Their increasing availability speeds the process by which people can experiment with their desires and choose and develop their behaviour and their identities.

SEXUAL ACTS, DESIRES AND IDENTITIES

Let me distinguish here between (a) sexual behaviour, (b) sexual preference or leaning, and (c) sexual identity. Large numbers of men in some cultures, sub-cultures and settings routinely have sex with other men. Their preferences or predispositions, however, lean toward women. That leaning might vary in strength from mild to very strong. The frequency of their having sex with other men may range from rarely to quite often, but they do not identify themselves as homosexual or gay. They may behave homosexually sometimes or often, but they are not homosexual or gay in terms of their identity. AIDS risk-reduction messages pitched to gays may sail right past such men. As far as they can see, the message has nothing to do with them. Are they all 'closet cases'? Are we to assume that these men are 'under construction' and will come out as gay in due course? This is unlikely, given prevalence figures such as Kinsey's, for same-sex experience among men. Similarly, a person may identify as gay or lesbian, usually have sex with members of the same sex, but still feel attracted to, and even have sexual relationships with, members of the opposite sex. Nevertheless, that individual identifies neither as 'straight' nor as bisexual. People who do identify themselves as bisexual may never have sex with members of one of their 'opposite' sexes. Therefore, identity, preferences and behaviour are very different, though they have some overlap. Ellis's viewpoint – with which many, if not most, social scientists agree – is that 'gay', 'lesbian' and 'bisexual' are personal and social constructions (Greenberg 1988). Where he differs radically is in his belief that *preferences*, too, are largely constructions.

Bisexual behaviour has likely existed as long as people have. 'Bisexual' as an identity and as a preference, however, is now rapidly gaining in popularity (Orndorff, forthcoming; Zepezauer, forthcoming). As has been true with 'straight' and 'gay', once such an identity or category exists as an accepted concept in the culture, many people try to fit themselves and others into one and only one category. They will say, for example, 'She had a relationship with a woman ten years ago, so she must be a lesbian', or, 'He used to have sex with other men for money, so he must "really" be gay.' Bisexual as an identity now adds a third category. What once was either/or (either straight or gay), now threatens to become either/or/or (either straight or gay or bisexual). The REBT viewpoint is both/and, not either/or. People have all kinds of sexual potentials, not just one kind. Placing oneself and others rigidly in one category or another is conceptually simple. It can sometimes have political advantages. It is one's prerogative to do so. Usually, however, it is an overgeneralization, and it may limit one's enjoyment and options in life.

NATURAL SCIENTISTS

REBT assumes that we humans have a biologically based tendency to explain and predict reality, to construct theories and develop ourselves in order to stay alive, suffer less and feel happier. REBT sees these motivational and evaluative tendencies as intrinsic, not learned. The assumption is that our attempts to force regularities on the world are psychologically prior to our observations of similarities. We naturally expect to find regularities. We like to produce explanations for phenomena, including our behaviour. We have a biological tendency not just to think, but to think about our thinking, and to make evaluations and predictions. We create theories about our observations and ourselves because far too many stimuli exist for us to consider them individually.

REBT sees people as natural theory-makers and scientists, but not necessarily good theory-makers and scientists. We have rational (self-actualizing) as well as irrational (self-defeating) tendencies. We often like and overemphasize easy, dramatic, grandiose or personalistic explanations. We tend to attribute special causes to events or behaviour. We want magic and miracles to be true and often refuse to look at evidence to the contrary.

To our detriment, in terms of problem-solving, we often enjoy easy and special explanations and feel completed by them. We think they are true because of the feelings we get when we believe them. We do not want to bother with all the complex factors that are antecedent to a particular event. We are not happy with the idea that many of the real causes of our behaviour seem difficult to change, complex, obscure or partly accidental. As soon as we construct an explanation that seems to fit with our (usually selective) observations, we may easily convince ourselves of its truth by ignoring some facts that do not fit. We may falsify – knowingly or unknowingly – facts that fit poorly. We may ignore or fail to see theories that fit more accurately. Because of these tendencies to invent easy, special explanations, and since there appear to be so many contributing factors, some of which are unknown or due to chance, Ellis (1979b) holds that it often proves self-defeating to look extensively for distant, historical explanations for one's behaviour.

According to the personality theory of REBT, people have an ability and tendency to make choices and commitments. The REBT viewpoint is that humans are uniquely purposive creatures, and our tendency to create purposes and then to define ourselves and the meanings of our lives in terms of purposes is our human core. Further, people can deliberately and creatively make choices. Once we change our intention, we can use that change to make other changes. Thus, we can construct, deconstruct and reconstruct our attitudes and behaviours based on circumstances and our hedonic desires, goals, and purposes in life. The kind of circumstances we notice and the information we look for and use in the environment to make these constructions is rooted in biologically based leanings.

REBT assumes that people actively and intentionally engage the environment. We *like* to think, imagine, plan, and attempt to explain reality and to make sense of things. We try to discover ways to reach our goals and avoid or overcome obstacles. We enjoy making bets on outcomes, and we like to be right. To explain our feelings and actions, sometimes we make up excuses or even invent things that never happened. In this process of plotting and scheming, we construct some parts of our personalities and build our habits, using social and cultural settings and our own inventions as raw materials. The principal goal of REBT is to teach people a method of strengthening this natural human process of self-determination and self-construction, to make it more effective and efficient, and to use it to solve personal and practical problems.

BELIEVING IS SEEING, AND THE PRESENT PARTLY CAUSES THE PAST

According to REBT's personality theory, reality is not simple, stable and linear. Instead, it often appears transactional and interactional. People construct reality largely relative to their goals and situations. REBT radically disagrees with the notion that one's history created one's present adjustment, such as homosexuality. Instead, REBT holds that people considerably create their own current adjustments *and* histories. We choose to accept the experiences we are given, and we seek out experiences and peers according to our preferences. We construct our life-span development every day.

As has been shown in voluminous research, our past memories are constructed and can be glaringly false (see, for example, Loftus and Ketcham 1994). We fill in memory gaps easily with whatever seems plausible or with what has been suggested to us, including things that never happened. Later we feel utterly convinced that we are remembering the whole truth and nothing but the truth. Because the future does not yet exist, our predictions about the future are entirely constructed. Yet most of us at times feel certain we are correct in our predictions about our personal lives. People who feel depressed and hopeless, for example, may attempt suicide because they are so sure they know the future as a fact. Our perceptions of the present are also prejudices and constructions. How we think and feel contributes to how we see and experience reality. We get ourselves into situations due to our goals and purposes. We notice aspects of reality selectively and give them importance based on our own motivations. Our current realities are an interaction of 'objective reality' and us. Not only do different people report the same objective event quite differently, but the same thing also happens 'within' an individual. In your current mood state, and with your current expectancies and preferences, how you see an event may differ markedly from how you would see it if you were in a different mood with different expectancies and preferences.

Children are neither blank tablets nor templates on to which parents and environment fit information, leading to personality formation and behaviour. Instead, like adults, children *bring themselves* to the events of their lives. They actively engage and shape the environment, create parts of it, and select parts of it for their own purposes. Children strongly affect the behaviour of their parents. Even new-born babies affect how the world responds to them (Birns 1965, Korner 1965, Bell 1968, Harper 1971, Lewis and Rosenblum 1974). People's temperaments, too, importantly determine what their world is (Eysenck 1981, Gray 1982, Cloninger 1986). People with anti-social behaviour are often depicted by the psychotherapy establishment as victims of poor upbringings and discrimination. Instead, careful study shows that criminals are delighted to adopt the 'victim' role. It can get them off the hook and give them more freedom to plan and execute their crimes (Yochelson and Samenow 1976). Such criminals laugh at therapists behind their backs. They compare notes with each other about how to *use* for their own purposes the prevalent belief system that your past makes you what you are.

HISTORY-TAKING IN REBT

In practice, REBT is largely ahistorical, believing in self-determination and self-construction. REBT sees one's past as influential, and of course personally important to people and worth listening to. Nevertheless, the past can operate only through oneself, in the present. This largely ahistorical and existential stance of REBT does not mean that Rational Emotive Behaviour Therapists have no interest at all in patients' histories. They do. Often, though, they view histories more as examples and products of the person's way of thinking, emoting and acting rather than as having a direct correlation with past events.

One's memories and reports of the past may be relatively pure versions of one's *current* mood state and belief system. History-taking in REBT also gives the clinician ideas about how devoutly the client holds what REBT considers to be a major self-defeating belief prevalent in Western culture :'one's past history is an all-important determiner of one's present behaviour and ... because something once strongly affected one's life, it should indefinitely have a similar effect' (Ellis 1962, p. 82). The stronger this belief, the less likely it is that the believer can change.

When a traumatic event – an objectively bad event outside the normal realm of experience – happens to a person, that person may subsequently show anxiety, depression, stress, or other symptoms as a result of that traumatic event: a condition known as 'post-traumatic stress disorder'. In the REBT viewpoint, the person's active constructivism and self-definition come into play in a complex fashion (Warren and Zgourides 1991). The person's evaluations of the bad event affect both the experience of the event and its aftermath. Even as it is happening, the history of trauma is partly a product of the individual. Later, the individual may continue to deconstruct and reconstruct the history to fit his or her current beliefs.

CONSTRUCTION WORKERS

People are builders: we each build ourselves on our individual biological foundations. Your foundation will limit and can complicate your efforts to build the personality and life you might desire. For example, if you are short, and you wish to become a professional basketball star, you will likely be severely limited. If you are male and want to be a woman and a mother, again your efforts will be obstructed. If your temperament is extremely sensitive and emotionally excitable – and was so even before birth, according to your mother – you will probably have to work much harder than the average person in order to succeed as a doctor in an accident and emergency department. If your sexual preferences lean in one direction from an early age, and if you long ago adopted a blueprint and have done extensive construction, REBT's constructivist personality theory holds that it will probably be difficult for you to change directions, assuming you want to.

Ellis's viewpoint, made clear earlier in this chapter, is that the large majority of people are innately plurisexual, whether leaning toward heterosexuality, homosexuality or bisexuality. He believes they can – with great work and practice and motivation – train themselves significantly in another direction of their choosing. Due to societal prejudices and penalties for homosexual behaviour, some of which were discussed above, relatively large numbers of homosexuals used to want to change their sexual orientation and behaviour and often sought therapy for that. As times changed, and homosexuals could more often live their lives free from fear, far fewer wanted to change. Also, it became more widely known that psychotherapy was ineffective at changing sexual identity and preferences. This, along with gay liberation's successful challenge to traditional therapy's viewpoint that homosexuality is a mental illness, may also have contributed to the fact that few homosexuals now seek therapy to change their sexual identity, preferences and behaviour.

The question yet to be answered is, how much do our innate biological predispositions determine the direction of our sexual leanings? Ellis himself believes, first, that in most people the inborn leaning one way or the other is very small. Second, he believes that people largely train and condition *themselves* rather than being trained or conditioned by parents and society. Many therapists and members of the laity believe sexual preference is determined at some point between conception and birth. They believe that training by society, much less oneself, has nothing to do with it. Yet others, the traditionalists, hold that one's upbringing – nurture – causes homosexuality by interrupting the course of nature. Much evidence contradicts the latter viewpoint, which appears to be waning as the genetic hypothesis is waxing; biological explanations for people's behaviour are now popular. However, to the nature and nurture hypotheses, Ellis adds a distinctive third hypothesis: that people construct, train into and condition *themselves* into their sexual preferences and identities; and they do this based, usually, on small initial leanings.

WHO CHOOSES?

In their positions on the question of the relative input of nature, nurture and self into the output – sexual preference – REBT practitioners probably can be found all over the map. The question itself has nothing intrinsic to do with the practice of REBT. In REBT, clients – not therapists – choose therapy goals. A client may state that her goal is to write the 'Great American Novel' and she feels inferior and depressed because she has failed – thus far – to write it. Even if the REBT practitioner thinks she is unlikely to reach her goal, the practitioner would rarely question the goal. REBT assumes it is not the failure and the frustration that lead to the client's depression and inferiority feelings; instead, it is her irrational beliefs *about* her failure to write her novel that causes her disturbance. The REBT practitioner would help the client to detect and dispute her irrational beliefs that produced her guilt feelings and sense of worthlessness. After her irrational beliefs were successfully tackled and her disturbed feelings mitigated, the client might or might not stick with her goal of writing the Great American Novel. It would be up to her. The therapist would not try to dissuade her from her goal.

How does this apply to homosexuality? If, for example, a client trained herself as a lawyer and identifies herself as one, and she could just as well have trained herself as and identify herself as a doctor, so what? This is irrelevant to therapy. What if she doesn't want to remain a lawyer? If, for example, she blocks herself from a career change, that would be a problem worthy of therapy – if the client wanted to work on it. She might choose to work on other kinds of problems. But what if she doesn't want to remain a *lesbian*? Would a REBT practitioner help her to become heterosexual?

As in the Great American Novel example above, the REBT practitioner respects people's goals. The difference between the Great American Novel example and the lesbian example is this: most of the culture, including most parents, relatives, teachers, neighbours, religious authorities and legal and mental health authorities (the latter until 25 years ago) do not call it a mental illness, a crime, or a sin to want to write the Great American Novel. Very rarely would one be fired from work, banished from one's family, or attacked on the street for writing, or trying to write, the Great American Novel. Thus, because of the large amounts of pressure from many sources, even in the most developed nations, to 'be heterosexual', REBT practitioners would be very sensitive here. They would enquire into what underlies the client's statement that her therapy goal is to be a lesbian no longer, whereas they would rarely do the same if she said her goal was to write the Great American Novel.

In the lesbian example, therefore, the therapist would likely first enquire into many aspects of the client's thinking. These aspects could include: Does the client want to change or does someone else want her to change? What have been her sexual and self-identity histories? What are her sexual desires and what have they been? Was she once straight? Has she had sex with men? With women? Was relating sexually with men her 'cup of tea' at one time? Second, the therapist would likely point out to the client that being a lesbian is not a mental disorder, and that there are no convincing studies to suggest that any form of therapy – including 'conversion' or 'reparative' therapy – effectively leads homosexuals to change their sexual orientation. The therapist would explore why the person wants to change from 'being' a lesbian – however she defines it – to something else. For example, is she being made to feel guilty by her parents? Does she feel that she has failed herself, her parents, or her children? Does she unconditionally accept herself *with* her lesbian behaviour? If not, her motivation for wanting to change may be to feel more worthwhile as a person. Self-rating, then, would itself become the priority of therapy before the client's desire to become heterosexual could be effectively addressed. Has she decided that her present way of life is a sin? Does she want to become a mother and does she believe that it would be wrong for her, as a lesbian, to have a child? Has she been living largely 'in the closet' and has she now decided that it is too frightening and stressful to come out to other people and face the possibility of rejection and discrimination? Are there rumours about her at work or at school that frighten her with the possibility of rejection, job loss, assault? These, and probably other aspects of this 'case' are among those a therapist would likely assess.

If, for non-neurotic and non-coerced reasons, the client still wants to move from lesbian to heterosexual, some REBT practitioners would probably demur, feeling they have no skill in that area. Others would attempt to help the client to realize her goal. That therapist might lead off by asking, just as in the case of the woman who wants to write the Great American Novel, 'What stops you?' What does stop most of us from writing the Great American Novel even though we would like to? In most cases, we don't even try. Second, we 'cannot' in the sense of not having the talent. Our biological foundations cannot support that kind of construction, no matter how hard we try. The latter is something that we can only discover by trial and error, by effort, by trying, by experimenting. The same thing would be true of the woman who wants to 'be' straight. If, as indicated above, it is a preferential goal – that is, she does not absolutely believe that she 'must' change, and that it is awful and intolerable if she does not, and that she is a worthless person who can never be happy in life as a lesbian – then it is fine for her to have a go at it. If she 'fails', that is, works hard at it and remains lesbian, the REBT practitioner would help the client continue to accept herself unconditionally, and then help her focus on constructing the best possible life for herself. A core purpose of REBT is to encourage people to create meanings in their lives, to develop purposes, commitments and a philosophy of life. REBT openly and explicitly espouses a value system that promotes its criteria of mental health. These criteria include self-interest, self-direction, self-creation, commitment, involvement, flexibility, acceptance of uncertainty, scientific thinking, non-utopianism, self-responsibility for one's own emotional disturbances, long-range hedonism and scepticism. Heterosexuality, homosexuality and bisexuality are not on the list.

PLUSES AND MINUSES OF HAVING AN IDENTITY

Having an identity – such as 'gay', 'lesbian' or 'bisexual' – has its advantages. The founders of Alcoholics Anonymous, for example, saw that if alcoholism were a disease, particularly one that was genetically based, it would help alcoholics escape being blamed, persecuted and otherwise mistreated for their drinking. Harry Hay's original concept paper for the Mattachine Society explicitly compared it to AA as a service organization. If you identify yourself with a disease or other biologically determined condition that you have, and this disease or condition is not infectious, most people – including yourself – will be less likely to blame you or persecute you for it. If your disease or condition was 'caused' by a malfunction in your upbringing, that may also help reduce blame. Therefore, both the nature and the nurture hypotheses about the origins of homosexuality can have some utility in allowing homosexuals to be themselves. Research into the upbringings of homosexuals tends to contradict the nurture hypothesis. The nature hypothesis has at least a little research support. The latter hypothesis may also reduce therapy expenses and guilt on the part of oneself and one's parents.

However, the proposition that people condition *themselves*, albeit unintentionally, into their sexual preferences is quite different from either the nature or the nurture hypotheses, in their pure forms. Ellis does not believe that preferences are chosen; he does not believe they are caused by childhood experiences: he believes they are largely a product of self-conditioning, with a foundation of usually small biological leanings. Some people fear that any but the genetic explanation of homosexuality could lead to the conclusion that it is a conscious choice. If it were a choice – similar to how you worship and how you vote – then, given the societal prejudice against homosexuality, persecution might increase. Persecution, however, is not caused by the fact that people can worship and vote as they like. To have personal freedom should not require adoption of any particular scientific hypothesis. In any case, the genetic hypothesis does not automatically mean that homosexuals will be allowed freedom. If the 'homo' gene is found, efforts to eradicate the gene might follow. Also, some religions, such as Roman Catholicism, accept homosexual beings, but damn homosexual behavings. Similarly, most people probably believe that some combination of genes and upbringing causes alcoholism; yet they believe that people choose to drink and drive, and they jail those who do so.

Having a set identity does have some more definite advantages than those just discussed. If you are part of a recognized minority group, you have some safety in numbers and can militate for civil rights and other benefits. Having a set identity also makes communication more simple and convenient. It makes life more predictable.

Is there a downside to having a set identity? REBT sees several and has long argued that self-labelling is self-defeating and an overgeneralization. REBT recommends that people adopt a flexible identity, not an immutable one – an example of the latter is: 'I am an alcoholic', and an example of the former is: 'I am someone who now has an alcohol problem.' While identifying oneself as being one thing can have advantages, its permanence can lock people into a rut. The person who once 'was' a severe substance abuser (that is, who once severely abused substances) can grow out of that problem and leave behind that self-identity, can graduate from recovery groups and from the 'in recovery' identity, and can get on with life (Ellis and Velten 1992; Velten 1994a, 1994b). Similarly, one day you may want to experiment sexually. You may want to behave bisexually. Or heterosexually. Or homosexually. If you have an immutable identity, you will be less likely to experiment and you might miss satisfying and enjoyable relationships.

REBT's approach allows and encourages people to continue to change and to leave the past and past identities behind, if that is their desire. When Truman Capote said, 'I am an alcoholic. I am a drug addict. I am a homosexual. I am a genius,' he was only describing some of his behaviour. The danger in having a set label is that you may cramp your style. One day you may want to try something else, to reinvent yourself, and you will be stymied because you think you can only do what you 'are'.

REBT discourages self-labelling; it also promotes self-acceptance (rather than self-esteem). REBT considers that when people have a high regard for themselves, this is usually based on achievement or approval. If people disapprove of you and discriminate against you, consider what former American First Lady Eleanor Roosevelt said: 'No one can make you feel inferior without your consent.' You can enjoy life more if you accept yourself and are not prejudiced toward your own future.

CONCLUSION

REBT, as Albert Ellis continues to construct it, has several aspects that may prove appealing and useful to people who identity themselves as 'lesbian', 'gay', 'biscxual' or 'questioning'. REBT:

- teaches people ways to construct themselves in images of their own choosing, and to transcend some of their biological and social limitations;

- offers methods people can use to make themselves into radically changed and different beings;

- encourages people to make themselves less conditionable and suggestible and to think largely for themselves, no matter what the majority thinks;

- teaches people methods of achieving unconditional self-acceptance, so that they can minimize their dire needs for approval and success that often force them into constrictive conformity;

- teaches methods of accepting and forgiving others as people, rather than damning them, but at the same time working to change or cope with their poor behaviour; and

- shows people specific methods to reduce their horror, rage, self-pity, and complaining about poor and frustrating conditions, and instead, to accept gracefully what they find they cannot change at present, but to persist in working to change what they find they can change.

NOTE

1   A complete bibliography of Ellis's writings can be obtained from the Albert Ellis Institute for Rational Emotive Behaviour Therapy, 45 East 65th Street, New York, NY10021 USA.

REFERENCES

Adam, B. D. (1987) *The Rise Of A Gay And Lesbian Movement*, Boston, MA: Twayne.
Altman, D. (1971) *Homosexual Oppression And Liberation*, New York: Avon.
American Psychiatric Association (APA) (1968) *Diagnostic and Statistical Manual of Mental Disorders* (second edition), Washington, DC: APA.

American Psychological Association (1997) *Resolution On Appropriate Therapeutic Responses To Sexual Orientation*, Washington, DC: APA.

Bayer, R. (1981) *Homosexuality and American Psychiatry: the Politics of Diagnosis*, New York: Basic Books.

Before Stonewall (1986) (Videocassette), MPI Home Video.

Bell, R. Q. (1968) 'A reinterpretation of the direction of effects in studies of socialisation', *Psychological Review*, 75: 81–95.

Bernard, M. E. (1986) *Staying Rational In An Irrational World*, South Melbourne, Australia: McCulloch Publishing.

Bérubé, A. (1990) *Coming Out Under Fire: The History Of Gay Men And Women In World War Two*, New York: Free Press.

Birns, B. (1965) 'Individual differences in human neonates' responses to stimulation', *Child Development*, 36: 249–56.

Campbell, I. M. (1985) 'The psychology of homosexuality', in A. Ellis and M. E. Bernard (eds), *Clinical Applications Of Rational-Emotive Therapy*, New York: Plenum, pp. 153–80.

Cloninger, C. R. (1986) 'A unified biosocial theory of personality and its role in the development of anxiety states', *Psychiatric Developments*, 5: 167–226.

Dryden, W. (1994) *Invitation to Rational-Emotive Psychology*, London: Whurr.

Dryden, W. (1995a) *Preparing for Client Change*, London: Whurr.

Dryden, W. (1995b) *Facilitating Client Change in Rational Emotive Behaviour Therapy*, London: Whurr.

Dryden, W. and DiGiuseppe, R. (1990) *A Primer On Rational-Emotive Therapy*, Champaign, IL: Research Press.

Ellis, A. (1949) 'A study of the love emotions of American college girls', *International Journal of Sexology*, 3: 15–21.

Ellis, A. (1950) 'An introduction to the principles of scientific psychoanalysis', *Genetic Psychology Monographs*, 41: 147–212.

Ellis, A. (1951a) *The Folklore Of Sex*, New York: Boni/Doubleday.

Ellis, A. (1951b) 'The influence of heterosexual culture on the attitudes of homosexuals', *International Journal of Sexology*, 5: 77–9.

Ellis, A. (1952) 'On the cure of homosexuality', *International Journal of Sexology*, 55: 135–8.

Ellis, A. (1953) 'Is the vaginal orgasm a myth?', in A. P. Pillay and A. Ellis (eds), *Sex, Society, And The Individual*, Bombay: International Journal of Sexology Press.

Ellis, A. (1954a) *The American Sexual Tragedy*, New York: Twayne.

Ellis, A. (1954b) *Sex Life Of The American Woman And The Kinsey Report,*. New York: Greenberg.

Ellis, A. (1955) 'Are homosexuals necessarily neurotic?' *ONE*, 3(4): 8–12.

Ellis, A. (1956a) 'An operational reformulation of some of the basic principles of psychoanalysis', in H. Feigl and M. Scriven (eds), *The Foundations Of Science And The Concepts Of Psychology And Psychoanalysis*, Minneapolis: University of Minnesota Press, pp. 131–54. Also published in *Psychoanalytic Review*, 43: 163–80.

Ellis, A. (1956b) 'Use of psychotherapy with homosexuals', *Mattachine Review*, 2: 14–16.

Ellis, A. (1957a) 'Adventures with sex censorship', *Independent*, Issue 62: 4; Issue 63: 4.

Ellis, A. (1957b) *How To Live With A 'Neurotic'*, New York: Crown.

Ellis, A. (1957c) 'How homosexuals can combat anti-homosexualism', *ONE*, 5(2): 7–8.

Ellis, A. (1958) *Sex Without Guilt*, New York: Lyle Stuart.

Ellis, A. (1959) 'Critique', review of the book *The Homosexual In Our Society*, *Mattachine Review*, 5(6): 24–7.

Ellis, A. (1960) *The Art And Science Of Love*, New York: Lyle Stuart.

Ellis, A. (1962) *Reason And Emotion In Psychotherapy*, New York: Lyle Stuart.

Ellis, A. (1963a) *If This Be Sexual Heresy...*, New York: Lyle Stuart and Tower Publications.

Ellis, A. (1963b) *Sex And The Single Man*, New York: Lyle Stuart and Dell Books.

Ellis, A. (1963c) *The Intelligent Woman's Guide To Man-Hunting*, New York: Lyle Stuart and Dell Books.

Ellis, A. (1964) 'A guide to rational homosexuality', *Drum Sex In Perspective*, 4(8): 8–12.

Ellis, A. (1965a) *Suppressed Seven Key Essays Publishers Dared Not Print*. Chicago, IL: New Classics House.

Ellis, A. (1965b) *Homosexuality Its Causes And Cure*, New York: Lyle Stuart.

Ellis, A. (1976) *Sex And The Liberated Man*, Secaucus, NJ: Lyle Stuart.

Ellis, A. (1979a) *The Intelligent Woman's Guide To Dating And Mating*, Secaucus, NJ: Lyle Stuart.

Ellis, A. (1979b) 'The theory of rational-emotive therapy', in A. Ellis and J. M. Whiteley (eds), *Theoretical And Empirical Foundations Of Rational-Emotive Therapy*, Monterey, CA: Brooks/Cole Publishing Co., pp. 33–60.

Ellis, A. (1992) 'Are gays and lesbians emotionally disturbed?', *The Humanist*, 52(5): 33–5.

Ellis, A. (1995) *Better, Deeper, And More Enduring Brief Therapy The Rational Emotive Behaviour Therapy Approach*, New York: Brunner/Mazel.

Ellis, A., and Dryden, W. (1997) *The Practice Of Rational Emotive Behaviour Therapy* (second edition), New York: Springer.

Ellis, A. and Velten, E. (1992) *When AA Doesn't Work For You: Rational Steps To Quitting Alcohol*, New York: Barricade.

Ellis, A., and Velten, E. (1998) *Optimal Aging: Get Over Getting Older*, Chicago, IL.: Open Court.

Eysenck, H. J. (ed.) (1981) *A Model For Personality*, New York: Springer-Verlag.

Gerassi, J. (1966) *The Boys Of Boise Furore, Vice, And Folly In An American City*, New York: Macmillan.

Gray, J. A. (1982) *The Neuropsychology Of Anxiety*, New York: Oxford University Press.

Greenberg, D. E. (1988) *The Construction Of Homosexuality*, Chicago, IL.: University of Chicago Press.

Haldeman, D. (1997) 'Conversion therapy', *Division 44 Newsletter*, 13(3): 17. Washington, DC: American Psychological Association, Division 44, the Society for the Psychological Study of Lesbian, Gay, and Bisexual Issues.

Harper, L. V. (1971) 'The Young As A Source Of Stimuli Controlling Caretaker Behaviour', *Developmental Psychology*, 4: 73–88.

Human Rights Campaign (HRC) (1997) 'Making Reparations', *HRC Quarterly*, 17 (fall), Washington, DC: HRC and the HRC Foundation.

Katz, J. N. (1976) *Gay American History Lesbians And Gay Men In The U.S.A.*, New York: Meridian, 1992.

Korner, A. F. (1965) 'Mother–child interaction: One-way or two-way street?', *Social Work*, 10: 47–51.

Lewis, M. and Rosenblum, L. A. (eds) (1974) *The Effect Of The Infant On Its Caregiver*, New York: Wiley.

Loftus, E., and Ketcham, K. (1994) *The Myth Of Repressed Memory*, New York: St. Martin's Press.

Martin, D. and Lyon, P. (1972) *Lesbian/Woman*, New York: Bantam.

Orndorff, K. (ed.) (forthcoming) *Bi Lives: Bisexual Women Tell Their Stories*, Tucson, AZ: See Sharp Press.

Rovere, R. H. (1959) *Senator Joe Mccarthy*, New York: Harper & Row.

Shilts, R. (1993) *Conduct Unbecoming Lesbians and Gays In The U.S. Military*, New York: St. Martin's Press.

Smith, D. (1982) 'Trends in Counseling and Psychotherapy', *American Psychologist* 37: 802–9.

Sprenkle, D. H., Keeney, B. P. and Sutton, P. M. (1982) 'Theorists who influence clinical members of AAMFT: A research note', *Journal Of Marital And Family Therapy*, 8: 367–9.

Summers, A. (1993) *Official And Confidential*, London: Victor Gollancz.

Velten, E. (1994a) 'Recovery options in private practice, agency, hospital and community settings', *California Psychologist*, 27(3): 29.

Velten, E. (1994b) 'Rational recovery and mandated self-help and treatment', *Journal of Rational Recovery*, 6(5): 3.

Walen, S. R., DiGiuseppe, R. and Dryden, W. (1992) *A Practitioner's Guide To Rational-Emotive Therapy* (second edition), New York: Oxford University Press.

Warner, R. E. (1991) 'A survey of theoretical orientations of Canadian clinical psychologists', *Canadian Psychology*, 32(3): 525–8.

Warren, R. and Zgourides, G. D. (1991) *Anxiety Disorders A Rational-Emotive Perspective*, New York: Pergamon.

Wiener, D. (1988) *Albert Ellis, Passionate Skeptic*, New York: Praeger.

Yochelson, S. and Samenow, S. E. (1976) *The criminal personality. Vol. I: A profile for change*. Northvale, NJ: Jason Aronson.

Zepezauer, M. (ed.) (forthcoming) *Bi Men's Lives: Bisexual Men Tell Their Stories*. Tucson, AZ: See Sharp Press.

Conclusion

Christopher Shelley

The many issues pertaining to homosexualities, both public and private, are among the most contentious in our contemporary European and North American societies. As we move into the next millennium, debates relating to same-sex marriage, legislative protection of lesbians and gays against discrimination, dissolving the systemic homophobia and heterosexism within the education system, adoption rights for same-sex parents, the ordination of homosexual clergy, and so on, are among the central issues of public debate. The increased visibility of gay men and lesbians in all forms of media, the workplace and other parts of the local community has certainly helped to keep these issues in the forefront. Nevertheless, the social, visible and external aspects of these debates must also be balanced with the personal, interior and less visible aspects. The disciplines within and drawn from psychology have attempted to cast greater light on these matters, as Roger Horrocks has pointed out, but the light of 'Diogene's Lamp' has not revealed a particularly desirable state of affairs. The question remains, though, what shall we do with the information we have received?

The accounts offered in this collection have provided, I believe, a significant step towards a better understanding of psychotherapy and homosexualities from contrasting perspectives. Moreover, the theoretical differences between the schools discussed in this volume all share a common denominator; that is, a potential to inform the practical and spiritual work of the psyche for those people who live as non-heterosexual without compromising the integrity of their sexual orientations and identities. Whereas systemic prejudice against the homosexualities has been an explicit part of the theorizing and practice of many models in psychology, we are able effectively to deconstruct these currents and make use of these systems without homophobia and heterosexism. The representation of homophobia and heterosexism in psychology may, as Joanna Ryan has argued, move towards resolution when each individual practitioner is able to explore and reveal his or her own feelings through countertransference. For many, this would be a valuable first step.

A number of issues have been raised within this volume which will not be solved without concentrated effort. For example, cross-cutting issues such as racism, ageing, experiencing a disability, or other forms of marginality need further clarification and dialogue within the sphere of this debate. We might ask ourselves, how can psychotherapy accommodate lesbian or gay individuals who are also members of a racial minority? How does the psychic life of elderly gay men compare with the therapeutic needs of an adolescent lesbian? How can psychotherapy build bridges with social institutions so as not to ignore fundamental aspects of context and ideology? And what of those professionals who continue to argue an illness paradigm? Further work in fostering understanding, dialogue and change regarding all of these questions would be welcome indeed.

Index